FLY for FREE

FLY for FREE

30 Strategies for Free and Budget Air Travel

BRUCE SHORT

Budget Luxury Travel
TRAVEL MORE, FOR LESS.

Fly for Free: 30 Strategies for Free and Budget Air Travel

Copyright ©2025 by Bruce Short

Published by Bruce Douglas Short, Budget Luxury Travel Pty Ltd

All Rights Reserved by Budget Luxury Travel Pty Ltd, including the right of reproduction in whole or in part in any form. No part of this publication may be produced, stored in a retrieval system, or transmitted in any other form or by any means, electronic, mechanical, photocopying, recording, or otherwise, without the publisher's prior permission.

While every care has been taken to ensure the accuracy of the material contained herein at the time of publication, readers should note that the rules of airline loyalty systems vary from airline to airline, are subject to change, and are at the discretion of each airline.

The laws governing credit rating systems vary from country to country. Each person's financial circumstances are different. Before acting on any matters related to credit cards, as discussed in this book, individuals should obtain independent financial advice.

Neither the author nor the publisher will bear any responsibility or liability for any action taken by any person, persons or organisation on the purported basis of information contained herein.

Without limiting the generality of the foregoing, no person, persons, or organisation should take any action on reliance of the material contained herein. Instead, they should satisfy themselves independently (whether by expert advice or otherwise) of the appropriateness of such action.

Contact the publisher at: budluxtravel@gmail.com

First edition, 2025

Printed in Australia

ISBN: 978-1-7641835-1-2 (Hard cover)
ISBN: 978-1-7641835-0-5 (Paperback)
ISBN: 978-1-7641835-2-9 (eBook)

Editing by David Aretha
www.DavidAretha.com

Cover design and interior formatting by Becky's Graphic Design®, LLC
www.BeckysGraphicDesign.com

This book is dedicated to my wife and favourite travelling partner, Lynda, and to my four children, Graham, Ryan, Larissa and Daniel, whose achievements inspire me daily.

Contents

PREFACE 1
INTRODUCTION 3
    Welcome 3
    About Us 3
    Our Mission—Luxury Travel for US$70 per Day 14
    About You 15
    The Structure of this Guide 15
    Currency and Naming Conventions 17
    Contact Information and Free Stuff 19

1. FREE FLIGHTS: EARNING POINTS & MILES

1.1 Airline Loyalty Programs

Loyalty 22
Standard Features of Loyalty Programs 24
Unique Features of Loyalty Programs 25
Our Terminology 25
Benefits of Collecting Points 26
Benefits of Collecting Status Credits 26
Examples of Programs 30
Trump Card Features of Loyalty Programs 34
Desirable Features of Loyalty Programs 35
Our Star Ratings 37
Program Star Ratings 38

1.2 Selection Strategy

Selections 42
Your Airline Portfolio 43
Primary Airline 44
Secondary Airline 47
Tertiary Airlines 47
Always Earn Strategy 50

1.3 Credit Card Strategy

Turn the List Upside-Down	52
Free Flights in Four Months	53
Exercise Caution	54
Why Banks Make Offers	54
Step-by-Step Guide	57

1.4 Payment Strategy

Payment Systems	66
Optimal Payment Method	67
Household Budgeting	70

1.5 Retail Strategy

Earn Points from Retail Partners	72
Set Yourself Up	73
Enter Via the Airline Site	74
Travel Expenses	75
Household Expenditure	76
Third-Party Loyalty Programs	79

2. FREE FLIGHTS: MANAGING POINTS & MILES

2.1 Checking Strategy

Keep It Simple	84
Check Credit Card Earnings	85
Check Initial Set-ups	85
Check One-off Transactions	85
Check Primary Airline Transactions	86

2.2 Expiry Strategies

Types of Expiry Policies	88
Activity-Based Expiry Policies	88
Issue-Based Expiry Policies	89
No Expiry Policies	91
Expiry Policies	93
Points Transfer Strategy	94

CONTENTS

3. FINDING THE BEST VALUE CASH FLIGHTS

3.1 Search Strategy

Research Tools	100
Traps to Avoid	102
Document Options	104
The Search Procedure	105

3.2 Budget Airline Strategy

Budget Airlines	107
Geographic Coverage	107

3.3 Return Strategy

The Study	112
The Results	112

3.4 Cheapest Day Strategy

The Study	118
The Results—Domestic	118
The Results—International	119

3.5 Cheapest Time Strategy

The Study	121
The Results—Domestic	121
The Results—International	122

3.6 Booking Strategy

How Far Ahead to Book	123
Booking Method	126

4. USING POINTS & MILES TO MAXIMISE SAVINGS

4.1 Valuation Strategy

The Numbers Will Set You Free	132
Treat Points Like Foreign Currencies	132
Types of Point Valuations	133
Valuation Method	135
Table of Point Valuations	135

Examples of the Use of Valuations	137
Performing Your Valuations	139

4.2 Redemption Strategy

It's What You Do With Them	141
Redemption	143
Maximising Redemption Value	143
Tell Him He's Dreaming	145
Perform Your Sanity Check	145
Airlines Highlight Bargains	146

5. FINALISING BOOKINGS: LUXURY & SAFETY

5.1 Body-Clock Strategy

Timing for Comfort	158

5.2 Upgrade Strategy

When to Pay for an Upgrade	162
Cost of Business vs. Economy	163
The Cost of Upgrades—Points	164
Cheaper Options than Business	165
Alternative Approaches	166

5.3 Pack Light Strategy

Benefits of Packing Light	168
How to Avoid Checked Baggage	171
Couples Can Compromise	172
Packing Guidelines	173

5.4 Seating Strategy

Features of the Best Seat	178
Using SeatGuru	180
Choices for Each Seating Configuration	181

5.5 Lounge Strategy

Lounge Benefits	185
Gaining Access	188
Lounge Access Ratio	190
No Lounge? Then What?	192

5.6 Safety Strategy

Zero Tolerance for Poor Safety	194
Safety Ratings	194
Criteria for the Ratings	195
Overall	196

6. STEP-BY-STEP IMPLEMENTATION PLAN

6.1 Earning Points & Miles

Step 1: Selection Strategy	199
Step 2: Credit Card Strategy	200
Step 3: Payment Strategy	200
Step 4: Retail Strategy	200

6.2 Managing Points and Miles

Step 1: Checking Strategy	201
Step 2: Expiry Strategy	201
Step 3: Point Transfers Strategy	201

6.3 Find the Best Value Cash Flights

Step 1: Search Strategy	202
Step 2: Budget Airline Strategy	202
Step 3: Return Strategy	202
Step 4: Cheapest Day Strategy	202
Step 5: Cheapest Time Strategy	203

6.4 Using Points to Maximise Savings

Step 1: Find the Best Value Flight for Points	203
Step 2: Valuation Strategy	203
Step 3: Redemption Strategy	203

6.5 Finalising Bookings—Luxury and Safety

Step 1: Body Clock Strategy	204
Step 2: Upgrade Strategy	204
Step 3: Pack Light Strategy	204
Step 4: Seating Strategy	204
Step 5: Lounge Strategy	204
Step 6: Safety Strategy	205

Step 7: Booking Strategy ... 205

7. ADVANCED STRATEGIES
Introduction to Advanced Strategies ... 207
Flying Strategies ... 209
Points Purchasing Strategy ... 209
Itinerary Strategies ... 209
Connection Strategies ... 210
Miscellaneous Strategies ... 210

7.1 Flying Strategies
Simplicity Strategy ... 211
Fly:Free Ratio Strategy ... 213
Consistency Strategy ... 217
Couples Strategy ... 223

7.2 Points Purchasing Strategy
Purchase Points? ... 228
Compare Cost to Valuation ... 229

7.3 Itinerary Strategies
Transport Strategy ... 234
Hub Strategy ... 240
Route Strategy ... 245

7.4 Connection Strategies
Layover Strategy ... 250
Stopover Strategy ... 258

7.5 Miscellaneous Strategies
Round-the-World Strategy ... 262
Gift Cards—Extension of Retail Strategy ... 264

CONCLUSION
Objectives Revisited — 267
Other Budget Luxury Travel Guides — 272
Free Stuff — 272

APPENDICES
Appendix A: Key Features of Airline Loyalty Programs — 275
Appendix B: How We Allocate Stars to Loyalty Programs — 278
Appendix C: Point (Mile) Valuations by Major Currency — 280

ABOUT THE AUTHOR — 284

Preface

The two most important days in your life are the day you are born, and the day you find out why.

MARK TWAIN

I WAS YOUNG WHEN I realised that I was born to explore. I travelled in my home country of Australia when I could, but I dreamt a lot about international travel in my teens. I bought a European travel guide many years before I could afford a flight. Eventually, I embarked on my first overseas trip in my 20s.

Luckily, as an explorer, I wasn't born in the 15th century. I would have had to travel on one of those rat-infested sailing ships. Instead, I was born into an era when I could travel around in a titanium tube at 40,000 feet, eat prawn cocktails, and deal with a G&T.

I was also born to discover the truth through numbers. My 40 years as a CPA were no accident. I love numbers. In this guide, I have combined my love of travel with my passion for uncovering truth through data analysis.

By analysing the numbers associated with travel, my wife Lynda and I continue to learn how to stretch our travel budget across many more destinations. It has enabled us to travel in relative luxury on a budget. We call ourselves TALTs. Tight Arse Luxury Travellers!

Travelling with family and friends strengthens our relationships and builds joint memories. Lynda and I enjoy exploring the world with the people we love.

I hope you enjoy this book and that it inspires you to pursue your travel dreams. Get out there and see more of the world!

—Bruce Short
On the Beach | Australia | 2025

> *Twenty years from now, you will be more disappointed by the things you didn't do than by the ones you did do. Explore, dream, and discover.*
>
> MARK TWAIN

Introduction

Once a year, go somewhere you've never been before.

THE DALAI LAMA

Welcome

Welcome to our guide to free and low-cost air travel. This is one of a series of guides designed to help you travel in luxury on a budget.

The purpose of this introduction is to:

- Assure you that we have the credentials to offer you valuable advice. Based on our firsthand experience, we can explain how to fly for free most of the time and purchase the remaining flights at a low cost.

- Inform you of the structure of this guide, which will help you navigate over 30 strategies for obtaining free and bargain-priced flights.

About Us

Our company publishes guides designed to help you save money. Our publishing brand, *Budget Luxury Travel*, may sound like a contradiction. That's because our society has been conditioned to think comfortable travel must be expensive. Decades of travel industry marketing have created that impression. All *Budget Luxury Travel* guides aim to make luxury travel affordable.

What are our credentials? Why should you devote a few hours to reading our crap? Because we can provide you with a great deal of information about travel and its associated statistics.

When I was a young kid, I was always fascinated with numbers. It was not uncommon for my mum to catch me adding up columns of phone numbers in the local phone book. In those days, printed books of such things were available. She told me, *"You are so smart that if you greased your bum, you could probably slip into the next world."* Thanks for those loving words, Mum. I was unsure if she was referring to my attitude or how I handled figures. But I always knew I understood things better by analysing the numbers.

Our guides do not involve couch surfing, camping, or backpacker hostels. We do not recommend hardship as a way of travelling on a budget. While we travel on a budget, we do so in relative luxury.

Extensive analysis of the numbers and decades of experience have shown us how to get more travel for much less money.

Financial Credentials

On the money front, I am a Fellow of CPA Australia and was recently honoured for 40 years of membership. I have a Bachelor of Business with an accounting major, a Graduate Diploma in Accounting and Finance, and a Master of Business Administration from the University of Technology, Sydney. I have worked as a finance executive for over four decades. Yes, that means I am chronologically challenged. However, it also means I have a good understanding of financial matters.

My financial roles have helped businesses make more money, partly by getting more for less. Our guides are concerned with getting more travel for less money.

Now, I know what you're thinking. OMG. I have just bought a travel guide from some CPA nerd. I'll bet he always carries a pen. He has probably never left his office. Let me reassure you. Yes, you've bought a travel guide from a CPA nerd. And I like to carry two pens and a calculator. But I have *often* left my office to travel worldwide.

INTRODUCTION

Why We Travel

Lynda and I were well-travelled before we met and have travelled extensively together over the last 30 years. While we each have individual interests, we share a common interest in travel and adventure. My career and love of travel have caused me to travel frequently. Every trip has taught me new things about nature, geography, history, our fellow humans, and many other things.

I have taken at least 1,000 flights. While many were for business, others have taken us to over 70 countries. That has caused me to ask myself, "Why do we put in such a large effort? And why are so many people doing the same or wishing they could?"

The reasons we choose to travel are because travel can:

- Satisfy our human need for *adventure*.
- Be shaped to explore and expand our *unique interests*.
- Provide *education* in an enjoyable and effective form.
- Provide *excitement*, often due to the inevitable unexpected events that occur along the way.

My parents worked hard to make ends meet, so we didn't travel much when I was young, although the idea was frequently discussed. My parents always seemed to have a travel brochure on the kitchen bench, and I would paw over them and dream about travel from a young age. Meanwhile, we travelled locally during school holidays but seldom left my home state.

My introduction to adventure through travel occurred when I was 16. I had the opportunity to spend a month of my school holidays on an excursion through the centre of Australia. I took it for granted that I could go and wondered why only half the kids in my year came. I now know that my parents made sacrifices to afford my trip.

We encountered a rare weather event along the way, and the ordinarily arid desert in the outback was flooded between Adelaide and Uluru (formerly known as Ayers Rock). The road was unsealed back then and became impassable when we were over 1,000 kilometres from civilisation in any direction.

We camped near our bus until the floodwater subsided. Luckily, we had sufficient food on board. Sleeping in the open and being awakened by a one-metre-tall Brolga (a small crane) pecking at my head was very exciting.

Days later, we eventually reached Uluru in time to witness the breathtaking sight of the enormous rock formation lit up by the sunset, a bright red and orange hue against the darkening blue sky. It was a sight I'll never forget.

Nor will I forget sneaking out of our campsites with my mate to play pool against the local boys at a pub just outside of nowhere.

After that trip, my love of seeking adventure through travel never left me. I still find travelling through my own country very satisfying, but in 1975, overseas shores beckoned. But I couldn't get there. Air travel was an economic barrier. It was costly when I left school.

All my grandparents were born in the UK, and London was the first place I wanted to visit. But air travel was costly in the 1970s. A Return ticket to London from Sydney cost A$1,300 at the time. That may not sound significant until I point out that $1,300 in 1975, adjusted for inflation, is equivalent to $12,900 in 2025. I didn't know much about inflation at the time, but I knew that while my first full-time job paid A$55 per week, I wouldn't be flying to London anytime soon.

I have been passionate about flying for free or at a low cost ever since.

I found that I could use travel to expand my unique interests, and you can do that, too.

Growing up, my dad and uncle often took my cousins and me to the speedway at the Sydney Showground. This experience planted the seeds of a lifelong interest in cars and motor racing, resulting in trips to renowned motor racing tracks worldwide, including Monza (Italy), Spa (Belgium), Silverstone (UK), and Indianapolis (USA).

Driving American muscle cars across large sections of Route 66 gave our three sons and me a unique perspective on the great USA.

Lynda and I love road trips and have driven in diverse environments, ranging from the twisting Sa Calobra Road in Mallorca to crazy traffic in Thailand, around many Caribbean islands, and along Europe's back streets and motorways.

Think of how you can enjoy your interests through travel. Even though work trips allowed me to play poor golf through the lava fields of Hawaii,

INTRODUCTION

golf is unlikely to drive my future itineraries. But what better adventure for a keen golfer than to play on the world's iconic courses?

The great thing about travel is that it opens many options for anyone to pursue their interests. I spent hours in Bali proving that I can't stand up on a board for long. However, competent surfers can enhance their experience by taking their sport worldwide.

I particularly enjoy learning about history. I can't imagine never having been to the many ancient historical sites worldwide. For us, they have ranged from the famous, such as the Roman Colosseum, Stonehenge, or Machu Picchu, to the lesser-known, such as the perfectly restored Medieval town of Rhodes on the Greek island of the same name and Admiral Nelson's pirate-fighting base in Antigua.

You cannot explore the many modern historical sites unless you travel. For example, the historical surrender of the German military to France in WWI was more interesting when we visited the railway carriage in a French forest, where the surrender was signed. It was fascinating to learn that the Germans used the same railway carriage when it came time for the French to surrender in WWII. Seeing such things brings history to life.

It is one thing to learn about the Cold War between the USSR and the West, but another to visit a nuclear bunker for the potential use of Maggie Thatcher's emergency government outside London.

In Malta, we visited an underground command centre, from which the Allied generals directed the invasion of Italy in WWII. It was locked up for 50 years, preserving it as it was during the war.

Reading about the French Revolution is interesting. It means more after seeing the Palace of Versailles and the French Loire Valley Chateaus. When confronted with the opulence, knowing many in France were starving when the Chateaus were built, it is far easier to understand the revolution than relying solely on written accounts.

Whatever your interests, you will enjoy exploring them internationally. The strategies outlined in this book for obtaining free and low-cost airfares will likely enable you to follow your interests worldwide more frequently.

The central place religion has always occupied throughout the world is better appreciated when you enter Notre Dame Cathedral in Paris or the Sheikh Zayed Grand Mosque in Abu Dhabi.

I particularly enjoy following the UNESCO list of World Heritage Sites and try to bag them wherever we go. They have all been selected according to strict criteria. Occasionally, I will visit one and wonder how it made the list, and then I learn about it and eventually understand. Most of these sites are essential parts of human heritage and well worth visiting.

Natural wonders have provided our most prominent travel memories: beaches from the Dominican Republic to Hawaii, waterfalls from Tasmania to Victoria Falls in Zimbabwe, and national parks from Kruger, South Africa to Yellowstone, USA.

Visit the national parks worldwide. Who can predict what you may see? No one could have planned for us to see hundreds of spinner dolphins jumping around our snorkelling boat when we snorkelled at Lanai Island in Hawaii. We didn't expect to experience the explosive power of a lion sprinting from our side to make a kill when we walked with "placid" lions that had been rescued and brought up by humans in Zimbabwe.

Lynda did not predict a monkey would use her head as a post when jumping between boulders on the Rock of Gibraltar. Pleasant? Maybe not. But it is the part of our Gibraltar adventure she talks about the most.

Using the tools in our guides, including this one on airfares, you can drastically reduce travel costs and enjoy many more places, including a magnificent array of national parks. Our country has lovely national parks, but they differ significantly from the wonders we saw in Yosemite in the USA or Ngorongoro in Tanzania.

Lynda and I love trekking in our own country and recently spent three months hiking dozens of wilderness trails in Tasmania. However, international travel has opened many opportunities.

These have included climbing Mount Kinabalu, the highest peak in Borneo. While it was hard work, there is no substitute for seeing the sunrise peak over the side of the mountain as you strive to get to the top. We have also hiked along the cliff-edge trail at Camino del Rey near the Spanish south coast and have hiked the Nepalese Himalayan Annapurna Trail.

I have hiked to the top of Kilimanjaro, the bottom of the Grand Canyon, across Papua New Guinea on the Kokoda Trail, over the Peruvian Andes on the Inca Trail, and crunched crampons into a glacier at 5 a.m. in Mt Cook National Park, New Zealand.

INTRODUCTION

We have done a little sailing. Lynda and three of our then-young children embarked on a glorious week sailing a rented catamaran through the Whitsunday Islands near the Great Barrier Reef in North Queensland. After using our Zodiac to explore Hill Inlet at the end of Whitehaven Beach, arguably the world's most beautiful beach, we wound the outboard up to full throttle as we returned to our catamaran to make dinner. Many stingrays raced alongside, speeding past many times faster than the boat could go. They were playing with us in a scene that deserved to be in a David Attenborough documentary. You can't plan that. But when you travel widely, adventures will present themselves.

We have had other local sailing adventures, but boating took on a new level of excitement when we sailed with close friends among the Croatian islands. We will never forget backing up to a pier on a new island each night, learning a unique European mooring method, and finding restaurant owners touting their menus even before we had tied off.

Whitewater rafting can be fun anywhere, but there was something more exciting about doing it in Bosnia-Herzegovina. We flipped one over on our son, set against devastatingly beautiful scenery in New Zealand. And if you like rafting at home, you will find it much more interesting in the Zambezi among the crocodiles.

Many people enjoy scuba diving and build their whole trip around dive sites. I get that. I earned my scuba diving ticket while wreck diving in the Bahamas, Puerto Rico, and the US Virgin Islands. But I have never been able to shake that fear of a shark appearing out of nowhere. I should never have watched Jaws when I was young. That giant rubber shark looked convincing back in the '70s. But whatever you love, you will find much more variety when you pursue your interest in various foreign countries.

And then there's the fishermen. If you love fishing at home, you will love it more if you take your gear to faraway places. I am not much of a fisherman, but even I caught a piranha in the Amazon when it committed suicide on the primitive gear my river guide rigged up. And then there was the two-metre parrot fish in Hawaii. The guide caught the fish; I had to reel it in. If I can enjoy bizarre fishing stories and am not even a fisherman, imagine the experiences a competent fisherman could have.

Whatever your interest, you can expand it by going international.

And then there is the priceless educational value that only travel can provide. Most of the reasons travel can educate are self-evident. It is an obvious way of learning about foreign cultures, religions, history, and cuisine. But while you can seek to educate yourself in these and many other areas, much of the education comes from being confronted by realities you may not otherwise consider.

My international adventures started when I was a young executive. My employer flew me from Sydney to Perth for a work-related assignment. A special deal allowed me to return via Hong Kong, and my employer permitted me to take leave to take advantage of this option. I found myself in a foreign country for the first time.

Hong Kong was still regarded as a British territory at that time, having been so for almost 150 years due to settlements established following ancient wars. As part of China, Hong Kong uniquely blends British and Chinese culture. An excursion by hovercraft from the then-British Territory to mainland communist China added excitement.

Bicycles were Canton's (Guangzhou's) primary mode of city transport in the 1980s. Our bus somewhat brutally parted a sea of bicycles to turn any corner. We returned to the port by steam train, which was already antiquated by Western standards.

During a more recent visit to China, I observed a remarkable transformation. The main arteries are now ten-lane highways, and thousands of cars have replaced bicycles. When I commented on the change to a hotel staff member, she proudly told me that China was building two coal-fired power stations each week, which led me to think, *"Something is not right about this."*

In 1980, the Chinese economy was only 25% larger than the Australian economy. The Australian economy has grown significantly. All Aussies know that this is primarily due to digging things out of the ground and sending them to Chinese factories, smelters, and power plants. China has been value-adding to those materials and selling them back to the world, including Australia. As of 2025, the Chinese economy is 10 times that of Australia's. Did we get the strategy wrong? This is an example of unexpected education that can come from travel. Seeing is believing.

We never intended to see a decimated forest in Tasmania, a half-metre-

INTRODUCTION

high pile of plastic bottles on an Indonesian beach that the local restaurant owners clear daily, or a communal village in Asia catching and selling 10-centimetre (four-inch) tuna because that is all that they have left.

We didn't look for the extraordinary number of homeless people living under bridges in Chicago, villagers without limbs in Cambodia after ploughing bomb-studded fields, or guides' excitement when a rhino was spotted in Tanzania because few are left. And then find the rhino has had its horn cut off by conservators so that he didn't get killed by poachers looking to supply people with "medicine."

Phew! That was a downer. Sorry guys! However, the point is that travel has an enormous educational value that goes beyond what you will find in a brochure.

Seventy-five per cent of travel is pure joy, and twenty per cent is hard work. However, taking in what you see during the other 5 per cent is life-changing.

My adventures have never stopped since that school trip to the interior of Australia and that first overseas trip to Hong Kong. And my quest to find ways to cut travel costs has not stopped either.

When travelling, you never know where your next adventure will come from. There are many methods to cut travel costs, all of which are valid. But this guide will emphasise that following our methods requires at least some planning. I also subscribe to the saying that the journey is more important than the destination. Many adventures arise from the journey.

For example, I was once arrested with friends at the bottom of the Grand Canyon without knowing I had committed an offence. The charge sheet said it was for *"Disturbing an Archaeological Resource."* My mates and I were rock climbers in those days, and we had climbed a face to reach a cave to escape a storm. We did not realise the cave we found was an undiscovered shelter for the ancient Anasazi. Archaeologists were flown in. We entered a plea bargain. It was exciting, albeit expensive.

I don't recommend getting arrested for some excitement, but you will usually hear more travellers' tales of the unexpected than you will about their perfectly executed plans.

Lynda and I have crammed great variety into our travels. Those travels have been undertaken for various reasons, including quite unusual ones. For example, I have been to Korea to buy a shipload of plastic (I said shipload). Even on business trips, I often took side excursions on my own time, such as visiting the DMZ (Demilitarised Zone) between North and South Korea.

When travelling for business, Lynda and I found ourselves at a ball in the former palace of the Prince of Romania and at a *Game of Thrones*-themed corporate event that occupied the entire castle next to the walled city of Dubrovnik.

We could each fill a book with travel stories, and I will use some of our Travel Stories in this guide to illustrate some key points.

Cost is the most common barrier to travelling as much as many would like to. This guide, along with its companion volumes, can help solve that problem if it applies to you.

Rest assured that the advice in this guide is based on extensive firsthand experience and thorough analysis. We have analysed our database of over 15,000 flights to supplement our knowledge and confirm conclusions that align with that experience.

Learn from Our Screw-Ups

It is also important to note that we have screwed up and been screwed over many times. We have gained the experience needed to save you from the same fate.

We arrived in Croatia in the summer heat, wearing the winter clothes we had on when we boarded in Sydney. We assumed our bags were on the same trip, but they took a lovely trip elsewhere.

I have slept on the side of a mountain, freezing all night because the rented bag was not as advertised. Our mate refused to call the bag by that name and, on principle, would only refer to it as *"a thing."*

We were bumped off our flight to the Canary Islands. The flight was oversold. We were sent to a crap hotel while they worked on fixing the problem. Again, our bags left without us to enjoy a holiday alone.

In Singapore, we were denied entry to a plane bound for Siem Reap, Cambodia, because we did not have the credit card used to pay for the flight. There were no disputes about payment or my identity, but I did not check the airline's box. We bought a second ticket and still managed to see Angkor Wat.

INTRODUCTION

We forgot to check our flight time from Buenos Aires to Santiago, Chile. When we arrived at 6 a.m., the flight had been rescheduled to 2 p.m., making it a long day at Buenos Aires airport.

Lynda and I signed up for what we thought would be luxury accommodation in Grand Bahama. However, we received a room that was such crap that we came to call it the Flintstone Cave.

We learned that a flight confirmation number is not enough. We could not afford to miss a flight from Albania to Brazil for a family wedding. But even though we had a flight confirmation number, we were told at the check-in counter that we could not board because the ticket had not been issued. Since then, we have always verified that we have a ticket number, even if we already have a confirmation number.

On a recent trip to Vietnam, we saved thousands of dollars on the flights but forgot to check visa requirements, resulting in a high cost for emergency visas.

We have been scammed by many. This includes a taxi driver in Estonia, a pretend parking attendant on the way to Gibraltar, a crooked concierge in Florida, and various travel and booking agents. There are many people out there trying to take advantage of you and your money. So, it is time for some payback. We have learned from both successes and mistakes.

We can impart decades of learning about saving money on luxury travel.

If you carefully study the books in this series and implement the strategies, we can promise you a lifetime of rewarding luxury travel on a budget. There is no better place to start than with the subject of airfares.

Free and low-cost flights are an important part of our approach. Saving money on flights is essential, as you must preserve those funds for trip costs that can only be paid in cash.

We live our advice. By following the processes we share in our series of guides, we have travelled widely on a budget in relative luxury. This guide focuses on our strategies for obtaining free flights and minimising the cost of the rest.

The luxury option is sometimes expensive, but we economise elsewhere to stay within our overall trip budget.

Sourcing free and low-cost flights is a crucial part of the strategy.

Our Mission—Luxury Travel for US$70 per Day

Our mission at Budget Luxury Travel is to help our readers afford luxury travel. Our guides aim to show readers how to travel in luxury for US$70 per person per day. That budget includes all fares for planes, trains, ferries, buses, car rentals, ride-sharing services, taxis, and public transportation. It also includes all accommodation plus entry fees to attractions.

Our budget includes a limited amount of eating out while recognising the importance of trying local cuisine. Our travel guides include accommodation options that allow you to cook and eat as you do at home, but that is a subject for another guide in this series.

In keeping with our luxury theme, we also show you how to avoid potentially unpleasant parts of air travel.

Long-haul flights typically connect cities near your home and your end destination. Those fares can consume a large part of your travel budget. We will show you how to utilise airline loyalty programs to secure flights at no cost. We will also show you how to purchase the rest at bargain prices. In this guide, we outline over 30 strategies that, once learned, will provide a lifetime of free and low-cost air travel.

Minimising the cost of airfares will allow you to travel on a budget without compromising on comfort. We recommend allocating some of your airfare savings to luxuries, which will help you enjoy your trips even more. If your travel budget gets out of control, the credit card bill will temper your excitement when you get home. Follow our strategies to prevent a cost overrun.

Consider an example of the effect of free flights on a budget for a shorter trip. Let's suppose you are planning a three-week holiday in the UK, and you live in Sydney. The cost of one Economy Class Return flight from Sydney to London is approximately US$1,500. That equals US$71 per day ($1,500 / 21 days) when averaged over the entire trip. Given our overall objective of travelling at US$70 per person per day, you can see how essential it is to obtain your longest flight for free.

Travelling is not carbon neutral, but travelling more will increase our collective knowledge of the planet, which can only result in more attention to the environment. Travel also helps us learn to tolerate our differences. Our guides are our small contribution.

About You

If you don't wish to increase your luxury travel or save money when travelling, this book is not for you. Others, please read on.

You *can* travel in luxury on a budget. It is much easier to do so if you get some flights for free and the rest at a low cost. We will show you how to spend less of your hard-earned dollars on airfares.

You may be single, have children, or be in a relationship with a wife or girlfriend. You may have a husband, a boyfriend, or both. You may be younger, in your midlife, or older. You may be a full-time worker or retired. The strategies outlined in this guide apply to all demographics.

Air travel costs are related to the number of seats flown. The advice applies regardless of who is in the seat. Therefore, the savings provided by this guide apply to all.

We hope you enjoy the book. We want to help you achieve your travel dreams.

The Structure of this Guide

Section 1: Free Flights—Earning Points or Miles

We start by explaining how loyalty programs work. Most of you will already be familiar with this, but it's a good time for a refresher. We then help you select airlines associated with loyalty programs with the right features. We have evaluated many programs and share our conclusions here. You can use our criteria to assess many others.

Our action plans will help you rapidly grow your bank of frequent flyer points and show you how to improve your point balances through everyday activities.

Section 2: Free Flights—Managing Points or Miles

Earning points is one thing. Ensuring your points are credited to your accounts is another. We will show you what to check and provide some ideas on how to ensure those points do not expire before you can use them.

Section 3: Finding the Best Value Cash Flights

However, it will still be necessary to buy flights some of the time because:

- You will not always have the right type or quantity of loyalty points.
- Using the strategies in this guide, you will often find flights at such bargain prices that it is wiser to pay cash. Sometimes, it's better to hold onto your hard-earned points or miles for an occasion when they can be redeemed for a higher value.

We have included a systematic step-by-step process to minimise the cost of the flights you must buy. We show you the best way to search for flights, optimise between Return and One-Way flights, the best days and times to fly, the role of budget airlines and the best time to book.

Section 4: Using Points or Miles to Maximise Savings

Once you know how to find the best value cash flight and have earned and managed many points, you will want to spend those points wisely.

Understanding the value of points or miles is essential. We provide point valuations for numerous airlines. Assigning values to points will enable you to make better decisions, such as when to use the points or when to pay cash instead.

We will explain how to maximise your savings when redeeming points for free flights.

Section 5: Finalising Bookings—Luxury and Safety

Our Budget Luxury Travel guides aim to maintain an element of luxury. Therefore, we will help you to:

- Choose the departure time to provide you with the most comfort.
- Find inexpensive upgrades to Business Class.
- Determine the packing trade-offs that suit you.
- Get the best seat allocation when travelling in Economy Class.
- Gain free or low-cost access to airport lounges.

We have included a safety section that outlines how to determine which airlines to avoid, regardless of their low prices. There is no point saving money on a flight to Paris if it might land prematurely, nose-first, on the side of a mountain in Bangladesh.

Section 6: Step-By-Step Implementation Plan
After being inundated with money-saving ideas, you may want to make a booking but not know where to start. We provide a systematic, step-by-step process for booking most of your flights for free and the rest at a low cost.

Section 7: Advanced Strategies
The final section of this guide outlines a range of additional strategies. They appear towards the back of the guide because they are not part of the fast track to getting you flying for free or at budget prices.

The strategies in this section are valuable but can be implemented after completing the step-by-step implementation plan in the previous section.

We cover a range of strategies that will increase the points you earn from flying. We also guide you through techniques that integrate your flying with other forms of transportation and show you how to save more money and points by implementing changes to your route planning.

We also show you how to improve your flight connections, making travel more enjoyable.

Finally, we cover how and when to save money by buying points and how to obtain better value fares using Round-the-World tickets.

Currency and Naming Conventions

This guide uses Australian dollars for all prices and values unless otherwise stated. We are teaching principles here that are not affected by small currency fluctuations. Just make rough conversions in your head as you read.

We use the term *points* for all awards that earn you free flights. Many readers use the term *miles*. Airlines each have their unique terminology.

We use *status credits* to describe awards that will affect your status level and luxury privileges in a loyalty program.

As Australians, we often use Australian examples to illustrate a strategy. However, the strategies and principles outlined in this guide apply worldwide.

FLY FOR FREE

TRAVEL STORY
Results of Our Strategies
Travel Around-the-World on US$70 per Day

As I wrote this introduction, we concluded a 132-day trip around the world, covering 19 countries in Asia, Europe, and South America. We used luxury accommodation and visited every sight we wanted, regardless of the ticket price. The cost? Less than US$70 per day per person.

US$70 per day included flights, accommodation, ground and water transport, tourist site tickets, dining out a little more than when at home, and all incidental travel costs. Our guides show you how to spend the same on most day-to-day food and alcohol as you do at home.

We can only adhere to our US$70 per day budget using the strategies outlined in our guides.

One crucial tactic to keeping overall travel costs down is to avoid the cost of almost all long-haul international airfares. While most free fares on our last trip were in Economy Class, some were in Business Class. When we bought flights for cash, we did so at a low price.

The retail cost of the flights on that trip would have been US$9,914 per person. US$9,914 divided by 131 days would add US$76 per person per day to the total trip cost. We would have had no chance of sticking to our US$70 per day total budget if we had spent US$76 per day just on airfares. Instead, our flight costs averaged just US$14 per day. More details about these flights can be found towards the end of this book.

We regularly apply the strategies outlined in our guides to travel on a budget of US$70 per person per day while maintaining reasonable standards of luxury.

Contact Information and Free Stuff

After over 1,000 flights through 70 countries, we continue to learn. We welcome suggestions for improvement for future editions. Please email us at budluxtravel@gmail.com

We have developed several Excel templates for travellers. We refer to them throughout the guide, and a list appears in the Conclusion. If you would like them, please refer to www.budluxtravel.com and if you have any difficulties downloading the files email budluxtravel@gmail.com.

1

Free Flights: Earning Points & Miles

THIS SECTION OF THE BOOK focuses on obtaining your longest flights for free.

The chapters in this part outline:

- *Airline Loyalty Programs*—learning how airline loyalty programs work.
- *Selection Strategy*—choosing the airlines with which you will accumulate most of your points.
- *Credit Card Strategy*—flying for free in four months.
- *Payment Strategy*—continually topping up your points by choosing the best payment methods.
- *Retail Strategy*—earning points from your suppliers when making routine purchases.

After reading this part, you will know which airline loyalty programs to support, how to accumulate many points rapidly and how to replace them as you use them.

1.1 AIRLINE LOYALTY PROGRAMS

I don't want to belong to a club that would accept me as one of its members.

GROUCHO MARX

Why Read This Chapter?

Airline loyalty programs hold the key to obtaining free flights. Here, you will better understand how airline loyalty programs operate. This understanding forms the foundation of knowledge we will build upon, enabling you to obtain free flights.

You will learn the answers to the following questions:

- Which airline loyalty program features are the most important?
- Which programs provide the best value?

Learning the answers to these questions will help you transition from passively collecting points to implementing a plan for flying for free.

Loyalty

Let's talk about loyalty.

My mum asked me to get groceries from her car boot one day. When I opened the boot, I found she had bought me a very cute Labrador pup. I called him Dino, after the Flintstone cartoon dog. That may sound demeaning to a modern-day dog owner, who is likelier to call his dog Horatio. No matter what sort of day I had at school or what I had done wrong, which was usually a lot as a 12-year-old, Dino forgave me and greeted me every afternoon like he had not seen me for months.

One day, our teacher showed us Origami, the ancient Japanese art of paper folding. I wasn't interested because it didn't relate to my planned future career as a chemist. But I admit it was more relevant to a future scientist than was Macbeth.

My mates and I discovered that if we did a lousy job of a paper crane, it would look more like a quite strong paper cube. The next natural step was to tear a hole in the top, fill it with water, and throw it at unsuspecting kids.

I filled my Origami water bomb and ran into the school canteen before the water leaked out. In the same year that a man got lobbed onto the moon, just because we could, I lobbed a water bomb at a kid, just because I could. They didn't see it coming but stepped aside just in time for it to sail past and hit a teacher. Everyone thought it was hilarious. Except for the teacher. She sent me to the form master.

I impressed myself with the defence I delivered. I thought I sounded like a 12-year-old barrister. It appears all he heard was, *"Bla, bla, bla . . ."* Then he said, *"Put out your hand."* The one-metre-long cane swished through the air at warp speed. It ripped across the end of my fingertips—press repeat.

In the 2020s, any teacher using a cane on a kid would be arrested. However, the social norms were different in 1969. A common parental saying was, *"Spare the rod and spoil the child."* Even though I had loving parents, I couldn't tell them I had been caned because then I would get into trouble for getting into trouble.

I told Dino all about it instead. He was friendly and a great listener. He never disagreed with me and completely understood my point of view. Dino never took anyone's side but mine. Now, that's loyalty.

In the case of airline loyalty programs, the airlines and their partners award points that can be redeemed for free flights. However, they are not entirely selfless like Dino.

The airlines sell the points at a profit to banks and retailers. The retailers offer them as incentives to encourage you to buy their products and services so they, in turn, can make a profit. However, you will profit, too, by working through the plan and strategies presented in this guide.

Your profit will be in the form of free and budget air travel. You can engineer this system of loyalty programs to achieve a greater benefit than the airlines originally envisioned. But first, to work with the system, you must understand it.

Standard Features of Loyalty Programs

All airline loyalty programs share the following commonalities.

- They award points and status credits every time you board a paid flight. You will receive frequent flyer points and status credits shortly after your flight's departure date. A *no-show* will not earn points or status credits.

- The more expensive the fare you purchase, the more points and status credits you earn. Flying Business Class will earn more than flying Economy Class. Flexible fare types attract more points and status credits than inflexible types.

- Airline loyalty programs sell points to *partners*, including retailers, credit card companies, and travel industry businesses, who use the points to reward their customers. Credit card companies offer many points to attract new customers and incentivise existing cardholders to use their cards more frequently.

- The way you use points significantly affects their value.

- All the points look the same on your account and have the same potential redemption value as others in the same account.

- Airlines do not measure your loyalty by the number of frequent-flyer points you have.

- Airlines care more about how often you fly with them than they do about how much you shop with their partners. If you earned all your points by buying groceries, an airline would not consider you a loyal customer.

- Points can be redeemed for free flights.

- Flyers earn frequent flyer points and status credits simultaneously. You can earn points in many ways, but with limited exceptions, you can only earn status credits by flying. Airlines use status credits to measure the value of their customers.

- Status credits provide luxury privileges when flying. Airline loyalty programs rarely sell status credits. You can only earn status credits by flying. The status credits help airlines categorise their customers into loyalty groups. The more status credits you have, the higher your status and the more luxury privileges you will receive.

- You will gain entry to a new status level as soon as you reach the applicable number of status credits. The status credits you earn in one membership year also determine your status category for the following membership year.
- With limited exceptions, you will not earn status credits on free flights.

Unique Features of Loyalty Programs

Each program has:

- Its unique terminology. The lowest membership level may be *Blue* in one loyalty program, *Bronze* in another, and *Member* in another. The highest membership level will be designated by grander sounding names such as *Platinum* or *Gold Elite*.
- Its unique currencies (e.g., *Miles* instead of *Points*, *Tier Segments* instead of *Status Credits*).
- Its rules regarding extra luggage allowances, boarding queues, and preferred seating.
- Different point earning rates for flying on a given route.
- Different point redemption rates on a given route.
- Different policies regarding point expiry.

Our Terminology

In this book, we use the term points generically to represent what you can trade for free flights. Many airlines refer to points as *Miles*. Some airlines have invented their terms, such as *Avios*, in the case of British Airways. However, they all refer to the awards that can be traded for free flights.

In this book, we use the term *status credits* generically. The term refers to the various measures airlines use to determine your status level. Every airline has a different measure, and rather than calling them status credits, they may use terms such as *Segments*, *Tier Segments*, *Flights*, or *Status Points*.

An appendix titled Key Features of Airline Loyalty Programs provides a list of terms used by popular airlines.

We will use the terms *Primary Airline, Secondary Airline,* and *Tertiary Airline.*

Primary Airline refers to the airline on which you will focus most of your point-earning activities.

Secondary Airline refers to the airline with which you typically hold the next most significant point balance.

Tertiary Airlines refers to other airlines with which you will hold minor but important balances.

We discuss this categorisation of airlines in detail in a later chapter.

Benefits of Collecting Points

We recommend focusing your efforts primarily on points. Points are necessary to keep us on budget, whereas status is a luxury. However, note that a higher status with an airline will earn you more points when flying than someone with a lower status on the same flight. However, most of your points will be gained through non-flying activities.

Both points and status credits are valuable. But sometimes you must choose which one to maximise. In those cases, we prefer to maximise points.

Benefits of Collecting Status Credits

We always prioritise earning points over earning status credits, as our primary objective is to facilitate free flights for more Budget Luxury Travel. However, status points are worth collecting and should not be ignored. This is particularly the case for your Primary Airline, where they can mount to a helpful quantity.

Airlines will not declare you a good customer based on your points balance. You may have earned all your points through credit card spending and retail purchases and rarely paid the airline directly for a flight. Therefore, airlines have invented status credits to identify loyal paying customers.

Airlines prefer customers who pay for many airfares in cash. They retain their loyalty by providing them with luxury benefits. The level of luxury benefits is determined by the number of status credits, not by the number of points. Remember, you advance through the loyalty program tiers by earning more status credits, which can only be earned by flying.

The benefits of collecting enough status credits are:

- Free lounge access.
- Priority check-in.
- Priority boarding.
- Additional baggage allowances.
- Free seat allocation.
- Additional points when flying.

In our view, the most significant benefit of higher status is free lounge access. As a bonus, the points you earn flying will also be heavily boosted at that membership level. All loyalty programs have levels above the lounge access level; however, the level that provides lounge access is the most important. The levels beyond that give access to extra privileges and higher point loadings. However, beyond the lounge access level, you reach the point of diminishing returns. We forgo pursuing those higher levels, and if they happen to come along, then that's okay.

Status credits can also provide less predictable benefits. Airlines are much more likely to upgrade a Moonrock Frequent Flyer than a lowly Wooden Spoon Frequent Flyer.

Lounge Access

When travelling, I try to follow a pretty good dietary regime. That is, until there is excellent free food to eat. Then I eat like a pig. *Snort!* I love free stuff. If you are in a lounge and two shoes are sticking out of the trifle, that is probably me licking the jelly off the bottom.

Lounges are not just comfortable places to sit while waiting for a flight. You can shower in transit between flights and feel fresh when you get on the next leg.

It is nice to wait in a pleasant lounge. The alternative is getting buttock cramps in a hard plastic seat among a crowd.

Other Benefits of Status

The status level that provides lounge access also provides the right to bypass the long queues of other people boarding Economy. If you have a higher status, you get to wait in the shorter Business Class people's queue. (Do not go looking for short businesspeople. I meant the line is shorter.)

Flying will rarely be comfortable, but there is no point in starting your discomfort early. When it comes to achieving status levels, focus on getting lounge access. After that, prioritise maximising points. Any further gain in status will be welcome but incidental.

Earning Status Credits

Examples of the number of status credits you can earn appear below. The more expensive the ticket, the more status credits you will earn. All airlines provide schedules on their websites that show the number of status credits they will award for each flight. However, reading these schedules is boring. Do not bother reading any other than for your Primary and Secondary Airlines. For now, note that cheaper fare types will earn fewer status credits. More expensive fare types will earn more status credits.

It is worth noting that if you buy someone else a ticket, the traveller will get the points and status credits.

If you regularly travel with someone else, only one of you needs to hold status, as the accompanying person also receives benefits when travelling with you, such as lounge access, shorter queues, and extra baggage allowances. Buying a Business Class ticket for cash to earn status credits while putting your partner in the back of the plane in Cattle Class on points may make logical sense. Please seek advice from a marriage counsellor before taking this step. We will discuss this further in the *Couples Strategy* section later in the book.

Status credits expire on each anniversary date, resetting your balance to zero.

EXAMPLE
Airline Loyalty Program Status

The Effect of Fare Type on Status Credits

The more expensive fares provide more status credits.

You would earn enough credits to become a Qantas Frequent Flyer Gold member, the level that provides lounge access, by purchasing three Return Business Class tickets on the Sydney-Singapore route in the same membership year. However, you would require nine Return Discount Economy Class flights on the same Sydney-Singapore route over the same period to reach the same Gold level. It's not easy, so it is unlikely that most people will be able to achieve high status with more than one airline in the same year.

The number of status credits awarded is much lower on short domestic flights.

STATUS CREDIT EXAMPLES	
Fare Type	Qantas Status Credits Awarded
Example A: Sydney to Singapore Return	
Non-Refundable Discount Economy Class	80
Fully Flexible Economy Class	120
Standard Business Class	250
Example B: Sydney to Melbourne Return	
Non-Refundable Discount Economy Class	20
Flexible Business Class	90

Examples of Programs

The following sample of loyalty programs was selected because:

- They have enough variation to display the various attributes of most airline loyalty programs, no matter where you live.
- Qantas is important when flying to and from Down Under.
- British Airways is an excellent example for UK and European readers.
- American Airlines is a suitable example for North American readers.

The loyalty programs for many other airlines are summarised in a table in appendix A.

After working through this section, you will be equipped to understand the operation of all loyalty programs.

Qantas

Australians are very creative when it comes to naming things. For example, in 1932, we opened the famous bridge that crosses Sydney Harbour. We called it the Sydney Harbour Bridge.

Luckily, we had 41 more years to choose a more creative name for the world-famous Opera House in Sydney, which opened in 1973. We called it the Sydney Opera House.

The Australian management at Qantas needed a name for their frequent flyer program. They racked their brains to come up with something inspiring. Eventually, in a burst of Australian creativity, Qantas called their frequent flyer program the Qantas Frequent Flyer Program.

Qantas is an essential airline for Australians because it is one of the few airlines that allows Australians to earn points using credit cards to pay for their purchases. It is also one of only two airlines where Australians can easily earn points from an extensive range of retailers and through credit card use.

Australians can earn Qantas Points by purchasing fuel from BP or Ampol and groceries from Woolworths.

You will be awarded *Bronze Status* for signing up.

FREE FLIGHTS: EARNING POINTS & MILES

Qantas Frequent Flyer may be the only airline loyalty program in the world that sometimes charges a fee for joining. However, there are many ways to waive this fee. Australians can join the free Woolworths Rewards loyalty program, which includes a complimentary Qantas Frequent Flyer membership.

To reach *Silver Status,* you must earn 300 Status Credits in a membership year. The primary benefits available to Gold members include complimentary lounge membership, priority check-in, and priority boarding. You must earn 700 Status Credits in a single membership year to reach Gold.

After you have achieved a status level, you can keep it by earning slightly lower Status Credits each membership year: 250 for Silver and 600 for Gold.

Program Summary—Qantas:

- Program Name: *Qantas Frequent Flyer*
- The things you earn that count toward free flights are called *Points.*
- The things you earn toward higher status levels are called *Status Credits.*
- Status level required for complimentary lounge access: Gold at 700 Status Credits.
- Maintain levels: 250 Status Credits for Silver, 600 for Gold.
- Additional points for flights: Silver +50%, Gold +75%.
- Point expiry policy: all points expire after 18 months of account inactivity.
- A unique Qantas program extension called Points Club is worth reviewing on the Qantas website. It provides additional benefits if your points from non-flying activities reach defined thresholds. These include earning status credits on reward (free) flights and providing another potential path towards lounge access.
- Alliance: *Oneworld.*

British Airways

Okay. Stiff upper lip, chaps. British Airways is an excellent airline. It is a Oneworld partner with great reach and a generous frequent flyer program.

British Airways and Qantas are each members of Oneworld. They provide an example of how the big airline alliances work. If you book through the Qantas site, you can book many BA-operated flights using Qantas Frequent Flyer points. We often find great British Airways Business Class bargains using our Qantas points. Tally-ho!

Program Summary—British Airways:

- Program name: *Executive Club*.
- The things you earn that count toward free flights are called *Avios*.
- The things you earn toward higher status levels are called *Tier Segments*.
- Status level required for complimentary lounge access: *Silver* at 600 Tier Points or take four flights.
- Maintain the above level: repeat the entry criteria each year.
- Additional points for flights: Bronze +16%, Silver +32%.
- Point expiry policy: 36 months of account inactivity.
- Alliance: *Oneworld*.

American Airlines

If you live in the USA, this airline is useful. It is also important for globe-trotters, regardless of their home location. I like American Airlines because they have a helpful local service desk in Australia and fly over a vast network. They are an enormous airline with impressive coverage to match.

American Airlines calls its loyalty program *AAdvantage*. Note that it is simply a single *A* followed by the word *Advantage*. If you say you are a member of AA, people will think you are a member of Alcoholics Anonymous. By the way... a big shoutout to my mates.

American Airlines uses the term *Miles* when referring to things that earn you free flights. Miles equate to our generic term, points.

In place of our generic term, status credits, American Airlines uses the term *Loyalty Points*.

Like all airlines, AAdvantage has a few status levels. When you earn

FREE FLIGHTS: EARNING POINTS & MILES

15,000 Loyalty Points, they start you with minor benefits. Gold at 40,000 Loyalty Points will get you upgrades. Gold members also qualify for a free checked-in bag. Some Aussies just said, "Big deal." But bags are not always free of charge in the rest of the world, y'all, so settle.

Like almost all loyalty programs, you would be awarded more *Miles* (points) at each extra status level compared to passengers with a lower status level on the same flight.

For example, Gold members would get 40% more miles than members with the basic membership, even though they are on the same flight and may have paid the same fare. This bonus increases to 120% for Executive Platinum members, which applies to Loyalty Points exceeding 200,000.

At the entry-level of 15,000 Loyalty Points, you get five vouchers for free seat selection. Now, Aussies, settle down again. We understand that you believe seat selection is free for everyone. That is just in Oz. Most citizens of the world must pay to choose their seats.

Many status levels entitle you to check in additional luggage. Goldies may take one additional piece, and Executive Platinum may take three. I don't know why anyone would want three extra bags, but I suppose some people prefer to change their underwear many times per day.

The American Airlines mileage expiration policy is good. You only need to have one transaction on your Miles account, and the expiry date for all points in the account gets pushed out to 18 months from the date of that last transaction.

Program Summary—American Airlines:

- Program name: *AAdvantage*.
- The things you earn that count toward free flights are called *Miles*.
- The things you earn toward higher status levels are called *Loyalty Points*.
- The status level required for complimentary lounge access is not applicable. The USA system is unique because it involves payment for lounge access. In the USA, there is no such thing as a free lunch. However, flyers with higher status with another

Oneworld alliance member can get free lounge access while flying with American Airlines.

- Additional points for flights: Gold +40%.
- Point expiry policy: 18 months of account inactivity.
- Alliance: *Oneworld*.

Other Airlines

Refer to appendix A for a summary of the key features of many other airline loyalty programs.

Trump Card Features of Loyalty Programs

Did that word make you flinch? We are not talking about the Donald here. The term *Trump Card* refers to an expression used in many card games, in which certain cards are potent and referred to as Trump Cards.

The most important thing you need to know about any loyalty program is the extent to which there are opportunities to earn points other than by flying. The Trump Card features for loyalty programs are:

- Credit card sign-on bonuses.
- Rewards for ongoing credit card use.
- Rewards from retailers for routine purchases.

These features are Trump Cards because:

- You will earn more points from these non-flying activities than from flying.
- Due to geographic limits, some countries only have one or two airline loyalty programs that offer these opportunities.

It is essential to select Primary and Secondary Airlines with the Trump Card features. This is discussed in detail in a later chapter titled *Selection Strategy*. The availability of these features for each airline will depend on the country in which you live.

Credit Card Sign-on Bonuses

Credit card sign-on bonuses refer to the large one-off rewards awarded for signing up for a new credit card. Follow the steps detailed in a later chapter titled *Credit Card Strategy*, and you will quickly earn many points.

Rewards for Ongoing Credit Card Use

If you have the right credit card, you can earn points every time you use it. It is essential to join an airline loyalty program partnered with credit card providers offering this benefit. We discuss this in detail in a later chapter titled *Payment Strategy*.

Rewards from Retailers for Routine Purchases

Many airlines have a list of retailers participating in the associated loyalty program. These retailers are typically active in the geographic area where the airline is based. Your primary focus should be loyalty programs that work with local retailers. We will discuss this in detail in a chapter titled *Retail Strategy*.

Desirable Features of Loyalty Programs

Your Primary and Secondary Airlines should be selected based on the Trump Card features discussed above. However, other desirable features should be considered in the following circumstances:

- You live in a part of the world where you have a choice of airlines offering the Trump Cards, e.g., the USA.
- You are selecting your Tertiary Airlines.

Aside from the Trump Card features, other desirable features are discussed below.

Network Coverage

Network coverage refers to the extent of an airline's and its partners' geographic coverage.

If an airline is part of a large alliance:

- You can use that airline's points to fly on partner-operated flights. This offers a wide range of global routes to utilise your points. That would not be the case if your points were with an airline

that is not part of a major alliance. If Timbuktu Airlines is not part of a comprehensive network, flying with them is unlikely to be an excellent option for accumulating points.
- Airline alliances allow airline partners to combine services to get you to your desired destination, including Round-the-world tickets, which can provide great offers. More about this later.
- If you have status with your chosen airline, you will get benefits when travelling with alliance members, including lounge access.

If an airline is part of Oneworld or Star Alliance, the loyalty program points provide access to a large geographic area. The Sky Team alliance is not as extensive, but still very useful.

You will find that most larger airlines, and many smaller ones, belong to one of these three major alliances. Members appear below:

- <u>Oneworld</u>: *Alaska Airlines, American Airlines, British Airways, Cathay Pacific, Fiji Airways, Finnair, Iberia, Japan Airlines, Malaysia Airlines, Oman Air, Qantas, Qatar Airways, Royal Air Maroc, Royal Jordanian Airlines, Sri Lankan Airlines.*
- <u>Star Alliance</u>: *Aegean Airlines, Air Canada, Air China, Air India, Air New Zealand, ANA, Asiana Airlines, Austrian, Avianca, Brussels Airlines, Copa Airlines, Croatia Airlines, Egyptair, Ethiopian Airlines, EVA Air, LOT Polish Airlines, Lufthansa, SAS, Shenzhen Airlines, Singapore Airlines, South African Airways, Swiss, TAP Air Portugal, Thai Airways, Turkish Airlines, United Airlines.*
- <u>Sky Team</u>: *Aerolineas Argentinas, Aero Mexico, Air Europa, Air France, China Airlines, China Eastern, Delta Air Lines, Garuda Indonesia, Kenya Airways, KLM, Korean Air, Middle East Airlines, Saudia, Tarom, Vietnam Airlines, Virgin Atlantic, Xiamen Air.*

Point Expiry Policies

Some policies make it easy to avoid the expiry of points. A later chapter on the *Expiry Strategy* provides a detailed coverage of these policies.

The Fly:Free Ratio

This ratio measures the number of flights you must buy for cash to earn enough points for a comparable free flight. The lower the ratio, the better. These ratios are outlined in a later chapter, *Flying Strategies*.

The Lounge Access Ratio

This ratio measures the relative ease with which you can achieve a status level that provides lounge access. This ratio is also outlined in a later chapter, *Lounge Strategy*.

Our Star Ratings

The ability to earn points from credit cards and retail businesses in your local area is crucial when evaluating loyalty programs. Programs with those features automatically become the best choice when selecting your Primary and Secondary airlines. Therefore, we have excluded these Trump Card features from our rating system because the primary purpose of our Loyalty Program Star Ratings is to assist you when choosing your Tertiary Airlines.

The ratings may also be helpful if you live in a geography such as the USA, which has multiple airlines associated with credit card sign-on deals and retail partners.

Please note that we may not have rated airlines with inadequate safety records. The safety scores are explained in a later chapter. Those who plan on rolling the dice with those airlines may not live long enough to implement our program, in any case.

We have ranked each airline based on each factor and granted them Rating Stars. This process has enabled us to provide an overall quality ranking for each loyalty program. Our criteria will help you assess airlines that are not on our list. Feel free to email us if you would like an assessment of your loyalty program. Our list of assessed programs is constantly growing.

The methods used to determine star ratings are consistent across all loyalty programs. The determination of the number of stars for each factor is outlined in an Appendix.

Program Star Ratings

Rating the above factors gives each airline loyalty program an overall Star Rating out of 16.

Below is a comparative table for some of the loyalty programs studied.

These ratings will change subject to the weighting you place on each item (our weightings are described in an appendix). In addition, the Lounge Access and Fly:Free ratios will change depending on the sample of flights selected for the base data. However, the choice of sampling data will not turn a poor rating into a great one.

FREE FLIGHTS: EARNING POINTS & MILES

RATINGS OF LOYALTY PROGRAMS		
AIRLINE	**LOYALTY PROGRAM**	**OVERALL RATING** *Stars*
Superior Group		
British Airways	Executive Club	14
Swiss	Miles and More	13
Austrian Airlines	Miles and More	12
Cathay Pacific	Marco Polo	12
ITA Airways	Miles and More	12
Lufthansa	Miles and More	12
United Airlines	Mileage Plus	12
Malaysia Airlines	Enrich	11
Qantas	Frequent Flyer	11
Satisfactory Group		
Air Canada	Aeroplan	10
Air Europa	Suma	10
Air France	Flying Blue	10
Alaska Airlines	Mileage Plan	10
American Airways	AAdvantage	10
Emirates	Skywards	10
Qatar Airways	Privilege Club	10
Singapore Airlines	KrisFlyer	10
Virgin Australia	Velocity	10
Delta Air Lines	Sky Miles	9
Inferior Group		
Air New Zealand	Airpoints	< 9
Thai Airways	Royal Orchid	< 9
Hawaiian Airlines	Hawaiian Miles	< 9
Southwest Airlines	Rapid Rewards	< 9
Etihad Airways	Guest	< 9

TRAVEL STORY
Some Early Inspiration

Get More Travel for Less Money

We had terrific trips before most of the strategies in this guide were developed. However, we used many plastic items, referred to as Australian dollars.

Lynda and I have almost always travelled independently and have tried many tricks to get the best deals. By independent, I mean travelling without using a travel agent and only relying on tour operators for local excursions.

In our twenties and thirties, we had already travelled individually to many places, particularly in our own country, Asia, and North America. But our first major trip together was to the Greek Islands via Italy. It was our honeymoon, so it was destined to be remarkable.

The trip was inspirational to me for another reason. I found a deal offered by Alitalia (now ITA Airways) that provided a free side trip to Egypt. Airfares, accommodation, and a tour of the pyramids were all covered. The airfare was the same as that of other airlines to Rome and Athens, but Alitalia included the side trip for free. To see the pyramids for nothing awakened my bargain-hunting spirit. It is fitting that the sight of this surviving ancient wonder inspired me to consider how we can see the whole world. We remain on that life's journey.

On that trip, we spent significant money on a Formula One race in Monza, visits to the wonders of Rome, fried swordfish, and beautiful cliffside accommodations in Santorini. But the free trip to the pyramids set me on a travel deal hunt that has never stopped. Getting it for free greatly appealed to a bargain hunter like me.

During the laser show over the Great Pyramid of Giza, I thought, *I bet I have inspired my beautiful new bride to believe I am a genius for getting this for nothin'*. I looked aside at her gorgeous, tanned legs, and my eyes followed her slim figure to her blonde hair. I brushed it aside so she could give me a well-deserved, admiring look. But she was in a deep state of jet lag sleep. Oh well. The show was good, and I was left alone to wallow in my scabbing success.

1.2 SELECTION STRATEGY

Free stuff is not important. Love is.
Luckily, I love free stuff.

Why Read This Chapter?

You will learn how to structure a portfolio of loyalty programs, which will serve as your vehicle for accumulating points and maximising your free flights.

Selections

I used to get torn away from the Chess Club in late primary school to play various sports, at which I was total crap. The kids were lined up against the wall until the teacher nominated a few kids to start things. Then, the team selections began.

The primary selections chosen by the teachers always consisted of the same few kids who acted as leaders. Those were the kids who excelled at football, were also skilled at cricket, and enjoyed swimming. They were necessary if the team was going to win. Those guys were like the steak on the plate. They were the protein of the outfit. They were core business.

The secondary selections were picked by their mates, the leaders. They were picked out of the lineup early. In my southern Sydney shire, they always had names like Johnno, Dicko, Stevo, Danno, and Robbo. You know the type—the popular, fun guys. Those guys were like the chips on the plate. Everyone liked them. The teams could score well with them.

The Tertiary Selections were not great sportsmen. They were not important individually, but they could help as a group. They could be sent to the outfield and might occasionally stop a ball from hitting the boundary. They were just a little bit useful. They were like dessert—unnecessary but good to have.

Then there were the rest. They were my mob. We were not part of the main meal and were called various names, many of which are now out of print. We were the uncoordinated ones who would swing three times at the ball and miss by a more significant margin each time. We were like the green beans to the selector kids. No one wanted us, but someone had to have us, as the teachers said there could be no leftovers.

It is not that I wasn't good at anything. My forte was operating the school bank. Unfortunately, that didn't seem to have the same cachet with the girls as winning the 100-metre sprint.

Just as a sports team needs to make suitable selections, you need to take care when selecting which airlines to support.

Your choice of Primary Airline requires focus. Making the right choice is necessary if you are going to win. It will be the steak on your frequent flyer plate, the protein of the outfit, and core business. It is essential to pick the right Primary. Your choice will massively affect your chances of winning the free flight game.

The Secondary Airline is also a necessary part of the lineup. You will score well with it. It can make a significant difference.

Tertiary Airlines are not individually essential, but can help as a group. You will need several of them. They will make a difference in the number of free flights you will achieve.

Then there are the rest. Don't sweat over those, but if they offer points you cannot direct towards your Primary, Secondary or Tertiary Airlines, take them anyway. You can't predict the future, and those points may become helpful. Besides, some loyalty programs have no expiry criteria for their points. Expiry policies change occasionally, and the industry appears to be moving more towards eliminating expiries.

Your Airline Portfolio

You will build your most significant point balance with your Primary Airline.

Forty per cent of loyalty schemes require account activity within set periods to prevent points from expiring, and another 40% require the points to be used within specified periods. Maintaining activity in multiple accounts simultaneously while preventing points from expiring is challenging. Even if you are a frequent traveller, it is best to consolidate most of your points to a small number of airlines.

The criteria many consumers use to select an airline are likely to include things like:

- I have heard of the airline.
- Last time I flew with the other airline, the meal was served in a cardboard box.
- Mum always said the airline is safe.
- The food was hot last time, and so was the hostie.
- The flight is leaving at my preferred time.
- The flight is direct or has fewer stops.
- I have a status with this airline, allowing me to enter the lounge.

These and many other considerations can be factored in. But for a TALT, when selecting a flight, the primary considerations, with the heaviest weighting, should be:

- Can I get a free flight?
- If not, what is the cheapest viable option?

Primary Airline

Your Primary Airline is where you will focus most of your point-earning activity. It is also the airline where you will accumulate the most status credits.

Using an airline with "national carrier" status makes sense in many countries. This usually guarantees an optimal combination of the following:

- Many partnerships with local credit card issuers that offer bonus sign-on points (refer to *Credit Card Strategy*).
- The ability to accumulate points using a credit card at no cost (refer to *Payment Strategy*).
- Many partnerships with local retailers (refer to *Retail Strategy*).
- Comprehensive coverage for flights departing from or arriving in your country.
- A comprehensive domestic coverage.
- Membership of a large airline alliance.
- Financial stability over the long term, with the likelihood of a government bailout if they run into trouble.

By far, the most crucial consideration when choosing your Primary Airline is that you must be able to earn points from *non-flying* activities. You will always earn more points from credit card sign-on bonuses, credit card usage, and retail activities than from flying. Opportunities to earn points from credit card suppliers and retailers should be your first selection criterion when deciding on your Primary Airline.

National Airlines

National airlines, such as Qantas in Australia, Emirates in Dubai, or British Airways in the United Kingdom, will likely be protected by their respective governments. This applies even though many so-called national carriers are privately owned and listed on a stock exchange. Some airlines are national symbols and sources of national pride. Those airlines are likely to get government financial support if required.

EXAMPLE

Selection Strategy

Primary Airline—The Insurance Provided by National Flag Carrier Status

In 2001, one of Australia's largest airlines, Ansett, went broke. We had half a million frequent flyer points, which suddenly became worthless.

However, consider what happened when COVID-19 put the airlines under pressure in 2020. The Australian government stepped forward and gave the private shareholders of Qantas a tremendous gift from the Australian taxpayer. The government should have received partial ownership of the airline through a share issue and later sold its shares on the exchange. Qantas is a publicly listed company with no government ownership. Why should taxpayers bail out wealthy shareholders? The answer is national pride. Qantas is an Aussie icon.

At the same time, it appeared that Virgin Australia was on the brink of collapse. The same Australian government watched Virgin Australia get sold to the private equity wolf pack for a few cents on the dollar. Why? Virgin was not a source of national pride. The Australian public was like Rhett Butler. Frankly, my dear, they did not give a damn. Virgin was almost gone with the wind. On this occasion, point holders like us got lucky when the new owners honoured the Virgin Australia Velocity points.

A national carrier will often be a good choice as a Primary Airline, providing its loyalty program includes ample opportunities to earn points from sources other than flying.

Making Your Primary Airline Selection

By now, you will be clear that we recommend that Australians select Qantas as their Primary Airline.

USA residents are spoiled for choice. United Airlines, Delta Air Lines, and American Airlines have extensive coverage. If we lived in the USA, we would probably choose one of the above three. However, there may be a route that you travel often. You could focus on the airline that services that route well.

It is easier for a Sydney resident to decide which airline to support than a New York resident.

Sometimes, choosing an airline from a nearby country may make sense. For example, you may select an airline based in a European country next to yours or a US airline if you live in Canada.

The most significant consideration is how closely a loyalty program is tied to credit card companies and local retailers. Based on these credit card and retail point-earning opportunities in your country, decide which one will be your Primary Airline. If it's also the *national airline,* that's a bonus, ensuring your points are unlikely to be lost if the airline encounters financial headwinds.

It is also essential that your Primary Airline is part of one of the world's three big alliances: Oneworld, Star Alliance, or SkyTeam.

When we use Qantas points to fly on a Oneworld partner airline, the booking will be made on the Qantas Frequent Flyer account using Qantas points. However, we could end up on any Qantas partner airline for any leg of the trip. When we cannot reach our destination on points, we usually get most of the way. We then make a separate booking for the last short leg. For the final leg, we can often use a small number of points we have saved with a Tertiary Airline from a different alliance.

Secondary Airline

The main objective of nominating a Secondary Airline is to provide opportunities to earn points from retailers that are not partnered with your Primary Airline.

Consider it a bonus if you can find a Secondary Airline that also:

- Flies routes not covered by your Primary Airline. This often means choosing an airline with good domestic coverage.
- Is a member of a large alliance that differs from your Primary Airline.

If you have two equal choices, consider the Budget Luxury Travel star ratings of airline loyalty programs.

Tertiary Airlines

Everyone should have a Primary and Secondary Airline, they should focus the remaining flying activity on a defined set of Tertiary Airlines. These will come into play when:

- You must fly on a route not serviced by your Primary or Secondary Airlines or their alliance partners.
- You wish to fly on an airline offering a great cash deal. Sometimes, you may prefer to pay cash and save points for another occasion. This may apply even if you have enough points to fly for free. If you decide to pay cash and cannot fly with your Primary or Secondary, it would be best to fly with one of your selected Tertiary Airlines.

When choosing your *Tertiary Airline(s)*, ensure you have:

- At least one airline in your portfolio that belongs to each of the Oneworld, Star Alliance, and SkyTeam alliances.
- Reasonable confidence that you can avoid the expiry of points.
- Considered our ratings of loyalty programs.
- Included any airline with a policy of never letting points expire (refer to the list in this guide).

Focus on your choices of Primary and Secondary Airlines for now. You do not need to choose your Tertiary Airlines until after reading this guide.

EXAMPLE
Selection Strategy

Our Primary, Secondary and Tertiary Airlines

Qantas is our Primary Airline, as it meets all the main criteria.

It has the Trump Card features:

- Credit card companies in Australia most commonly offer Qantas points for sign-on bonuses and credit card use.
- Qantas has the broadest range of retail partners.

Virgin Australia, our Secondary Airline, is not part of any big alliance. However, we chose Virgin because it is allied with Australian retailers that are not allied with our Primary Airline. That factor is so important that we even ignored our low overall Star Rating of Velocity, Virgin Australia's loyalty program.

We selected Singapore Airlines, Delta, Hawaiian, and United for our Tertiary Airlines.

Singapore was included because:

FREE FLIGHTS: EARNING POINTS & MILES

- It is a Star Alliance member. When we book with any Star Alliance member, we can nominate the Singapore Airlines KrisFlyer number to consolidate our points.
- We have had good flying experiences with Singapore Airlines.
- The KrisFlyer loyalty program has a high Budget Luxury Traveller star rating.

We have included Delta as a Tertiary Airline because:

- It rates highly on our Star Ratings.
- It is a SkyTeam Alliance member.
- It offers a points program with a no-expiration policy.

We included Hawaiian and United because they are risk-free. They have a no-expiry policy.

Note that the above choices ensure:

- We have membership in the three largest airline alliances.
- We can easily avoid the expiry of Qantas and Virgin points by a single transaction with Woolworths and Coles supermarkets.
- We only need to manage the Singapore Airlines account because United, Hawaiian and Delta have a policy of never allowing points to expire.

SELECTION STRATEGY

Focus your point-earning activities on one Primary Airline. Ensure your Primary Airline offers numerous point-earning opportunities with credit card companies and retailers. Ideally, your Primary Airline should have broad geographic coverage, be a member of one of the big three alliances and be financially strong.

> Select a Secondary Airline to widen the number of retailers and credit card companies from whom you can earn points.
>
> Add Tertiary Airlines to ensure you have at least one airline in your portfolio that belongs to each of the Oneworld, Star Alliance, and SkyTeam alliances. Add other airlines if they have a "no expiry" policy for their points. Consider the Budget Luxury Traveller Star ratings when making your selection.

Always Earn Strategy

Even though we encourage you to form a portfolio of loyalty programs, never let a point-earning opportunity pass, even if you are flying on an airline outside your portfolio.

Make sure you consistently earn points when you pay to fly. Don't let an earning opportunity pass because you may be flying with a new airline. Join their loyalty program before booking, and ensure your partner does the same. Only make an exception if the airline is allied with one of your Primary, Secondary or Tertiary Airlines and you intend to nominate one of those loyalty programs.

Never buy an airfare without registering for points. This strategy is so straightforward that it requires little explanation. But many points are lost because people do not follow it. You have nothing to lose. Make sure you earn points of some kind on every paid flight.

If you think you may not use that airline before the points expire and cannot nominate your Primary, Secondary, or Tertiary Airline, earn the points with that airline anyway. You cannot see the future, and it costs nothing to join and earn.

It will be rare for you to be on an airline with a loyalty program but not part of one of the three largest airline alliances. However, it does happen. When it does, collect points from someone, anyone, *every* time.

Collect every point you can.

FREE FLIGHTS: EARNING POINTS & MILES

> **ALWAYS EARN STRATEGY**
>
> Every time you pay cash for a flight, ensure you have joined the airline's loyalty program and claimed points. If you have a partner, encourage them to join as well. Never let a point-earning opportunity pass.

1.3 CREDIT CARD STRATEGY

> **Psychologist:** *"Have you made progress with your inability to wait for things?"*
>
> **Patient:** *"Yes, Doctor. I recognise now that I used to be too impatient. And that I don't have time for that anymore."*

Why Read This Chapter?

You may be impatient and want to start working on your free flights. Here, you will learn how to use credit card incentive programs to kick-start your lifetime of flying for free. You will learn how to get enough points for a free intercontinental return flight four months from now simply by performing the five specific steps in this chapter.

Turn the List Upside-Down

There is a long "to-do" list on the way to flying for free. I considered slowly building up to the most significant step on the list. And then I remembered the power of turning the list upside down.

One morning in 1992, I was 6,000 feet in the air, falling towards the planet at 190 km per hour, lying helpless on my back like an upended turtle. I didn't measure the speed, but 190 km per hour is the terminal velocity for a skilled skydiver in free fall in the correct position; however, I think an upended turtle may fall faster.

It started after I had recently become single for the second time and was bored on the weekends because I didn't have my kids, Graham and Ryan. A mate was in the same situation. We decided to draw up a list of exciting things to do. We put the least bold activities at the top and added increasingly high-adrenaline activities as we worked our way down.

The list started with hiking, skiing, white-water rafting, and rock climbing. It then progressed through canyoning, scuba diving, bungee jumping, alpine mountaineering, flying planes, hang gliding, and skydiving. We pledged to get started.

Later that week, he rang. "I've booked us."

"Good work," I replied. "What are we doing—rock climbing?"

He replied, "We're enrolled in an accelerated free-fall course at the Sydney Skydiving Centre on Saturday."

He had turned the list upside down. I didn't sleep for the next few days.

After several jumps and the threat of being taken off the course for my safety, I figured out how to perform various free-fall manoeuvres while keeping my face down rather than up. Eventually, I was allowed to jump without the instructor flying near me, and after about 20 solo jumps, we progressed to the following item on the list. But we were working our way up the list rather than down.

It was a great confidence booster as we progressed through the rest of the list over the following years. We might never have progressed to skydiving had we not turned the list upside down. The secret was to jump in at the deep end, which we are about to do in this chapter.

The *Credit Card Strategy* is the boldest step towards flying for free. It requires commitment and will give you the fastest progress. Rather than starting slowly with the easy tasks, I decided we should jump in and show you how to obtain many points quickly.

This way, you will fly for free in a few months, building your confidence and enthusiasm. Once you have had this taste, there will be no stopping you, and the rest will seem easy.

It's time to turn the list upside down.

Free Flights in Four Months

The *Credit Card Strategy* outlined in this chapter will quickly help you earn many points. Approval for a new credit card will earn you enough points for a free long-haul flight without doing anything else. If you act on this today, you can fly for free in four months.

The average time to complete the application and approval process and receive your card is one month. To be awarded the sign-on incentive, most cards require that you use the card for three months.

You can earn many points simply in exchange for some administrative time. Sticking to the *Credit Card Strategy* will incur zero interest and limited fees. You will also avoid the ongoing annual fees that banks try to charge us.

Be confident that the following facts apply:

- *Fact 1:* All banks try and suck people into as much debt as they are capable of repaying, so they can make as much profit as possible, which includes luring customers to sign contracts that include excessive charges. Their only concern is that you can keep making the payments. They rely on asymmetry of information, meaning they have more knowledge about finance than most of their customers.
- *Fact 2:* We can turn the bank's unscrupulous practices against them to get free flights.

Exercise Caution

My lifetime of asking people to be careful with their money makes me want to caution you.

The techniques we discuss here are like giving a power saw to someone who has only ever used a handsaw. A power saw can be helpful. However, it can be dangerous in the hands of a klutz. Sorry to our intelligent readers, but we assume you lent this guide to a klutz. And the thing about klutzes is that they can be camouflaged as intelligent people. Yes, we mean you, Professor.

Credit card providers charge exorbitant interest rates, three to five times the average housing loan rate. Follow this guide to avoid these excessive interest charges.

You must follow the complete process we will outline, including the one at the end that says, *"Now cut up that spanking new card."* Sorry, Professor, but we will remind you of that later.

Credit card providers make squillions from customers who don't pay them off. And I know. Because, like many of us, I have been a credit card klutz in one phase of my life, too. Lynda would say I am still a klutz at navigation and cooking, but no longer a klutz of the credit card variety. We use the credit card system to get where we want to go. No. I don't mean in life generally! We use the credit card system, among other methods covered later, to fly across the world for nothing.

Why Banks Make Offers

Banks love to hook new credit card users. They love them. A casual look at bank profitability and the size of their credit card activities confirms that billions are involved. According to the US Federal Reserve, 80% of credit card companies' profits arise from the exorbitant interest rates charged.

Fifteen per cent of credit card profitability comes from fees, primarily for late payments. Isn't it incredible how much of their business relies on a computer program charging late fees just because it can?

Source: https://www.federalreserve.gov/econres/notes/feds-notes/credit-card-profitability-20220909.html *for information on credit card profitability in the USA.*

Suppose you owe $1,000 and pay seven days late. If the cost to the credit card company is interest of about 5% per annum, that equates to a cost of 96 cents in this example. However, a late fee of $20 is typical. No administrative expenses are incurred, as the computer program automatically charges your account. What a rort! No other big business would be allowed to engage in this unethical price-gouging behaviour. Banks regularly abuse the privileged position they have been handed in our society—it's time for some payback.

The retailers also pay merchant fees covering the system's operating costs. Our society is so dependent on credit cards that any merchant who refuses to accept them risks going out of business.

What is the actual number of billions the industry is making? It is X. Where X is large. We are too busy travelling for free to find an exact number. However, when banks paid us less than 1% on our term deposits during Covid, they still charged 17% on card balances. And many of the *free* benefits are covered by an annual fee anyway.

The offers of free points, simply for getting a credit card approved, are genuine. But the banks play the averages. They know the average person gets stuck in debt. Your parents may have told you that if a deal looks too good to be true, there must be a catch. Good advice, parents. Parents are more often right than wrong.

But, parents, listen to this. Credit card providers are generous to new cardholders because they rely on them, on average, to have a growing unpaid balance. Then, the companies can charge an exorbitant interest rate. They know that some of us will not get sucked in. They don't care. A significant percentage of credit card users accumulate substantial balances. Those victims pay for the benefits provided to the rest of us.

People who follow a method like the one in this book incur costs for credit card companies. Who cares? I don't. You don't. And the banks don't. The banks are cleaning up by playing the averages and charging excruciatingly high interest rates to those who get it wrong. That includes most of their customers.

The good news is that incredibly lucrative industries attract great competition. The competition between financial institutions to exploit innocent people is intense. They offer all sorts of incentives to suck us in. This competition in the credit card industry presents an opportunity on which to capitalise. They give away stuff to get you to sign up because they know 94% of people say to themselves:

"I can control my spending on the card. I will never pay interest. I will pay the card off before the interest-free period expires."

But do you know how many people fail to keep this promise to themselves? It's 86%! Okay, those last two percentages were among the 53% of statistics in the world that are made up on the spot, but you get the idea.

Banks must give away free items to all new cardholders so they can charge most of them for years. They do not care if a minority works the system. Ensure you are in the minority and do not lazily join the exploited majority after getting the new card. You don't need to hide anything from the banks. They know a small number of people win. But, just like a casino, they hope the small number of winners brag about it so they can suck in the rest. When trying to catch a barramundi, you don't worry about the cost of the bait, even if you may lose some.

Credit card providers are so keen to make money from us that they incentivise everyone to sign up.

They know that when they cast their net in the sea of people drifting through life, they will catch lots of the victims they want. They also know they will see some smarty-pants exploiting their incentive scheme. Banks profit excessively from the overall system. They do not care if a few smarty-pants people game that system.

Step-by-Step Guide

Step 1: Search

Offers are easy to find.

As outlined in a previous chapter, you must select your Primary Airline. Sometimes, the selection process requires knowledge of the best sign-on bonuses.

Use Google to find offers. You can find deals in any country by entering something like *credit card frequent flyer offer [insert country name]*. You only need one. Which one? The one that satisfies the following criteria:

- They must offer many points as a sign-on bonus, and the points must be associated with your Primary Airline.
- They must offer points for using the card (e.g., one point for each dollar charged to the card).
- They must either waive the annual fee for the first 12 months or reduce it to a low amount. You should avoid paying the undiscounted fee, commonly close to A$400. If you cannot find one with a zero first-year fee, do not wait. It's okay to pay something. You should not need to pay the full fee, as it is common for companies to offer a reduction in the first year.

Amex cards usually offer significant sign-on bonuses. However, the annual fee is typically high, and many merchants charge a fee to accept American Express. You will have to weigh that up. We recommend sticking with a Mastercard or Visa card. We rarely use Amex, but we make exceptions.

Note that you will only pay the annual fee when you sign up. You should have cut up the card by the time of the yearly review. The only exception would be if you decide to keep the card for use in implementing the *Payment Strategy*, discussed in the next chapter. Discounts usually only apply to the first year. Unless you decide to use this card to implement the *Payment Strategy*, you must cut up the card before the following undiscounted annual fee falls due. You too, Professor!

EXAMPLE
Credit Card Strategy

Two Offers Compared

To assess the value of any point offer, you must know the value of points. Later in this guide, we provide valuations for the points of many airlines. For the following discussion, please accept that Qantas points have a value of 2.5 Australian cents per point (A$0.025). Those already using Qantas points may think the value per point is overstated. But stick with me. Finishing this guide will teach you how to realise that much value.

At the time of writing, some Australian credit card offers included the following. There were many others.

Offer A: One company offered 110,000 Qantas Frequent Flyer Points for an approved application. The offer included an annual fee of $170, payable by the new cardholder upon approval.

After lodging the application, paying the $170 fee, and completing the routine qualifying steps outlined below, this offer would have provided enough points to buy $2,750 of Qantas airfares.

Therefore, this deal provided a net value of $2,580.

Offer B: If the application were approved, the company would credit the applicant with 80,000 Qantas Points, subject to the qualifying spend discussed below. The first-year annual fee was $249.

This deal was worth $1,751.

Why take Offer B versus Offer A? Offer A requires the applicant to demonstrate a higher income than Offer B. Just accept the offer for which you can qualify.

EXAMPLES OF CREDIT CARD OFFERS					
Offer	Points Offered	Value of Points Offered		Card Fee	Net Value of Offer
		Calculation	Value		
A	110,000	110,000 x $0.025	$2,750	$170	$2,580
B	80,000	80,000 x $0.025	$2,000	$249	$1,751

Step 2: Apply

It is easy to apply.

Note that you must demonstrate your income to have your application approved. Most banks require a copy of your two most recent pay slips. The bank will guide you through the necessary documentation if your income is not readily apparent from two payslips. If neither you nor your partner has employment (or another source of income), then we recommend the following options:

- *Option 1:* Get a job.
- *Option 2:* Get a new partner.

According to government income statistics, many readers may have just thrown this book out the window. Income earners, please continue.

The banks are like rabid dogs waiting to feed on your wallet. But if you want a rabid dog to play with you, you must pet it on the head. Play it straight with the bank. Do not exaggerate your income. Ensure the payslips you provide match the income you declare on the application.

For example, you may know you usually earn $500 per fortnight in overtime. You may also have included that amount in your estimate of annual income. If so, make sure both payslips you provide show at least that amount of overtime. Usually, payslips also show a year-to-date amount. Ensure that the year-to-date figure accurately reflects the income you reported on your application.

Credit records are maintained and disseminated differently in each country. However, rejected credit card applications may still appear on your credit report. One rejection is not a big deal, but it's better not to have any rejections. Make sure your applications count. Only apply if you are confident that you meet the criteria. Ensure that all required documentation is included and that your application is complete. Disclose all the relevant financial data accurately.

If you have an existing credit card that you wish to keep, before you lodge your new application, ask your credit card company to reduce the limit on that existing credit card. Your credit exposure will be considered when you apply for a new credit card to get sign-up bonuses. Banks will assess your application based on your credit limit, regardless of the current balance. If you have a card with a $20,000 limit, that card will be assessed as a $20,000 debt even if the current balance is zero.

When applying for a new card, ask for a low limit. You can still spend as much as you like on the card by paying it in advance. For example, if you intend to buy a $15,000 item, but your credit limit is $10,000, pay a large part of the $15,000 off the card before you use it. You will still get the points when the $15,000 purchase is debited to your card. Remember, our objective is to earn points, not to borrow money.

Step 3: Qualify

Following approval and receipt of the card, qualifying for the points is a snack!

Most credit card offers require you to spend a minimum amount on the card, which is easy to satisfy. A typical requirement is to spend about A$6,000 of *eligible expenditures* within three months of card activation. This would mean charging A$2,000 of *eligible expenditures* on the card each month for three months.

Suppose the bank offers 90,000 points for signing up. If you achieve the minimum monthly spending, you can expect to be awarded 30,000 points in each of the first three months.

Never buy anything that you wouldn't have purchased if you did not have the card. The banks want you to rack up some debt you cannot repay. They want you to overspend and never pay off the card. But we intend to get you out as soon as possible after you have earned your points.

Couples typically spend around $1,000 per month on food and other groceries. If you do not, you will likely spend significantly more on eating out. You can also use your card for that. Spending a few hundred dollars monthly on petrol is normal. Tap your card for that, too.

When tapping at most retailers in most countries, there are no merchant fees for Mastercard or Visa cards. However, you can quickly verify this by tapping and immediately checking the charge to your card. Tap for your groceries, grog, transport, and petrol. When you are in the qualifying spend period, don't be scared off by the odds and ends of fees. They are more than covered by the benefits.

If necessary, pay a few utility bills with the card to reach the minimum spend. If your deadline is approaching, pay your utility bills in advance and place them in credit. However, don't pay via BPay, as this typically does not meet the definition of eligible expenditure. Pay by phone, which will probably incur a small fee. You will still receive the points even if paying in advance.

If you pay your council rates (local taxes), water rates, or utility accounts by credit card, you will typically incur a fee of 1.5% to 2%. Avoid this if you can. However, if you need to do this to reach the minimum spend, do it. Consider what you are gaining.

Suppose you tap $4,000 over three months and pay $2,000 in bills. Who cares if you pay a 2% fee on the $2,000? That's only $40. That's a small amount compared to the value of a sign-on incentive.

Note that while the definition of *eligible expenditure* includes most day-to-day spending, it does not involve drawing cash advances from the card or using it for online gambling. Regular users of online gambling need to read a different book!

Step 4: Bank the Points

Don't let the banks get you.

Refer to the example of *Offer A* above. If you do nothing more than get approved and spend $6,000 within three months of that approval, you will earn 110,000 points.

However, if you are not paying attention, you could find yourself paying the usual exorbitant interest rates on unpaid balances. Twenty per cent per annum is not uncommon. However, you only pay interest if you have an outstanding balance beyond a specified date. If you follow this guide, you will never have a balance that attracts interest.

If you pay for something with the card, you should transfer money from your bank account in the same week. First, so you cannot forget. Second, so you do not feel like you suddenly have more money. That's how the bank wants you to feel. Then, you will overcommit and be playing their game.

Paying the card immediately means you will never have an unpaid balance. You will never get charged any interest. You will never feel like someone has given you money, and you won't over-commit.

Do not delay your payment solely because an interest-free period may be available. The banks do not offer you this interest-free period out of the goodness of their cold electronic hearts. They offer it to take the urgency away from making a payment. They are relying on you to delay paying and eventually forget. How else would they earn all those late fees and interest charges upon which their business is based? Pay as you go. Weekly payment is a good habit.

Banks rely on you to miss a payment date. They want to slug you with late fees and excessive interest. If you have not paid the card in full by the due date, it will often be because you were busy that day and forgot. When that is the case, you will, by definition, also fail to make the minimum payment. Remember, 15% of credit card company profits come from fees, most of which are late payment fees.

You do not need a balance to get your bonus points. If the debit has been processed on the card, you will qualify. They don't care if you paid off the card the day you bought that pink latex suit. However, you cannot return the latex suit for credit and still get the bonus. They're onto that one.

Stop using the card as soon as you have made three months of qualifying purchases. Check your frequent flyer statement to ensure all your points have been credited. Then, call the credit card company and cancel the card.

Step 5: Cut Up that Card

Now! Cut up the card! When you see the sign-up bonus points in your frequent flyer account, cut that sucker up. But first, phone the credit card company. You will be transferred to the Customer Retention Department, which will aim to persuade you to keep the card. Before you call, please go into the bathroom, look into the mirror, and practice saying, "*Thank you, but I want to cancel the card.*"

Often, they will try to talk you out of the cancellation. Why? The banks must lend us money for their business to survive. That's their *only* purpose. Credit cards are just another way of lending us money.

Consider what a disaster it would be for the modern world if the banks failed to lend people money. What would happen to the economy if the banks stopped convincing us to borrow money to buy stuff we don't need? The banks would get smaller. The companies that produce unnecessary products would shrink. The rich people who own the means of production would become less wealthy. Bankers would become less wealthy. The rest of us would not need as much money.

The above scenario would ruin productivity and reduce the GDP of many countries. People would spend time at home with family and friends instead of working overtime or impressing their boss by staying late. Then, everyone would pay less tax, and we would be unable to support so many politicians. And what about the companies that operate landfills? What are they supposed to do?

Customer Retention officers play an essential role. However, don't let them win at their job when they speak to you. Say, "*Thank you, but I want to cancel the card.*" When the card has been cancelled, cut it up.

We have gone through this process many times over the past several years. On one occasion, about 10 years ago, I spoke with one particularly persistent yet polite Customer Retention officer. He asked, "Why do you want to cancel the card?" I told him the interest rate was too high. I did not want to say, "*Because I only signed up for the points, and now that I have them, I want to get ready to do it again with a different bank.*"

He responded by cutting the interest rate from an eye-watering percentage to a less unreasonable one. Then I said the annual fee was too high. He waived the fee. Then I said I didn't want to go through this process yearly. He waived the fee for life. We agreed to reduce the limit to a minimal amount so that it would not interfere with any new applications. We still have that card, and it costs us nothing. We carry it as our backup card when travelling. Try your luck.

Consider Repeating Steps 1 to 5

If you decide to repeat steps 1 to 5, consider your future borrowing intentions. As everyone's financial circumstances differ, it is recommended that you seek independent advice from a financial advisor.

The application terms typically state that after 12 months, you can return to the original institution to obtain another card. If you decide on a second card, we recommend considering a different bank, as numerous options are available.

Both you and your partner can apply for a card in the same year. Your partner's card will not affect your credit rating, but if you both apply for a card in the same year, it may affect some future finance applications made as a couple.

Companion cards are a good idea. A companion card will ensure that all eligible expenditures made by both partners will help the applying partner achieve the qualifying spend. It is worth the small fee because a companion card has no additional effect on anyone's credit record. Attaching a companion card to your account will not affect your companion's credit rating. This is because the companion is not responsible for the debt.

However, never lodge credit card applications in joint names. A joint application will affect both people's credit records. It has the same effect as if two partners had applied individually for one card each. This is because, under a joint application, each partner is jointly and severally liable for the total debt.

The application will appear on your credit record, so you should limit this activity to one card per person per year. This is particularly true if you plan to be active in the credit market soon, such as when applying for a housing loan. Discussing your plans with your financial advisor is recommended. They can advise whether applying for a credit card suits your unique circumstances.

One new card per person, combined with the other strategies in this guide, is adequate to get most people flying for free. We recommend that you do no more than that. Completing the process just once will kick-start your point collecting.

If you need a card to implement our *Payment Strategy*, outlined later, killing two birds with one stone would be wise. Try to apply for a card that offers bonus sign-on points *and* points when you use it. Only under those circumstances should you keep the card. You only need one card to execute the Payment Strategy outlined in the next chapter.

We will cover many more point-earning opportunities. However, in just four months, the *Credit Card Strategy* will get you halfway to our minimum objective, which is:

- At least one long international return airfare for you and your partner.
- Plus, many free shorter flights.

This is the first phase to get you on a long international trip without breaking your budget.

> ### CREDIT CARD STRATEGY
>
> Before proceeding, please consult your financial advisor, as everyone's financial circumstances are unique. Subject to advice regarding your financial circumstances, sign up for one credit card with sign-on bonus points, a discounted annual fee for the first year, and a companion card if you have a partner.
>
> You should cancel the card after spending the qualifying amount and checking that the sign-on bonus and points for usage have been received. A possible exception is if you need the card to implement the Payment Strategy. If you already have a credit card, reduce your limit on that existing card to ensure that your overall credit card limit does not increase.
>
> See your financial advisor regarding whether you should repeat the Credit Card Strategy and, if so, how long you should wait between applications.

1.4 PAYMENT STRATEGY

> **Psychologist:** *"What is your favourite memory of travelling with your parents?"*
>
> **Patient:** *"Dad paid."*

Why Read This Chapter?

You learned in the last chapter how to build an impressive number of points in one initial burst of activity. Here, you will learn how to replenish your point balances relentlessly and automatically at zero cost. You only need to change the way you make your existing payments.

By taking the actions in earlier chapters, you will have earned an initial load of points by getting the right credit card approved. Here, you will learn how adopting a suitable payment method for everyday purchases will regularly top up your points balance.

Payment Systems

My mum had her system for paying bills and refused to change it. My sister tried to convince her that there were easier ways. However, she was independent in her late eighties and refused to try a new payment method. She would go to the bank with her trusted passbook, withdraw cash, walk down the street to buy groceries, and then pay her utility bills at the Post Office.

One day, she briskly walked past a police patrol car with her shopping trolley. Knowing Mum, she would have started the following dialogue with a wisecrack to the policeman sitting in the car. He replied, *"I'll arrest you for speeding with that thing if you don't slow down."*

Mum quipped, *"What are you going to give me? Life? Big deal. Two years,"* and continued to the Post Office to pay those bills. No one was going to change her payment method. She was wrong about the two years; as I write, she is 98.

You may have your favourite payment method, but I am about to convince you to change. The reward? More free flights.

Optimal Payment Method

Identify which Mastercard or Visa card you will keep for the long term. This card should enable you to earn points on your daily spending. Use it for all payments that do not attract a transaction fee. The card you use should earn two to three cents worth of points for every dollar charged to it. Refer to our valuation table in the *Valuation Strategy* chapter for the point values of various airlines.

You want points—points, points, and more points. And you do not want to pay a high annual fee. No one will think you are James Bond because you have a *Titanium Alloy* card. Titanium Alloy cards are just plastic that attract whopping annual fees. Even though some advertising may imply that such cards come with a lot of prestige, you will not receive a promotion or make new friends because your debt is associated with a black or platinum-coloured card.

You will rarely be charged a merchant fee for using a Mastercard or Visa card. When you are charged a fee, the value of the points earned will almost always exceed the value of the transaction fees. For ease of management, use a single card for all day-to-day purchases.

Make an exception if you are making a large one-off purchase. In that case, determine the transaction cost. Then, balance that against the value of the points you will earn and decide accordingly.

Most families must spend at least $3,000 monthly on regular bills, including food, transportation, alcohol, petrol, retail, and entertainment. You can tap for all these costs.

From monthly payments of $3,000, you should earn points worth $70 to $100. Most families try hard to keep their expenses that low, but without success. If you do not have children, you probably spend less on groceries and more on eating out and entertainment. Our monthly credit card debits average around $5,000. We earn one point per dollar, which translates to $125 worth of points (5,000 Qantas points at 2.5 cents per point). This is in addition to points provided by retailers, which we discuss under our *Retail Strategy*.

When travelling internationally or booking fares and accommodation with overseas suppliers, the earning rate is more than this.

The key is to channel all ongoing expenditures through the card.

Follow these guidelines to maximise points earned using your payment method. Every time you can pay for something with your Points-Earning Card without being charged a fee, you should.

- Any time there is a tap option, you should tap your Points-Earning Card. This will include groceries and fuel. You will almost always earn points when you tap with your points card and rarely pay fees.
- When making a one-off major purchase, check that the transaction fee is worth less than the points you will collect.
- Ignore the transaction fees as you strive to meet the minimum spend associated with the credit card sign-up bonuses covered elsewhere.
- Some routine bills, such as strata fees and municipal rates, may only allow you to use your card if you pay a fee. Therefore, consider using an alternative payment option that does not incur a fee.
- Amex is more often associated with fees for use. If you have an American Express card, that can be beneficial for reasons covered elsewhere. However, you will also need a Visa or a Mastercard. Treat the Amex as an extra card for occasional use rather than your main Points-Earning Card.
- You should also tap your card when travelling internationally in many locations. International spending attracts extra points with most cards. When you tap your card, you will likely receive a favourable foreign exchange rate in most Western countries. However, this does not always apply in third-world countries.

You will earn points from the *Payment Strategy* concurrently with the points under our *Retail Strategy*, discussed in the next chapter.

Check the terms of your Points-Earning Card. We expect that, in first-world countries, it will cost you significantly less than ATM conversion rates or the use of over-the-counter foreign exchange dealers. The easiest way to check is to make a small purchase and check the effect on your card.

FX rates and fees are too extensive to cover here, but they are covered in another of our guides.

EXAMPLE
Payment Strategy
Be Awarded Free Points for Credit Card Use

While our focus is Qantas points, Virgin Australia points are handy for domestic travel. Our Virgin Points usually allow us to fly around our country for free, enabling us to save Qantas Points for international travel. We get most of our Virgin Australia points through retail activities, which we will outline later. However, we collect some occasionally when we spot a bargain, such as a new credit card offer. After Qantas, Virgin Australia points are the second most frequently offered for new credit card approvals in Australia.

In the Australian context, you should earn at least one Qantas point or a Virgin Australia point for most dollars charged to your card. You should earn more points per dollar when buying from certain specific retailers. You usually earn less per dollar spent when paying utility bills. However, regardless of the earning rate, these free points accumulate.

In the Australian example, we value Virgin Australia Velocity Points at $0.020 and Qantas Frequent Flyer Points at $0.025 per point. Earn one Point per dollar spent for a benefit worth 2.0% to 2.5% of your purchased item.

Please note that when using our point valuation table, you should convert the Australian dollar (A$) to your local currency. Then, compare your country's credit card transaction fees to the value of the points you will earn when making your decisions.

Household Budgeting

Using a single card account for almost all your day-to-day transactions may not immediately appeal to some people who already diligently follow a budgeting system at home. However, it can help you maintain control over your household expenses. We will provide a summary here of how the *Payment Strategy* aligns with our household budgeting method.

Our method involves putting almost all expenditures on one point-earning card. I use the main card, and Lynda has a companion card. Groceries, petrol, grog, clothes, travel costs, eating out—you name it—go on the card. If we buy anything from a store or online, we almost always charge it to the card.

The exceptions are:

- If the credit card is a card that attracts high fees. In our environment, that generally only applies to utility and council bills, which we automatically debit to a bank account.
- A rare transaction where a credit card will not be accepted.

Periodically, but at least once a month, I allocate transactions to spreadsheet columns that align with our bank accounts. We maintain separate bank accounts for each expenditure type, including groceries, entertainment, travel, and other expenses. This provides an easy reference for comparing our progress with our long-term budget and identifying areas where adjustments are needed.

This book is not about budgeting; many valid ways to manage your finances exist. However, my point is that if you don't want everything in one bucket, it's easy to maintain separate accounts, even though you may initially charge everything to one card as a first step. Then, break it down on a spreadsheet and make payments to the card from each account.

FREE FLIGHTS: EARNING POINTS & MILES

> **PAYMENT STRATEGY**
> Pay for almost everything using a credit card that attracts points. Avoid excessive transaction fees on large one-off purchases. Your partner should use a companion card.

1.5 RETAIL STRATEGY

> *I am also just a girl, standing in front of a boy, asking him to love [shopping].*
>
> ANNA SCOTT, NOTTING HILL (1999 FILM)

Why Read This Chapter?

You will learn an additional method of regularly earning points. Specifically, you will learn how to maximise the points your retail suppliers award you. These points from retailers will be in addition to the points you earn from your payment method.

Earn Points from Retail Partners

The objective is to earn points from the suppliers you already use.

You can earn points from the credit card company and the supplier for a single transaction. Double dipping is standard.

To be clear, you should aim to get points from the bank when you pay for something using your card. Additionally, you should determine how you can earn points from the retailer for the same transaction.

Whenever approaching any transaction, you should ask yourself two questions:

- What payment method will I use to maximise points from the bank?
- How should I complete this purchase so the supplier will also award me points?

But don't stand in a payment queue in a store and embarrass yourself by asking these questions out loud. Instead, ask yourself these questions (in your head) as soon as you need to buy fuel, groceries, or any other retail item. Questioning how you will get points from the supplier at the next transaction will become second nature.

Set Yourself Up

At many retailers, you must show your loyalty program membership card to earn points. Australians, for example, often show their Qantas Frequent Flyer card, Virgin Australia Velocity card, FlyBuys card, or Woolworths Rewards card.

If you carry old-school plastic membership cards, you may not have one on you when you need it. We ensure we have downloaded the relevant apps and cards onto our phones and accumulate them in our phone wallet or a dedicated folder.

This sort of activity may seem a bit geeky. That's because it is. But, hey, you're the one who bought a book about how to get free stuff! Good on you!

You don't need to be bashful when dealing with the store staff. They are all over this stuff. They will see your 7-Eleven app coming from 20 paces. If FlyBuys are their thing, they'll usually ask before you pay. I think we get some respect from the people at the checkout. They see people refusing to scan and wonder why. It's like getting respect from a fellow Train Spotter when you turn up in a new anorak.

Don't wait until you're at the point of payment to consider this. Ensure the app is downloaded and set up before you leave home. If you already have the app, ensure you have located it on your phone and identified the barcode you need to scan. If you do not do this in advance, the pressure of having people waiting in line behind you may encourage you to skip the process. Be ready.

Loyalty program websites list their retail partners. Focus on the loyalty program websites for your Primary and Secondary Airlines.

We suggest creating a Partners Register as you review your Primary and Secondary airlines' websites. That Register will include all the partners through which you can earn points. It will show the number of points you will earn (e.g., three points per dollar spent or one point per litre of fuel purchased) and the preparatory steps you need to take.

Retailers often require a single step to activate point earnings on all future purchases. Most commonly, this will involve joining the retail store as a member and then scanning a barcode at the checkout.

Enter Via the Airline Site

For some suppliers, you can only earn points by making purchases online. To do so, log in to your airline website and click through to the retailer's site.

Many airlines have this feature. First, log in through your airline loyalty program website using your membership number. Click on the relevant retailer icon to be directed to the retailer's website. From that point, everything works as if your loyalty program were not involved, except that you will start earning points on your purchases.

Many airline loyalty programs have capitalised on the long-term trend toward online shopping. Next time you make a purchase, log in through your airline loyalty program, buy it online, and earn some extra points.

EXAMPLE
Retail Strategy
Earn Additional Points by Using Online Shopping

For example, you will earn additional points if you log in to your Qantas Frequent Flyer account and then click through to designated retailers that have an agreement with the airline. For an up-to-date list of retailers, go to the Qantas website.

Qantas Shopping supports various stores, each offering a different number of Qantas points per dollar spent. Note that we are not talking about a small number of retailers. Qantas's online shopping partners include 101 fashion retailers, 17 sports and sportswear retailers, 23 household goods retailers, and seven car hire and transport providers.

You can view the list on the Qantas website, but creating your own Register works better. We have provided an *Example Partners Register* in the "Free Stuff" section. There, you will also find a generic Excel template for a *Partners Register*, which you can adapt to suit the loyalty programs of any airline. We suggest you prepare one for your Primary and Secondary Airlines.

The average earning rate from online retailers is 3.5 Qantas Points per dollar spent. We add one more point by paying with our points card, earning 4.5 Qantas points per dollar spent. Qantas points are worth 2.5 cents each. We earn 11.25 cents worth of points for every dollar spent with selected retailers online. That's the equivalent of a substantial discount. But those discounts accumulate in our points accounts and pay for free flights.

Travel Expenses

Accommodation

Airbnb has allied itself with many airlines. Typically, you must log in to the airline loyalty program first and then click through to the Airbnb site. If your airline is part of such an alliance, you will earn points on your bookings.

Many hotels offer points in their hotel loyalty program. If you often stay with your favourite hotel brand, stick with the hotel points. If not, check whether you can earn airline points by providing your airline loyalty program number.

Some hotels must be booked directly through the airline's website to qualify for airline loyalty program points. If booking this way will result in the same price as the best deal you've found, then why not book through the airline site?

Another guide in this series values hotel chain points and compares them to the values of frequent flyer points. It is too much to handle here. For now, establish whether you can earn points from someone whenever you book accommodation.

Car Hire

Check the websites of your Primary and Secondary Airlines for information about their alliances with car rental companies. For example, Qantas has partnerships with Avis and Budget.

Ride Sharing

Check with your Primary and Secondary Airlines and your favourite ride-share websites to see if your airlines are partners with ride-share companies, such as Uber. We had to register with Qantas to receive points from Uber. Since then, it has been on autopilot, and we receive points from qualifying rides.

Household Expenditure

Fuel

Whether you call them service stations, gas stations, or garages, they commonly offer points for fuel purchases.

Of course, always buy your fuel from the cheapest source. Do not change your buying pattern to suit point accumulation. However, ensure you are organised so you receive points from someone every time you fill up. Again, you will pay with your points card, but we seek additional points from the vendor.

Usually, fuel purchases attract some points per litre or gallon of fuel purchased. You may also earn points for each dollar spent on overpriced groceries at the convenience store. We rarely buy groceries at gas station convenience stores because of their premium prices. However, most of us pick up the odd item. You may have a coffee habit when you stop for fuel. You may as well get points on all of it. So long as you scan your membership barcode at the checkout, the rest is automatic.

Many merchants have a simple system to ensure they only give points to those who value them. Some require you to download their app and sign up for their propaganda emails. Subscribe to the emails. Many suppliers send you emails with buttons to click, offering extra points for your next purchase. Accepting these emails runs against the common desire to reduce inbox traffic. However, opening them and clicking where indicated will earn you extra points.

Importantly, continue to purchase your fuel from the most cost-effective source. Ensure you are set up to earn points from someone, regardless of where you buy fuel.

Groceries and Liquor

Earning points on grocery purchases is essential, as we spend a significant amount at the supermarket. Also, check the websites of your favourite grog shops.

Energy

Check the websites of your electricity and gas companies.

Of course, you need to buy your energy at the best price. However, check online to see if your electricity supplier offers airline loyalty points. Often, they require you to complete a simple online linking step to start earning points on existing expenditures.

This is not about changing electricity suppliers to get points. It's about ensuring you receive the points on bills you already pay. Often, all that is required is some one-off administration.

Streaming Services

Some streaming services, which you may already be paying for, offer points. You must register to receive them.

EXAMPLE
Retail Strategies

Earn Points from Fuel Suppliers

The set-ups for each fuel supplier in each country will differ. However, an Australian example will give you an idea of what you must do to earn points from fuel purchases.

- BP is allied with Qantas Frequent Flyer. You must go to the BP website and register for BP Rewards to earn points. After that, when buying fuel, you must scan the Qantas Frequent Flyer barcode from your card or app on a special scanner at every BP checkout desk.

- When you register with BP, you must provide your email

address. BP will send you marketing emails. Do not ignore or delete these emails without opening them. You usually get to click a button that provides various point bonuses. I recently earned triple points for the subsequent three fills. You may also earn five times points on your next tank. I am referring here to a tank of petrol. You don't have to buy a tank with tracks and a cannon. That would be just silly.

- 7-Eleven is a partner of Virgin Australia Velocity. Download the 7-Eleven app and enter your Virgin Australia Velocity member number. The app also offers a valuable feature called Price-Lock. It locks in the lowest price of any 7-Eleven outlet within a defined geographic area. When you pay for fuel, show the attendant the barcode on your app. You will automatically get the lower price. Importantly, you will also get Virgin Australia Velocity Points.

- Ampol provide Woolworths Rewards points. Download the Woolworths Rewards app. Scan the Woolworths Rewards barcode from the app when you make a payment. You can set up your Woolworths Rewards program to ensure that Woolworths Rewards are automatically converted to Qantas Points.

Earn Points from Grocery Suppliers

In Australia, Woolworths is one of the biggest grocery retailers. Its loyalty program is Woolworths Rewards.

Australian grocery shoppers can join Woolworths Rewards online. The Rewards provided by Woolworths can be converted to Qantas Frequent Flyer points. You must go to the Woolworths website to set up the automatic conversion of Woolworths Rewards to Qantas Points.

In any country, the systems will be similar but with different suppliers.

- Join all the grocery chain loyalty programs in your geographic area.
- Put the necessary membership details on your phone.
- Develop the habit of scanning when you pay at any major grocery store.

Grocery retail chains often have special deals so that you can get even more points. For example, in the case of Woolworths, the company offers a program called Everyday Extra. Subject to a small monthly subscription, you may nominate one shop per month and get 10% off that shop. It is easy to come out in front. But importantly, you will also earn double points on all purchases. And if Woolworths offers a special of 10 times the standard number of points for a limited period or on certain items, then members of Everyday Extra will get 20 times the usual number.

Earn Points from Energy Suppliers

For example, Energy Australia will provide Virgin Australia Velocity Points. However, you must log in to your Energy Australia account and link it to your Virgin Loyalty Club (Velocity) account.

Red Energy offers Qantas Frequent Flyer Points.

Earn Points from Streaming Services Suppliers

Binge and Kayo's streaming services offer Qantas Frequent Flyer Points in Australia. To gain points from our Binge subscription, we had to log in to our Binge account and follow a linking process. To earn points from our Kayo subscription, we first needed to log in to our Qantas Frequent Flyer account and click through to the Kayo website.

You may miss such free points if you fail to complete a Partner Register.

Third-Party Loyalty Programs

Most airlines and retailers design and operate their loyalty programs. To achieve this, they must establish a purpose-built, complex organisation. Some prefer to outsource the entire activity.

In response, a small number of businesses offer outsourced services. Here, we refer to these as *Third-Party Loyalty Programs*. Retailers can purchase points from a third party and offer them to their customers. The third party takes care of all the administration associated with the program.

Third-party loyalty program organisations differ from country to country. End customers typically have several options for redeeming third-party points. One standard option is to swap the third-party points for those of an airline loyalty program.

Retail loyalty programs usually allow you to accumulate points indefinitely, so long as your account is active. One transaction every year or two is usually enough.

Consider opening one account per household, all held in one person's name, and attaching extra cards to that account. That way, you are more likely to keep the account active, as more people will work on it. If you have adult children, siblings, or parents not interested in collecting points, consider giving them a card linked to your account and training them to use it. Note that these are not payment cards. They simply ensure that purchases attract points, no matter how the purchases are paid for. The points will be credited to the account holder of the third party loyalty card.

EXAMPLE
Retail Strategies

Use Third-Party Loyalty Programs to Earn Points

In Australia, the FlyBuys organisation is the most extensive Third-Party loyalty program.

Retailers like Coles supermarkets and Bunnings hardware stores have opted into the FlyBuys program. Each dollar you spend at a participating retailer earns you two FlyBuys points.

The customers then have two options.

Option 1: Convert the FlyBuys points to a direct cash discount at the checkout. Coles allows the conversion of 2,000 FlyBuys points to a $10 discount, which provides a $0.005 value per FlyBuys point.

Option 2: Convert 2,000 FlyBuys points to 1,000 Virgin Australia Velocity Points. Velocity Points are worth $0.020 each. This provides a higher value of $0.010 per FlyBuys point.

Customers should add the electronic FlyBuys card to their phone wallet and remember to scan the FlyBuys barcode at the checkout. The retailer's checkout staff will remind the shopper, and if the shopper uses self-service, the retailer's robot will remind them.

Review Marketing Emails from Selected Suppliers

Australian retailers, including Shell, Bunnings, Liquorland, Kmart, Target, and Coles, frequently send email offers to FlyBuys members. These offers are released randomly but are common around major holidays, such as Black Friday and Christmas.

A typical offer will be something like the one that came out the week I wrote this section. Coles suggested spending $50 weekly for the next four weeks and collecting *10,000 Bonus Points*. In this example, 10,000 bonus points, plus the usual 400 points for spending $200, equals 10,200 Fly Buy Points. These can be traded for 5,200 Velocity Points valued at $102 (5,200 x $0.020). Spending $200 on necessary groceries for a $102 benefit is excellent!

I only became aware of this offer because I allowed the Fly Buys organisation to continue sending me marketing emails. If I unsubscribed, I would not be made aware of such opportunities.

Black Friday Offer

Here is another great example! While compiling some base data, I referenced my FlyBuys app for verification. While I looked at it, a Black Friday offer came through: *buy anything over the next five days and earn 30 times the usual FlyBuys points.*

Instead of getting the expected 500 FlyBuys points (one per dollar spent), a routine $500 shop would earn 15,000 points. These can be converted to 7,500 Virgin Australia points worth $150 (7,500 x $0.02). A $150 reward for $500 spent on essential groceries is the equivalent of a 30% discount.

> **RETAIL STRATEGY**
>
> Consult the websites for your Primary and Secondary airlines and compile a Retail Partners Register. Take note of the organisations you do business with that can provide you with points. Activate a link, download an app, or click through your loyalty accounts to earn points from retailers. Before making a purchase, determine if there is a way to arrange for the retailer to provide you with points and be prepared with the relevant app or card.

2

Free Flights: Managing Points & Miles

NOW YOU KNOW HOW TO accumulate many points.

You can increase the number of free flights in three ways:

1. *Earning Points:* Increase the number of points you earn.
2. *Managing Points:* Ensure you have received the points you deserve and avoid letting them expire.
3. *Maximising Point Values:* Understand the value of your points so you can redeem them at their full value.

The second and third ways are often underestimated.

In this section, we will outline how you should manage your points:

- *Checking Strategy*: Ensure your systems and setups for earning points are working correctly, and you receive all the points you deserve.
- *Expiry Strategy*: Ensure you have processes to prevent your points from expiring before you use them, such as our *Points Transfer Strategy*.

2.1 CHECKING STRATEGY

> **Flight Attendant:** *"Would you like some dinner, madam?"*
> **Passenger:** *"What choices do I have?"*
> **Flight Attendant:** *"'Yes' or 'No.'"*

Why Read This Chapter?

You will learn how to ensure that earned points get credited to your accounts.

Keep It Simple

Checking every transaction is not the best use of your time. Some point-earning activities should be checked, while others can be treated as *set-and-forget*.

After reading this guide, you may experience a rush of blood to the head. You may think you will become a points god and a status credit machine. You may think you'll check your rewards diligently and be as keen and efficient as a tax auditor. But you won't keep it up. Therefore, let the occasional point go. Let them go!

A couple of point-gods just said some unrepeatable things. However, it is better to be diligent with a few essential checks. Don't aim to be a detail hound. After the first month of enthusiasm, you will lose interest as the administration becomes unsustainable. Checking every transaction would be like being a proofreader of the first draft of the Old Testament, a task of biblical proportions.

It is better to diligently check a few critical things on an ongoing basis than to inspect everything thoroughly for the first month, lose interest after a short time, and then neglect to check anything.

You will earn many points from:

- Bonuses for signing up for new credit cards
- Ongoing credit card use

- Retailers
- Flying

You will earn points more often than you will complete transactions. For example, buying petrol from a service station is *one* financial transaction but *two* point earning transactions. You will earn points from the oil company, plus you will earn points from your credit card company. After you have set everything up, you can easily earn points over 100 times per month.

Check Credit Card Earnings

Over the long term, credit cards will provide your most reliable source of points. Carefully check you have received the following:

- Your sign-on bonuses
- Monthly credits

Don't double-check that the points are credited for each daily credit card transaction. Instead, ensure the process is working and that you receive a lump sum of points from the credit card company monthly.

Then, periodically check your points account to see if anything stands out as an obvious problem.

Check Initial Set-ups

If you have linked your favourite retailer to your loyalty scheme, check what happens the first time you buy something at that retailer. If you receive the expected points on that first transaction, consider it a success and disregard checking that retailer again.

For example, you may set up an app for an oil company. Verify that the oil company has credited your points account after one fuel transaction.

Check One-off Transactions

Check one-offs such as your points for purchasing the $2,000 gold-threaded mohair hat with matching UGG boots. But don't bother checking the small transactions.

Check Primary Airline Transactions

Check the points earned from flying with your Primary Airline. Examine the website and determine how they calculated the number of credited points. It will be an excellent learning experience. That knowledge will enable you to make informed decisions. However, consistent with the *Simplicity Strategy* (covered later), only do that for Primary and Secondary airlines.

Many boarding passes are still in paper form. Take a photograph of those boarding passes before you arrive at your destination. It would be best if you did this because:

- As soon as you are off the plane, boarding passes seem irrelevant, and it is easy to lose them.
- The print fades very quickly.
- When claiming points the airline system has missed, some airlines may ask you to supply an image of your boarding pass. Some old-school systems require copies of the pass to be loaded onto their system.
- Many airlines will direct you to enter data on their system and provide you with immediate credit. However, sometimes, the data you must enter includes the seat number. You may need a copy of your boarding pass for that purpose.

If you are new to diligently collecting points, you may say, *"If only I had known about this a few months ago, before I took that flight."* Don't worry. You may be able to recover the lost points. Most airlines allow you to make a retrospective claim for flights. Usually, claims are restricted to flights taken up to six months before you join their loyalty program.

You may have some of your old boarding passes. Possibly, you received them electronically. They may be buried in old emails or elsewhere on your phone.

Create a habit of checking all the boarding passes against your frequent flyer accounts within a month of getting home. If any have not been credited, lodge a claim online.

For longer trips, check them in the order you took the flights to ensure you do not miss any. All our flight confirmations are stored in TripIt. We suggest visiting the App Store, downloading the free TripIt app, and following their directions to store all your confirmations. Most travel organisations conform to a file protocol. You usually only need to forward your flight and accommodation email confirmations to a specified email address. The Tripit system will identify the information came from your registered email address, examine the dates, and load the details into the correct trip in your app.

CHECKING STRATEGY

- *Check your loyalty program accounts.*
- *Check credit card sign-on bonuses.*
- *Check that you are getting monthly credits from the credit card supplier.*
- *Ensure your points have been credited by checking any new or changed set-ups with retailers.*
- *Check that points have been credited from large retail transactions.*
- *Keep your boarding passes and mark them off against your points accounts.*

2.2 EXPIRY STRATEGIES

I travel not to go anywhere but to go. I travel for travel's sake.

ROBERT LOUIS STEVENSON

Why Read This Chapter?

Until this point in our guide, we have been focused on earning points. However, points are not always durable. You must learn how to extend the life of the points you earn. Here, you will learn to store points over the long term and avoid losing them due to non-compliance with loyalty program expiry policies.

Types of Expiry Policies

You should ensure that you have a plan for maintaining your points. The plan will depend on the policies of your selected airlines. Expiry policies fall into three groups. They are:

1. *Activity-Based:* Points expire after a period of account inactivity. So long as you can generate a tiny amount of activity within a defined period, the points can last forever.
2. *Issue-Based:* Points expire a set period after the date they were earned. This is very restrictive and is the worst kind of expiry policy. There is nothing you can do to delay expiry under such a policy. You must use the points within the specified period or forfeit them permanently.
3. *No expiry*: Some airlines never allow the points to expire.

Activity-Based Expiry Policies

Approximately 40% of programs have a policy that allows points to expire a specified number of months after the last activity on the account. We refer to this type of policy as *Activity-Based*. Proper monitoring and management allow these programs to retain points indefinitely. You only need to earn a single point to restart the expiry period for all points on the account.

Generating Activity

For accounts with an Activity-Based expiry policy, you will need plans to keep the accounts active.

Transactions with retail partners in your home country can create activity on a loyalty program account, restarting the expiry period for all points on that account. You must identify a program partner and purchase something from them. For a program that requires annual activity, this could be as simple as using one supplier for groceries once a year or making a single fuel purchase that year.

Alternatively, you could use some points. That also counts as activity.

Many loyalty schemes have an online store. You only need to use points to buy a single item from that store. That will register as an activity, and the expiry clock will reset.

Keeping your Primary and Secondary Airline accounts active is usually straightforward. But it can be harder to keep Tertiary Airline accounts active if they operate in a part of the world that you do not frequent. You may do a one-off flight with Tibetan Yak Herders Airways. You may not use that airline again for a long time, and your local grocery store probably does not support Tibetan Yak Herders Airways. Those points may expire due to inactivity.

You must maintain your loyalty program accounts differently for airlines not based in your home country.

Buying Points

Many airlines allow you to purchase points. Although there are exceptions, this is rarely a good deal at standard prices. But you do not always need a good deal. Buy the minimum quantity allowed, and your account will reflect the activity. The expiration clock will reset for all points in that program. Refer to a later chapter on *Purchasing Strategy*.

Issue-Based Expiry Policies

A further 40% of loyalty programs have policies that allow points to expire a specified number of months after they were earned. This is not an excellent policy from a member's point of view because there is nothing you can do to stall the expiry of these points. If not used, points regularly drop off the account as they reach their age limits. We have named this type of expiry policy *Issue-Based*.

Note, however, that about 80% of Issue-Based expiry policies allow you 36 months to use points from the date the points have been earned. The airlines will allow you to book within the expiry period, but most also permit you to book well ahead. During the month preceding the expiry date, some airlines will enable you to book a flight up to 11 months in advance, extending the life of the points by up to 10 months. However, we don't like programs with Issue-Based policies as much as those with Activity-Based policies. With some management, points with Activity-Based loyalty programs can last forever.

Expiry dates suck! I'm glad those hundred-dollar notes my uncle hid in that gigantic chemistry set in his van did not have an expiry date. However, you can generally make loyalty programs with longer expiration dates, such as 36 months, work in your favour. We need a compelling deal before we favour airlines associated with an Issue-Based expiry policy, particularly if the policy requires using the points before 36 months from the issue date.

TRAVEL STORY
Expiry Strategy
Add to the Expiry Time of Your Points

Singapore is well-located as a stop for Australians on their way to Europe. We often use the *Stop-Over Strategy* there, which is covered later.

The newly developed area includes the Ce La Vi Bar at the top of the Marina Bay Sands Hotel. The electronic Gardens by the Sea is an essential sight for every visitor. It's also lovely to wander around the English Colonial heritage sites such as the old cricket ground, the Raffles Hotel, and the Peranakan Terrace Houses. As a WWII history enthusiast, I enjoyed visiting the Changi Prison Camp Chapel, memorial, and museum. And then there is the food. The Hawker markets are so unique that they have been added to the new UNESCO Intangible Cultural Heritage list.

Occasionally, we find ourselves on a flight operated by Singapore Airlines, one of the best airlines in the world.

Under the Kris Flyer program, unused Singapore Airlines points expire 36 months from the date they are earned. There is nothing you can do to stall the expiry. Use them or lose them.

We noticed that our Kris Flyer (Singapore) points would expire in three months. However, we had no plans to fly in the area until the following year. We booked before the last day of the 36 months. Singapore Airlines releases its flight schedules 11 months in advance. Therefore, in month 35, we booked a flight for departure in month 42, measured from the issue date. In this way, if you have points in an Issue-Based program with a 36-month expiry policy, you may be able to use them for flights up to 45 months from the issue date. However, check the expiry terms for your airlines, as all programs have different terms.

No Expiry Policies

The best expiry policy is no expiry. These policies state that all points will never expire. Less than 20% of programs have this policy.

The rationale for selecting a small group of Tertiary Airlines is that you will have fewer programs to manage. However, programs with *No Expiry* policies require no management. The points will sit in your account even as the nurse changes your diaper.

EXAMPLE
United Mileage Plus

Favour Airlines That Do Not Allow Their Points to Expire

For example, you can use your United MileagePlus points with United or one of its partners anytime. They will never expire, so the program account requires no management.

FREE FLIGHTS: MANAGING POINTS & MILES

Expiry Policies

Airline	Program	Expiry Policy Type	Months
Air Canada	Aeroplan	activity	18
Air China	Phoenix Miles	issue	36
Air Europa	Suma	activity	18
Air France	Flying Blue	activity	24
Air India	Flying	issue	36
Air New Zealand	Airpoints	issue	48
Alaska Airlines	Mileage Plan	activity	24
All Nippon Airways	Mileage Club	issue	36
American Airlines	AAdvantage	activity	18
Austrian Airways	Miles and More	no expiry	-
Bahamas Air	Air Miles	activity	24
Bangkok Airways	Flyer Bonus	issue	36
British Airways	Executive Club	activity	36
Cathay Pacific	Marco Polo Club	activity	18
China Eastern Air.	Eastern Miles	activity	18
China Southern	SkyPearl	issue	36
Delta Airlines	Skymiles	no expiry	-
Emirates	Skywards	issue	36
Etihad Airways	Guest	issue	18
Garuda International	Garuda Miles	activity	12
Hawaiian Airlines	Aloha	no expiry	-
ITA Airways	Miles and More	no expiry	-
Japan Airlines	Mileage Bank	issue	36
Korean Airways	Skypass Club	no expiry	-
KLM	Flying Blue	activity	24
Lufthansa	Miles and More	no expiry	-
Malaysian Airlines	Enrich	issue	36
Qantas	Frequent Flyer	activity	18
Qatar Airlines	Privilege Club	activity	36
Royal Brunei	Royal Skies	issue	36
Singapore Airlines	Krisflyer	issue	36
Southwest Airlines	Rapid Rewards	no expiry	-
Swiss Airlines	Miles and More	no expiry	-

Thai Airways	Royal Orchid	issue	36
Turkish Airways	Miles and Smiles	issue	36
United Airlines	Mileage Plus	no expiry	-
Vietnam Airlines	Lotus Miles	issue	36
Virgin Australia	Velocity	activity	24

If you and your partner have memberships with the same program and need to avoid expiry by showing some account activity, try transferring points from one account to another.

A few airlines allow points to be transferred between programs. For example, Singapore Airlines KrisFlyer will transfer miles to Virgin Australia points. If your points are about to expire, check if you can transfer them to an associated airline, which will restart the expiry time clock.

Management Tools

Tools are available to help you keep track of your points and alert you to pending expirations.

We recommend using the free version of TripIt to store your booking information. However, if you travel frequently, we recommend the paid version, TripIt Pro. It offers many additional features compared to the free version, including the ability to load more PDFs of your travel documents.

TripIt Pro includes a handy feature that tracks your points balances, records your membership numbers, and alerts you to points when an expiry date is approaching.

Points Transfer Strategy

Many store loyalty card systems will allow you to set up an automatic transfer from your store loyalty account to your airline loyalty account.

When available, automatic transfers to your Primary or Secondary Airline are the way to go if their expiry policy is <u>Activity-Based</u>. You will eventually transfer these points, so you have nothing to lose by setting up the auto-transfer. The benefit of doing so is that your airline loyalty program account will register activity frequently. You will never have to worry about your frequent flyer points expiring.

If you can accumulate points with a non-airline program (e.g., a store you often use) or a credit card program (e.g., Amex Rewards) and if those points do not expire, you could accumulate points there. Then, you could direct them to airline loyalty programs when needed. This requires memory and management, however.

If your Primary or Secondary Airline has an Activity-Based expiry policy, we recommend automatic transfers in most circumstances. Set up non-airline loyalty cards to convert loyalty points to frequent flyer points.

On the other hand, if the airline loyalty program has an Issue-Based expiry policy, it may be better to accumulate the points in your retailer's reward program and only transfer them to the airline program when you are ready to use them.

POINT TRANSFERS STRATEGY

If your airline loyalty program has an Activity-Based expiry policy, automate the conversion of retailer rewards to frequent flyer points. If the loyalty program is Issue-Based, consider accumulating points in your retailer's program or credit card program. Transfer them only when required for a specific flight booking.

EXAMPLE

Points Transfer Strategy

Use Automatic Transfers to Create Activity for Airlines with Activity-Based Expiry Policies

Both Qantas and Virgin Australia have Activity-Based expiry policies. Those airlines are our Primary and Secondary Airlines, respectively.

In Australia, you can automatically set up your Woolworths Rewards loyalty account to transfer Woolworths Rewards to your Qantas Frequent Flyer account. This transfer will occur every time you accumulate 2,000 Woolworth Rewards.

You can do something similar with the third-party loyalty program, Fly-Buys. The system can ensure automatic transfers to the Virgin Australia Velocity program.

If Australians have nominated Qantas and Virgin Australia as their Primary and Secondary Airlines, they should enable these auto-transfer features.

American Express

Use Manual Transfers to Add to the Life of Points for Airlines with Issue-Based Expiry Policies

When you use an American Express card, you can earn Amex Rewards points. These points can be transferred to the loyalty programs for many airlines, including Air Canada (A), Delta, British Airways (I), Qatar (A), Etihad (I), Qantas (A), Singapore (I), Air France (A), KLM (A), and Cathay Pacific (A).

The airlines marked with the letter (A) have an expiry policy that relies on account activity. A transfer from Amex can provide that activity and reset the expiry clock.

On the other hand, the airlines marked with the letter (I) have an Issue-Based expiry policy. If the Amex Rewards points are to be converted to an airline with an Issue-Based Expiry Policy, it would be better to hold the points indefinitely in the card account as Amex Rewards points. You can extend the life of the points by delaying the transfer to the airline loyalty program until you are ready to redeem them for a flight.

EXPIRY STRATEGY

If two deals are very similar, opt for an airline with a loyalty program that has a No-Expiry policy. If you use an airline with a loyalty program that has an Activity-Based expiration policy, determine how you intend to keep your account active. Deprioritise any airline with an Issue-Based expiry policy, particularly one that requires using points less than 36 months from their earned date.

3

FINDING THE BEST VALUE CASH FLIGHTS

WE LOVE TO USE POINTS and fly for free, but our points are not unlimited. We only want to use them when we can get good value. We prefer to pay cash if the flights are cheaper than the Target Redemption Value of our points. This will become clearer when we discuss our *Redemption Strategy* in the next part.

This section of the guide will help you spend as little as possible when purchasing flights with cash.

Sometimes, you will intuitively know some answers without working through each step in this part. For example, you may identify a very cheap flight, so it may not be worth spending your valuable time on further research. However, we will assume that your travel costs are high and that you are willing to use all strategies to reduce the cost.

This section will outline:

- *Search Strategy*—find the best value flights.
- *Budget Airline Strategy*—use budget airlines to reduce costs.
- *Return Strategy*—use return fares to reduce costs.
- *Cheapest Day Strategy*—identify which days of the week are the cheapest to fly.
- *Cheapest Time Strategy*—change your flight time to reduce cost.
- *Booking Strategy*—book at the optimal time using the most effective method.

3.1 SEARCH STRATEGY

If we knew what we were doing, it wouldn't be research.

Why Read This Chapter?

You will learn the role of search engines in widening your options when buying flights for cash or points. The wider your options, the better your chances of nailing a bargain.

Research Tools

I don't know about you, but sometimes my mind is like a web browser. Nine tabs are open, three are frozen, and I have no idea where the voices are coming from.

Thankfully, some great websites work more consistently than my brain. As a first step, we recommend using three or four search engines or online booking sites to find flights.

Online booking sites charge airlines a commission for bookings made through their websites. Their primary purpose is to sell you a flight. Important booking sites include Expedia and Booking.com.

Search engines may not generate revenue directly from airlines. They provide information on deals that are available through online booking sites. The search engines then charge the online booking sites for each lead they send when you click through. Google Flights, Kayak, Momondo, and Skyscanner are examples.

We recommend starting with Expedia or Google Flights, as these sites are generally user-friendly. They offer great tools to get your search into first gear. These and similar sites only require entering the start and finish destinations, as well as the travel date.

Use the Expedia filter to order flights by price, starting with the cheapest. Then, reset the filter to order flights by the shortest duration. This sets some reasonable initial boundaries within which to work.

Then try Google Flights, which will alert you to good-value flights on alternate routes. A great feature of Google Flights is the ability to enter up to five departure points and up to five arrival points.

Kayak's Explore feature can be found by scrolling down the home page. After you click on the globe, you can enter your departure airport. A map will then be displayed, and you will see the costs of the cheapest flights available for each surrounding destination. Consider the more affordable options that come up. Taking a budget flight to a nearby city and transferring by bus may be more cost-effective (refer to the *Transport Strategy*).

Each online booking agency has signed agreements with various airlines. No search engine covers all the airlines. The search engine will direct you to some great flights but may be biased by the commissions it earns. Each search engine displays the results differently and highlights various aspects. Pricing will vary between sites.

After experimenting with search engines and online booking sites, you will soon settle on the ones you like to use. Like you, our time is valuable, so we rarely look at more than two or three.

TRAVEL STORY
Search Strategy

Use Google Flights to Quickly Explore Multiple Options

One summer, we visited our son in the UK, as we often do, and toured the Scottish Highlands. The beauty of the many ruined castles on the edge of lochs is a wonder. The scenery around Glencoe is gorgeous.

The Isle of Skye has its unique charm, offering the most spectacular scenery we saw on that trip.

The Whisky Trail has been on our bucket list for many years and did not disappoint, even though it was much more commercialised than I expected. I had a romanticised image of heading down infrequently travelled Scottish lanes to boutique scotch makers. However, our tour visited some of the world's largest whisky makers, including impressive distillery tours and expansive gift shops. But it was still fun.

On our way to Edinburgh, we visited Balmoral Castle, the British Royals' summer residence. We had been to the Scottish capital many years before to see the spectacular military tattoo with its lone piper playing in the mist. Edinburgh is a beautiful city that is always worth a stopover.

Our next stop was Europe. Given that many European cities are connected by affordable and efficient bus and train services, there were numerous options for an arrival point. We used Google Flights to set our departure points as Edinburgh, Glasgow, Birmingham, Manchester, or London. We entered Amsterdam, Berlin, Paris, Brussels, and Nantes as potential arrival points. This provided 25 routes in one search. After that, we chose a few other arrival points on a new search. With 25 combinations per search, we quickly found a cheap option.

Tip: When using Google Flights, a "+" sign will appear to the right of the location name after you enter one departure point. Just click on that "+" sign to allow you to enter the names of other cities.

Traps to Avoid

The cheapest flight may not include what you need, and it may no longer be the best deal after you pay for the extras.

Most airlines do not include checked bags in ticket prices and typically charge between US$30 and US$70 per checked bag.

Often, you will have to pre-order and pre-pay for a meal if you want one.

Seating choice is often only available for an extra fee.

Additionally, you may be on a booking platform that quotes you in multiple currencies. The currency will always be declared, but it may be easily missed in the fine print.

Ensure you log in to the search engine in your home country so it's harder to get caught using foreign currencies. For example, in Australia, use expedia.com.au and be careful not to wind up on expedia.com. Even then, you must be cautious about which currency you are quoted.

TRAVEL STORY
Search Strategy

Check That Quotes Include All Costs

After visiting our UK-based son and his family, we planned to go to Vienna.

Vienna's most famous sites include Schönbrunn Palace and its extensive grounds, which are listed as a UNESCO World Heritage Site. The estate was first used as a hunting ground by the Habsburgs, one of the most powerful European families, in the 16th century. The palace was established as their summer residence in the 17th century.

While the French Palace of Versailles achieved fame as the home of Louis XVIII and Marie Antoinette during the French Revolution, Louis and Marie were not alone in enjoying ostentatious displays of wealth while the poor went hungry.

Many powerful European families competed to build such palaces. Schönbrunn is an excellent example of this competitive palace building.

Another notable Vienna site to visit is the Spanish Riding School. Spanish? Yes, Spanish. This riding school is dedicated to classical dressage and the training of Lipizzaner horses. We have not yet been able to schedule our visit to the Hofburg to see a performance, but we did tour the facility off-season, which is still worth doing. If you're passing through during the cooler months, consider booking a performance, but do so well in advance. We caught a similar performance by the Royal Andalusian School in Córdoba, Spain, and the beauty of the display brought tears to our eyes.

When planning our November departure from Birmingham for Vienna, we determined that a British Airways flight would cost A$682.

But hang on! Expedia was showing a Eurowings flight for just $192 for two. A closer look revealed that Eurowings would have charged Lynda $68 for her checked-in bag and $16 for her carry-on. They would have charged me $32 to take on my two carry-ons. The Eurowings price, including baggage, was $308. Hang on again! A closer look revealed that the quote was in US dollars. The total cost was A$462.

The BA flight was still more expensive, but was direct from Birmingham to Vienna. As Oneworld members, we could relax in the BA lounge with a complimentary breakfast before boarding. There would be no layover, and we would get a free meal again on the plane. The Eurowings flight included a 2.5-hour layover in Düsseldorf.

We would have had no free lounge access, necessitating payment for breakfast while waiting for the first flight. The Eurowings option would have cost us A$50 for two for an inferior breakfast with less comfort at airport prices. There was no free food on the flight. We would have had a coffee and a snack costing A$30 to help pass the time during our layover while waiting for the second flight.

The cost for the bargain Eurowings flight, including basic food, was now A$542. While it was still a $140 saving, we would have lost significant time, earned no applicable loyalty rewards, had no seat allocation, and experienced less comfort. If we sacrifice comfort, convenience, and a few hours, we want a more significant saving than $140.

The moral of this travel story is to ensure you include all the costs of your journey so you can compare them like for like.

Document Options

It is often tempting to dive in at the deep end and start working through the options in a less-than-systematic way. At first, you may be tempted to rush the process, thinking you will commit the best choice to memory and then try to beat it. It is better to proceed slowly and document the options as you go.

When researching flights, compile all the detailed information in a neat list in a consistent format. There will be too much data to keep track of if you do not keep careful records, in a structured format, as you research. Once you have written the best-looking options on your list, proceed to the next search engine and repeat the process.

I have included a Flight Research Template in the free stuff. To get the best result, diligently record your search results as you work through the steps described below.

The Search Procedure

- **Step 1a. Price the cheapest and the fastest.** Price the most inexpensive way you could make it work, considering the total cost of your journey, including baggage charges and food. Then, use your favourite search engine to find the fastest and most direct route. Record key facts and interesting options, including Airline, Departure Airport, Departure Time, Layover Airport, Layover Time, Arrival Airport, Arrival Time, and Price (in your currency, including baggage).

- **Step 1b. Check prices a few days before and after your chosen date.** Price these two options a few days on either side of your chosen date.

- **Step 1c. Use at least one other search engine or booking site.** If you find any better options, record similar information as described above.

- **Step 1d. When settled on a flight, check the airline's website.** When you think you have the best option, check the cost of the same flight on the operating airline's website. Record the result.

This is a good start, but you still have more work to do.

You can return to the job a day or two later by recording the results and continuing without losing your work. But if you do not keep a meticulous record, it is unlikely you will remember everything you have learned. Proceeding slowly while maintaining a detailed record is faster.

Please do not rush to book a flight simply because it appears to be a good deal. You will probably find a better one. Finish your research before you book.

> **SEARCH STRATEGY**
>
> Identify at least two booking sites or search engines you prefer.
>
> Use one of these to identify the cheapest cash flight you can work with and the most direct flight at a reasonable cost. Price the flights for cash for a few days on either side of your chosen date.
>
> Record the options. Use at least one more search engine to identify a better deal. Then, check the airline's cash price directly on the airline's site.

3.2 BUDGET AIRLINE STRATEGY

Travel and change of place impart new vigour to the mind.

SENECA

Why Read This Chapter?

You will learn the role of budget airlines in your overall cost-reduction plan.

Budget Airlines

Budget Airlines are often referred to as *Low-Cost Airlines*. Our definition of *"Low cost"* is based on those with that classification on airlineratings.com. When writing this section, we have included only airlines with a safety rating of at least six stars. We will discuss safety later.

The gap between the offers of *Full-Service Airlines* and Budget Airlines has narrowed in recent years, as most airlines have shifted to a user-pays basis for optional extras, such as baggage and seat allocation. However, some Budget Airlines in some regions are hard to beat in terms of price.

A significant portion of this guide focuses on leveraging airline loyalty programs. Budget Airlines emphasise low fares. They achieve this by cutting out every nonessential cost. Loyalty systems are often eliminated or compromised. Items frequently not included in the fare include meals, drinks, checked baggage, cabin baggage, seat allocation, and airport check-in assistance. Usually, most of these things can be purchased separately.

Some Budget Airlines may not appear in search engine results because they do not wish to pay commissions. Look out for this and check the relevant Budget Airlines' sites directly.

Geographic Coverage

So, how will you know which of the Budget Airlines are relevant? The scope of Budget Airline operations is usually regional rather than intercontinental. We have listed their areas of operation below.

These airlines undoubtedly offer low prices under certain circumstances. It is always worth checking those operating in the area where you intend to travel.

Budget airlines often offer deals that are well-suited for individuals on short trips who travel alone without checked luggage. These passengers may not value seating allocation or an in-flight meal.

For example, if a single person living in London regularly visits a friend or relative in a European city, it would be best to leave some toiletries and clothes at their relative's place. They could then travel on the most affordable flight and avoid all the additional charges.

We commonly use Air Asia to travel internally within Asia, as their prices are hard to beat, even after adding the charges for baggage and food.

If we cannot find a suitable flight using points, we often use Scoot to fly from Sydney to Singapore. This is usually half the price of our Primary Airline, Qantas, or our Tertiary Airline, Singapore Airlines.

If the budget airline has opted out of search engines, you may need to check prices directly on the airline's website.

FINDING THE BEST VALUE CASH FLIGHTS

BUDGET AIRLINES

Airline	SE Asia	Wider Asia	Australasia	Japan	Pacific Islands	India	China	Middle East	Western Europe	Eastern Europe	Northern Europe	UK-Ireland	North America	Sth/Cent America	Caribbean	Africa
Aer Lingus												X				
Air Arabia								X								
Air Baltic											X					
Air Botswana																X
Air Cairo								X								
Air Do				X												
AirAsia India						X										
Air Asia Indonesia	X															
AirAsia Malaysia	X															
Air Asia Philippines	X															
AirAsia Thailand	X															
AirAsia X	X															
AirAsia X Thailand	X															
Allegiant Air													X			
Avelo													X			
blu-express														X		
Breeze Airways													X			
Cebu Pacific	X															
Corendon Airlines									X							
Eastar Jet																
easyjet									X			X				
Eurowings									X							
Fastjet																X
Fly Dubai								X								
flyNas		X						X	X							
FlySafair																X
Frontier Airlines													X			
Go First						X										
HK Express	X			X												
IndiGo						X										
Israir								X								
Jazeera Airways								X								
Jeju Air		X														
Jet2									X	X		X				
TUI Fly Belgium									X							
JetBlue Airways													X			

109

FLY FOR FREE

BUDGET AIRLINES, CONTINUED

Primary Areas of Operation

Airline	SE Asia	Wider Asia	Australasia	Japan	Pacific Islands	India	China	Middle East	Western Europe	Eastern Europe	Northern Europe	UK-Ireland	North America	Sth/Cent America	Caribbean	Africa
Jetstar	X		X													
Jetstar Asia	X															
Jetstar Japan				X												
Jetstar Pacific					X											
Jin Air		X														
Juneyao Airlines							X									
Norwegian											X					
Philippine Airlines	X															
Ryanair									X	X		X				
Scoot	X															
Sky Airline														X		
Smartwings									X	X						
Southwest Airlines													X			
Spicejet						X										
Spirit Airlines													X	X	X	
Spring Airlines				X												
Sun Country Airlines		X											X	X	X	
Sun Express								X	X							
Swoop													X			
T'way Airlines		X														
Thai Smile	X															
Thomas Cook											X					
Transavia									X	X						
TUI UK									X			X				
TUIfly Germany									X							
TUIfky Netherlands									X							
Tunisair																X
Turkish Airlines		X														
VietJet Air	X															
Vietravel Airlines	X															
Viva Aerobus													X			
Volaris													X	X		
Volotea									X							
Vueling								X	X							X
Westjet													X			
Wizz									X							
Zipair				X												

BUDGET AIRLINE STRATEGY

Check which budget airlines operate within the region you plan to fly. If these airlines do not appear in your searches, they may have opted out of the search services to save money and lower fares. Check prices directly on the airline's website.

Ensure price comparisons include the extras, such as baggage, seat allocation, and meals, to the extent you need them.

3.3 RETURN STRATEGY

Passenger: *"I would like a return ticket, please."*

Operator: *"Where to?"*

Passenger: *"Back here, thanks."*

Why Read This Chapter?

You will learn how to reduce travel costs by optimising the balance between Return fares and One-Way fares. Getting that balance right can substantially cut your fares, whether you pay in cash or points.

The Study

A Return ticket is often cheaper than two One-Way tickets covering the same route on the same plane. We decided to quantify those savings.

We created a database of 1,600 fares on 20 airlines to compare the costs of two One-Way tickets versus one Return ticket. Both options would have put us on *the same pieces of flying hardware on the same days*.

To clarify, regardless of how we booked, we would have been on the same planes on the same day, whether we used one Return or two One-Way tickets. The only thing that would have been different would have been the booking numbers on the airline's computers and the amount of money or points deducted from our accounts.

Half of the theoretical bookings in our database were made for cash, and the other half were made with points.

The database includes international and domestic fares in Economy Class and Business Class.

The Results

The results of the study were:

- Very similar between Economy Class and Business Class.
- Different for domestic versus international fares.

- Very different depending on whether the payment method was cash or points.

The overall results are summarised below:

The passengers would end up on the same planes, whether they purchased two One-Way fares or one Return fare. Only the ticketing would be different.

All Domestic Fares

There were many anomalies. However, <u>on average</u>, there was no substantial cost difference between two One-Way tickets versus one Return ticket in the domestic markets. This applies whether paying by cash or points.

International Fares when Paying with Points

When booking using points, the number of points required for two One-Way tickets is usually similar to that needed for a Return ticket. Return tickets, <u>on average</u>, require only 9% fewer points than the equivalent trip using two One-Way tickets.

However, there were many anomalies. For example, 20% of Return tickets cost more points than the equivalent One-Way tickets!

International Fares when Paying Cash

On average, Return flights are 45% cheaper than One-Way fares when paying cash. For example, if the cost of two One-Way tickets were $1,000, the equivalent Return fare, on average, would be only $550.

Therefore, when paying cash to travel internationally, you should adjust your itinerary to maximise the Return flights and minimise One-Way flights.

EXAMPLE
Return Strategy

Make Subtle Changes to Your Itinerary to Incorporate Return Fares

Suppose you planned a one-week trip to Singapore from Sydney, followed by one week in London. Your proposed departure date from Sydney is 1st March.

Option One:

You could book three One-Way tickets:

Sydney-Singapore	One-Way	1st March
Singapore-London	One-Way	7th March
London-Sydney	One-Way	15th March

Option Two:

You will usually find it is much cheaper to book two Return tickets:

Sydney-Singapore	Return 1st March	Returning 15th March
Singapore-London	Return 7th March	Returning 14th March

It is worth pricing both options, whether using points or cash. In this case, Qantas quoted the One-Way fares for Option 1 at $3,467 and the Return fares for Option 2 at $1,726.

FINDING THE BEST VALUE CASH FLIGHTS

TRAVEL STORY
Return Strategy

Fly on the Same Planes on the Same Days at a Lower Cost

Option One:

The costs below are based on actual expenses for a trip departing from Sydney in September and returning in November.

To maintain consistency, we have used Qantas for flights in and out of Sydney, Air France for flights in and out of Singapore, and Swiss for flights in and out of Birmingham.

All prices are per person. The total cost of six One-Way flights would be $5,628.

OPTION 1: ONE-WAY FARES				
One Passenger				
	Date	Airline	A$	Fare Type
Sydney to Singapore	26-Sep	Qantas	893	One way
Singapore to Vienna	28-Sep	Air France	1,131	One way
Vienna to Birmingham	5-Oct	Swiss	346	One way
Birmingham to Vienna	22-Oct	Swiss	640	One way
Vienna to Singapore	27-Oct	Air France	1,594	One way
Singapore to Sydney	1-Nov	Qantas	1,024	One way
Six one-way fares		Total	5,628	

Option Two:

The second option would be to book on the same planes but use Return tickets. Only the ticketing is different. The quoted cost dropped by 33% to $3,430. Note that we end up on the same pieces of hardware on the same days either way. The only differences are the paperwork and the price.

OPTION 2: RETURN FARES				
One Passenger				
	Date	Airline	A$	Fare Type
Sydney to Singapore	26-Sep	Qantas	1,190	Return
Singapore to Vienna	28-Sep	Air France	1,760	Return
Vienna to Birmingham	5-Oct	Swiss	480	Return
Birmingham to Vienna	22-Oct	Swiss	-	Incl. in Return Fare
Vienna to Singapore	27-Oct	Air France	-	Incl. in Return Fare
Singapore to Sydney	1-Nov	Qantas	-	Incl. in Return Fare
Six one-way fares		Total	3,430	

Anomalies in International Fares

You should always compare the price of a Return ticket to the cost of two one-way tickets, whether you are paying with points or cash. While Return tickets are usually cheaper, there are many anomalies.

In our large sample, there were many more variances from the averages when comparing point flights than when comparing cash flights. When paying with points, the average saving on our database of Return tickets versus One-Way tickets was only 9%. But that was on average. The randomly selected flights in our database included incidences of savings of over 50%.

While Return tickets are cheaper than One-Way tickets 80% of the time, we found many examples where Return flights were more expensive than two One-Way tickets. Always compare the cost of a Return ticket to two One-Way tickets when booking flights.

Twenty per cent of the Return fares were more expensive than the equivalent One-Way tickets. These exceptions were much more frequent for points flights (27%) than for cash flights (14%).

RETURN STRATEGY

Engineer your itinerary to allow a choice between Return and One-Way fares when finalising bookings. For every booking, compare a Return ticket to the equivalent pair of One-Way tickets.

If you use a combination of cash and points, try to use the points in the One-Way sections.

3.4 CHEAPEST DAY STRATEGY

> *When should you arrive at the airport?*
> *You should be there already.*

Why Read This Chapter?

Suppose you can start your journey on any day of the week. Which day of the week should you plan on flying? The answer to this question is provided below, based on an extensive analysis.

The Study

The following conclusions are based on a sample of over 4,000 domestic and 5,000 international flights, which were spread across 15 airlines and encompassed 12 countries in North America, Southeast Asia, Australasia, the Middle East, the UK, and Europe. Every fare used in our database was the cheapest flight with that airline on that day.

We only included routes where flights were available daily over our nine-month sample period. We eliminated the week nearest to our bookings, as fares can be expected to spike closer to the booking date. We then fed the data into a database for interrogation.

We split our study between domestic and international travel. Half the data was for Economy Class and half for Business Class.

The Results—Domestic

The following conclusions are based on averages and only apply to <u>domestic</u> cash flights.

- Monday to Thursday are the least expensive days of the week to fly.
- Fridays, Saturdays, and Sundays are 14% more expensive than Monday to Thursday.
- Tuesdays and Wednesdays are 4% cheaper than Mondays and Thursdays.

Using averages understates the savings that can be achieved by flexing the day of travel.

Individual fares can vary significantly from Monday to Thursday in any given week. There are usually substantial differences between individual fares on Fridays, Saturdays, and Sundays.

Mondays, Tuesdays, Wednesdays, and Thursdays are not always the cheapest days. Before locking in your flights, you must check the flights for each potential travel day. But if you base your draft plans on flying Monday to Thursday, you will be stacking the odds in your favour when you finalise your bookings.

As mentioned above, the fare from Monday to Thursday is 14% lower than the average from Friday to Sunday. But if you take the cheapest fare of the week (typically on any one of Monday, Tuesday, Wednesday, or Thursday) and compare it to the most expensive fare (usually Friday, Saturday, or Sunday), the variances are usually double that.

The Results—International

The following conclusions are based on averages for <u>international</u> flights.

- The day of the week you fly matters less for international flights than for domestic flights.
- Monday to Thursday are still the least expensive days of the week to fly internationally (as for domestic).
- However, flying internationally on Fridays, Saturdays, and Sundays is only 6% more expensive, on average, than flying Monday to Thursday.

The findings are the same for international flights as for domestic flights. However, the percentage savings are much lower for international flights.

The conclusion is that when planning your trip, try to schedule your flights for Mondays to Thursdays whenever possible. Do not lock your flying days in until later in the process. Anomalies are common, so please review the actual fares. By constructing your draft plan based on flying on the days with the cheapest average fares, you will likely include lower costs in your final plan.

FLY FOR FREE

> **CHEAPEST DAY STRATEGY**
>
> If possible, base your draft plan on flying on Monday through Thursday. As your itinerary solidifies and you're ready to book, consider a wide range of dates. Price your flights before committing to an event that forces you to fly on a specific day.

3.5 CHEAPEST TIME STRATEGY

Time flies. But you are the pilot.

Why Read This Chapter?

In a later chapter, we cover the *Body Clock Strategy*, an important concept. However, we will consider price alone here. You will learn what flight times attract the lowest prices.

The Study

We broke the day into 24 time slots. Well, *we* didn't. The Egyptians did that about 3,000 years ago. We decided to stick with the Egyptians and examine the average cost in each of the 24 one-hour time slots.

We have only examined Economy Class cash fares.

The Results—Domestic

We found that some timeslots are more expensive than others on well-travelled domestic routes. The conclusion is the opposite of what many would expect: the most expensive flights are when the airport is *not* busy.

On average, the most expensive time to travel domestically is between 2 p.m. and 4 p.m. Flights cost approximately 30% more than the average for the rest of the day. Outside of that timeslot, the prices are remarkably consistent.

When airlines operate multiple flights within the same hour, one flight is easily deleted from their schedule to keep the remaining flights full. For example, if an airline has scheduled 10 flights in the early hours, it can cancel one flight to keep the other nine full.

Later, if they only schedule a single plane within the hour, they can do less to tailor their capacity to match the demand. That means there is a higher risk they won't be able to fill all their seats in that time slot. We suspect that is why flights are more expensive at less busy times.

When planning, avoid flying on domestic flights between noon and 2:00 p.m. This effect is quite strong from Wednesday to Saturday. The cost difference is less on Miser Mondays and Cheap Tuesdays. The higher cost period is longer on Sundays, from 11:00 a.m. to 4:00 p.m.

In summary, for domestic flights, avoid the middle of the day (noon to 2:00 p.m.), Monday through Saturday. On Sunday, avoid 11:00 a.m. to 4:00 p.m.

The Results—International

Our conclusion for international fares is that there is no consistency. Most long-haul international routes only have a small number of daily departures for a given airline. All the other factors affecting fares swamp the time-of-day effects. Of course, you may find a significant difference between two flights at different times for any given route, airline, or day. However, we could not find enough correlation across all flights to conclude that any time of day is *consistently* cheaper. There are more significant factors influencing the pricing of international flights.

> **CHEAPEST TIME STRATEGY**
>
> Check all time slots for international flights, as there are no consistently cheaper time slots. Avoid travelling on domestic routes between noon and 2 p.m., six days a week and 11:00 a.m. to 4:00 p.m. on Sundays.

FINDING THE BEST VALUE CASH FLIGHTS

3.6 BOOKING STRATEGY

Book 'em, Danno.

DETECTIVE STEVE MCGARRETT, *HAWAII FIVE-O*

Why Read This Chapter?

You will learn the answers to these questions:

- How far ahead should you book flights to achieve optimal pricing?
- Who should you involve in your booking process?

How Far Ahead to Book

We rely heavily on our planning process for long and complex trips. Our trip planning involves many considerations other than airfares. Consider that we:

- Use timeshare organisations. One way to get the best value out of those systems is to book far in advance (up to 13 months in some cases).
- Use various organisations through which we achieve free accommodation by exchanging our homes for other people's homes in different countries or states. These swaps must be organised well in advance.
- Use house-sitting organisations. These accommodations are typically provided free of charge in exchange for caring for a pet.
- Book far ahead to allow us to lock in bargain prices within our preferred dates for the best bus, train, and plane seats.
- Book far ahead to get the best deals on rental cars.
- Book early enough to get the best point-based flights. As discussed below, this availability decreases if we leave our bookings too late.

- Obtain tickets to events and sites likely to sell out early.
- Select from paid accommodation while a wide range is available.

Many will argue for nabbing last-minute specials or freewheeling through a country and booking as they go. However, booking at the last minute does not align with our holistic approach to travel planning.

We find that achieving the optimal result requires planning the route, accommodations, flights, trains, buses, and rental cars in advance of booking. Then we book the lot. Some great last-minute specials arise. Having total flexibility while travelling can be attractive. However, failing to plan or book ahead results in a poor overall financial outcome regarding total trip costs. That one cheap last-minute fare will be offset by many other costs that arise if you fail to plan. Failing to plan is planning to fail.

However, we decided to set aside our bias toward booking well in advance and calculate some unbiased numbers. The numbers show that, <u>on average</u>, booking at the last minute is not the most effective way to save money or earn points on airfares.

How far in advance should we book to secure the best airfare deal, whether paying with cash or points?

We analysed 1,200 fares on 12 airlines on 70 routes. The fares were divided into our usual categories: Economy and Business Class, Domestic and International, Return and One-Way Fares. For the Return fares, we assumed a return one month after departure.

The periods below relate to the time difference between booking and departure. We examined the prices of each fare when booking one to ten months ahead.

| BOOKING WINDOWS: INTERNATIONAL ||
| Optimal Time to Book ||
Period Between Booking Date and Flight Date	Prices Compared to Average
1 to 30 days	+50% more expensive
31 to 60 days	+25% more expensive
61 to 90 days	- on average
91 to 120 days	-15% less expensive
121 to 180 days	- on average

181 to 240 days	-15% less expensive
over 240 days	-10% less expensive

The conclusions for booking <u>international</u> fares for cash are:

- Particularly avoid booking less than one month ahead.
- Book at least 60 days ahead when you have a choice.
- The optimal times to book, from a pricing point of view, are 91-120 days ahead or more than 180 days ahead.
- Booking more than 120 days ahead makes it very likely that your flight schedule times will change, which will often upset other arrangements. Therefore, we recommend booking 91-120 days in advance. This achieves the optimal balance between flight availability and price on one hand, versus the likelihood of unplanned scheduling changes on the other.

BOOKING WINDOWS: DOMESTIC	
Optimal Time to Book	
Period Between Booking Date and Flight Date	Prices Compared to Average
1 to 30 days	+30% more expensive
31 to 60 days	+5% more expensive
61 to 90 days	-10% less expensive
91 to 120 days	-15% less expensive
121 to 180 days	- on average

The conclusions for booking <u>domestic</u> fares are:

- Avoid booking less than one month ahead.
- The optimal booking period, from a pricing point of view, is 61-180 days ahead.
- If you book too far ahead, you will likely be subject to scheduling changes. Lower the risk of these scheduling changes by booking earlier in the low pricing period, say 61-90 days.

Booking Method

Unless the fare is significantly cheaper through a booking agent, book directly with the airline operating the flight. As in other areas of life, always cut out the middleman if they do not offer a compelling benefit.

Use intermediary sites only for research purposes. Cutting out the middleman does not make a significant difference until things change, but changes in flight times are common and to be expected.

If you book through the airline, you can deal directly with them in case of a change or an issue. Introducing an intermediary complicates the process of obtaining refunds or making changes. If the fare is not cheaper, what is the benefit of involving an intermediary, such as Expedia?

I would rather deal with the airline directly than with an intermediary who cannot make decisions on behalf of either party. Intermediaries cannot decide on behalf of the airline or the traveller, which slows things down.

Before booking through the airline, ensure you and your travelling partner(s) have signed up for that airline's loyalty program. You can log in to any airline site using your confirmation number and surname for a single booking, and you do not need to be a member. However, as a member, you will receive more information.

Simply logging in as a member will provide you with a complete list of your bookings. And the next time you book a flight, you can log in and avoid the need to input your personal information. Most importantly, you must be a member to earn points.

TRAVEL STORY
Booking Strategy

Family Emergency

We had an occasion when we could not follow the *Book Direct Strategy*. The outcome demonstrates why it is advisable to follow this approach when possible.

We decided to visit the Canary Islands. The islands are part of Spain despite being located just off the coast of southern Morocco, approximately 1,700 km from the Spanish Mainland.

Attractions include the volcanic areas, notably Teide National Park, the dunes in Reserva Natural Especial de las Dunas de Maspalmos, and the beaches of Playa de Cofete. The islands are home to numerous natural wonders, including the World Heritage-listed Garajonay National Park on La Gomera.

We have yet to properly visit the islands, as we had barely arrived when we were urgently required to travel to Sydney due to a family emergency. Expedia had two seats available due to a cancellation. They were on a Qantas flight operated by Emirates. We were unable to book anything similar through either Qantas or Emirates. Due to the urgency, we could not use our normal *Layover Strategy* or *Stopover Strategy* described elsewhere.

The Emirates flight out of Dubai was late. Due to that delay, we missed the connecting Qantas flight in Melbourne and could not return home to Sydney at the planned time. Qantas did not want to know about the problem, as they regarded the delay as an Emirates problem. Emirates would not own the situation as it was booked through Expedia. Expedia could not help on the day as the airlines held all the cards.

With credit to all concerned, it did get sorted out. However, getting someone to take responsibility took us considerable time and effort.

No one can pass the buck if you book directly with the airline.

Caribbean Middleman

We were booked to travel from Nassau, Bahamas, to Grand Cayman. Due to our time-share arrangements, we had complimentary accommodation in Grand Cayman.

We were scheduled to be in Grand Cayman for a week, as there was much to do. It is one of the most developed parts of the Caribbean. In this case, we welcomed the excellent roads and facilities. Not to mention the crystal blue water and white sandy beaches. Seven Mile Beach is one of the most beautiful beaches in that region. Then there is Starfish Point, where you are guaranteed to see giant starfish in ankle-deep water despite the pressure on them from cruise boat tourists. And there is the excellent Blue Iguana Conservation Centre, where you can see tiny blue dinosaurs faking it as giant lizards.

Our ticket from the Bahamas to Grand Cayman consisted of two short flights connecting through Miami. We had to use different airlines for our in-flight and out-flight connections from Miami, but the long layover provided plenty of time to make the connections.

Cayman Airlines changed our flight. The flight time was changed by nine hours. The first flight would not arrive in time to get the connecting flight out of Miami that day. We would have forfeited one day of our longstanding booking on Grand Cayman and had to pay for an overnight stay in Miami.

We rebooked our flights with an alternative airline. Then we tried to get a refund of A$846 for the Cayman Airlines flight. We had to deal with Expedia as they were the people we had paid. Expedia then had to get the airline's permission to issue the refund. I waited on hold for 39 minutes, and the Expedia rep could not get through. Expedia would not provide a refund until the airline agreed to it. The airline would only deal with the party that had made the booking, which was Expedia.

Expedia said they would call back. Fine. They did when I could not take the call. Then, I did not hear from them again, so I called them back. Another 30 minutes wait. Again, they informed me again that they needed to obtain an answer from the airline. I followed up half a dozen times over the next three months.

By comparison, an American Airlines flight changed on the same trip.

Because I had booked directly with them, I could call American Airlines and make a new arrangement. As soon as I hung up, I logged into my AAdvantage account on the American Airlines website and could check that all the flights were correct.

Using intermediaries rarely provides a benefit, but it will complicate your life when something changes.

Exceptions to Booking Direct

Note that our *Booking Strategy* does include the words "unless you have a compelling reason to use the intermediary." Compelling reasons are rare, but they do occasionally arise.

A compelling reason to use an Intermediary once arose due to a situation: an unusual currency event. We tried to book a flight directly with Aerolineas Argentinas during a period of high inflation in Argentina. We had the opportunity to experience Buenos Aires (BA) by breaking our flight between Rio and Santiago.

Any good guide will give you a long list of things to see in Buenos Aires, but our favourite activity was walking the inner-city streets. Be sure to do the day trip to Colonia de Sacramento in Uruguay. It was the first city established in Uruguay and has been well preserved as a UNESCO World Heritage site. The river crossing is relatively short. Get an early ferry from BA, and you will have plenty of time to see this beautiful Spanish colonial city. Return to BA in the late afternoon.

You can explore most inner-city streets of BA without taking risks. Be more selective and cautious at night, but don't hesitate to venture out.

If we had booked directly with the airline, the flights would have been more expensive than booking them through Expedia.

At the time, Argentina's inflation rate was forecast to be 90% for the year. For Aerolineas Argentinas to make a booking, they had to quote the fares to the public in Argentinian pesos. Being a government entity, they could not express a lack of faith in their currency by publicly quoting fares in any currency other than Argentinian pesos. However, given the forecast deterioration in the peso's value, they had to collect a substantial number to ensure that the costs they would incur six months later would be covered.

However, we could buy fares in US dollars through Expedia. Why? We assume that the airline received US dollars by accepting bookings through Expedia, eliminating its local inflation risk. The fares were much cheaper on Expedia on that occasion, but that is rare.

> **BOOKING STRATEGY**
>
> Book directly with the airline unless you have a compelling reason to use an intermediary. On average, when paying cash, book international flights 91-120 days in advance and domestic flights 61-90 days in advance to secure the best pricing while avoiding excess schedule changes that can occur if you book even further ahead.

4

Using Points & Miles to Maximise Savings

You have now learned strategies to:

- Accumulate many points.
- Manage your points.
- Identify the best value cash flight.

This section will show you how to obtain the best value for your points. We will explore how and when to deploy your points to your best advantage.

This process involves using the *Valuation Strategy*, which allows you to treat your points like valuable foreign currency rather than something you received for free.

Then you should use the *Redemption Strategy*, which involves three steps:

- Step 1: <u>Find the Best Cash Fare.</u> Use the process outlined in the previous section to identify the lowest cash fare available for your intended route.
- Step 2: <u>Find the Best Points Fare.</u> Repeat the steps we used to determine the best value cash fare, but this time, look for the best value points flight. This step will be much simpler. When purchasing flights for cash, there are dozens of airline options available. Most of the time, when considering redemption of flights for points, we must only consider airlines in our portfolio.
- Step 3: <u>Decide Whether to Use Points or Cash.</u> This section provides you with the tools to make an informed decision.

4.1 VALUATION STRATEGY

The truth will set you free.

JOHN 8:32

Why Read This Chapter?

You will learn how to value loyalty program points. Being aware of their value will enable you to make better decisions when faced with the option of redeeming or acquiring them. Assigning a value to your points under various circumstances is essential, so you can maximise their value when you employ the *Redemption Strategy* discussed in the next chapter.

The Numbers Will Set You Free

Numbers don't lie. They are only one part of the decision-making process, but an essential one. I was routinely confronted with various ideas, opinions, and statements during my decades as a chief financial officer. These included some that were bad, good, or misguided, as well as brilliant insights and hard facts. Those decades taught me that it is hard to separate these categories without accurate numbers.

You need the numbers and *Valuation Strategy* in this chapter to make optimal decisions about using your points. The numbers will help you decide whether it's better to use points or cash on any occasion.

Treat Points Like Foreign Currencies

Remember, a point is not a point. It may be evident that a Mile (United), an Avios (British Airways), or a Point (Qantas) will not have the same value. It is also true that comparing an American Airlines Mile, a Cathay Pacific Mile, and an Emirates Mile is like comparing a US dollar, a Singapore dollar, and a New Zealand dollar. Just because some airline currencies share the same names does not mean they have the same value.

Think of when you last had a wad of foreign currency in your hand and were deciding whether to buy something. What was the first thing you did? You converted the foreign currency back to a currency you are familiar with.

If a Berlin traveller had to decide whether to buy a wooden elephant from a Thai market, she would ask how much it was. If the purveyor of wooden elephants said, *"One thousand Baht for you?"* the Berlin traveller would immediately calculate the equivalent in euros. The tourist could not make an optimal wooden elephant decision without converting the exchange unit to her familiar currency.

Our study has determined the point values for many major airlines. We have expressed the value of points in one uniform currency: Australian dollars (AUD) and cents. Just convert the Australian dollars to the local currency you are familiar with.

For the convenience of many readers, we have included similar tables of point values in an Appendix, expressed in US dollars (USD), pounds sterling (GBP) and euros (EUR), based on the FX rates stated in the tables.

Our valuations are based on samples. Different samples will provide different results, typically plus or minus 15%. That makes minor FX rate changes immaterial.

Types of Point Valuations

Business vs. Economy

For many airlines, the cash price of a Business Class fare is usually four times that of an Economy Class fare on the same flight. Yet the points required for a Business Class fare are generally only two or three times those needed for an Economy Class fare. That means you usually get a higher value per point when booking a Business Class fare.

One Way or Return Fares—International
You will also achieve different values depending on whether you redeem the points for One-Way fares or Return fares. The cash price of two One-Way flights is usually 50% to 80% more expensive than the same journey booked on one Return ticket. However, on average, a minor premium is charged for replacing a Return ticket with two One-Way tickets if you pay with points.

Domestic vs. International Fares
Some airlines offer better value for your points on domestic flights, while others provide better value on international flights.

Five Different Valuations
The differences described above give rise to five different valuations depending on the fare type:

- One-Way International Economy
- One-Way International Business
- Domestic Economy
- Return International Economy
- Return International Business

We do not recommend using points for Domestic Business for reasons discussed under the *Upgrade Strategy*, described later.

Weighted Average Values
Often, you can only use a single value when making decisions about earning points. When you earn points, you usually do not know which type of fare you will redeem them for in the future. Therefore, we have calculated a Weighted Average Redemption Value based on a likely percentage split between the five fare types.

Our weighted average value assumes that you will use points in the following ratio:

- 20% for Domestic Economy
- Zero for Domestic Business
- 60% for International Economy
- 20% for International Business

Note that the above weightings are based on points used, not flights booked. For example, International Business may only account for 10% of your fares but use 20% of your points. Our weighted average further assumes the split between One-Way and Return international flights will be 50/50.

Valuation Method

To arrive at our recommended redemption values, we took the following steps:

1. We loaded thousands of airfare cash prices (C) into a database. We selected the cheapest available flight for each randomly selected date.
2. We established the number of points (P) required for each of the same flights.
3. We established the value of supplementary payments (S) required to book a points flight.
4. We deducted the supplementary payment from the cash price to arrive at the cash difference (D) between a cash flight and a points flight (C—S = D).
5. We divided the cash difference by the number of points required for the same flight (D/P) to provide the cash equivalent value (V) per point.

Table of Point Valuations

For example, .025 in the next table means A$0.025 or 2.5 Australian cents.

If you are interested in an airline not on this list, you can perform your valuation using the template and procedure below. Note that an Excel version of the template is included in the Free Stuff.

FLY FOR FREE

REFERENCE TABLE — A$ AUD POINT (MILE) VALUATIONS

	Airline	Loyalty Scheme	One-Way International Econ.	One-Way International Bus.	Return Domestic Econ.	Return International Econ.	Return International Bus.	Weighted Avg Value
			A$	A$	A$	A$	A$	A$
	Air Canada	Aeroplan	.036	.042	.020	.016	.031	.028
	Air Europa	Suma	.035	.011	.021	.030	.009	.025
	Air France	Flying Blue	.033	.036	.014	.012	.012	.022
	Air New Zealand	Airpoints	.920	.920	.920	.920	.920	.920
	Alaska Airlines	Mileage Plan	-	-	.024	-	-	.024
	American Airlines	AAdvantage	.036	.024	.028	.018	.010	.024
**	Austrian Airlines	Miles and More	.024	.061	.007	.012	.030	.025
	British Airways	Executive Club	.027	.085	.010	.012	.026	.029
**	Cathay Pacific	Marco Polo	.038	.070	.016	.020	.049	.037
	Delta Air Lines	Sky Miles	.018	.013	.017	.015	.010	.015
**	Emirates	Skywards	.026	.039	.028	.016	.032	.026
**	Etihad Airways	Guest	.023	.015	.013	.013	.017	.015
*	Hawaiian Airlines	Hawaiian Miles	.020	.032	.013	.018	.023	.018
	ITA Airways	Miles and More	.024	.061	.007	.012	.030	.025
**	KLM	Flying Blue	.033	.036	.014	.012	.012	.022
	Lufthansa	Miles and More	.024	.054	.006	.012	.026	.023
	Malaysia Airlines	Enrich	.048	.055	.017	.038	.038	.042
	Qantas	Frequent Flyer	.028	.022	.019	.027	.020	.025
**	Qatar Airways	Privilege Club	.040	.195	.046	.031	-	.058
**	Singapore Airlines	KrisFlyer	.034	.057	.019	.019	.035	.032
	Southwest Airlines	Rapid Rewards	-	-	.019	-	-	.019
**	Swiss	Miles and More	.025	.069	.009	.012	.033	.027
	Thai Airways	Royal Orchid	.024	.033	.010	.021	.031	.024
	United Airlines	Mileage Plus	.035	.039	.017	.021	.020	.027
	Virgin Australia	Velocity	.022	.012	.016	.028	.012	.020

** For small countries (eg Switzerland) domestic definition includes directly neighbouring countries.
* For Hawaiian Airlines international definition includes flights to mainland USA.
Qantas: Includes 2025 devaluation.
Qatar Airlines: It is difficult to redeem points for Business Class - sample size was inadequate for valuation purposes.

How *Not* to Use the Valuations

Do not misinterpret these values to mean that one airline's loyalty system is better than another. The valuation of one point for one airline may be more than that of another airline. However, that is only part of the story. Each airline will require a different number of points for a similar flight.

Examples of the Use of Valuations

Here, we provide examples of how point valuations can be used to illustrate why the *Valuation Strategy* is so important.

EXAMPLE

Valuation Strategy

If The Value of Your Points is Worth More Than The Cash Price of a Flight, Then Pay Cash

We have provided a Target Redemption Value of $0.016 per point (1.6 cents per point) for Emirates Return International Economy flights. Let's discuss how you should use that value.

Suppose you can buy an Emirates Return International Economy flight for $500. If the airline accepts 60,000 points for the same flight, should you use points or cash?

To answer this question, multiply the points required by the Target Redemption Value (60,000 x $0.016 = $960). This means that, on average, you should be able to save $960 when redeeming 60,000 points on an Emirates Return International Economy fare.

However, in this example, you will save only $500. Therefore, you should pay cash and keep your points for an occasion when you can redeem them for their Targeted Redemption Value.

If you fly a mix of Business Class and Economy Class, you should expect a different redemption value between the classes.

You should also achieve different values for One-Way flights versus Return flights.

When making point acquisition decisions, you will not always know the fare type you will book with the points. Therefore, we recommend using the weighted average value.

EXAMPLE
Valuation Strategy

Using the Weighted Average Value to Evaluate Credit Card Offers

Suppose you were offered a credit card with a sign-up bonus of 100,000 Delta points (SkyMiles). How should you value that offer? If you are likely to use the points solely for International Business Class One-Way flights, refer to the table and value them at A$0.013 per point. That would make the offer worth A$1,300 to you (100,000 x A$0.013).

However, if you knew you would use the points exclusively for International Business Return flights, you would value the offer at $1,000 (100,000 x A$0.010).

However, you usually won't know what you'll use the points for when you earn them.

Therefore, we have made reasonable assumptions about the mix of flight types most people will take if they follow the advice in this guide. Using that mix, we calculated the weighted average value per Delta point as A$0.015 per point. On that basis, we would value the offer at A$1,500 (100,000 x A$0.015). Use this method to compare various offers.

Performing Your Valuations

You may be interested in an airline not listed here. As stated above, the Free Stuff includes an editable Point Valuation Template and instructions for completing valuations. The valuation method and an example of the format appear below.

		POINT VALUATION TEMPLATE				
		Qantas				
		International Economy				
				Cash Price	Points Required	Supplement. Payment
				C	P	S
				A$	Points	A$
	One-Way					
		From:	To:			
28-Feb	One-Way	SYD	SIN	751	25,200	147
7-Mar	One-Way	SIN	SYD	948	25,200	147
28-Feb	One-Way	MEL	LAX	1,177	41,900	223
7-Mar	One-Way	LAX	MEL	791	41,900	82
28-Feb	One-Way	SYD	HNL	953	26,000	216
7-Mar	One-Way	HNL	SYD	1,624	26,000	148
	Total Sample - Domestic One-Way Economy			6,244	186,200	963
	Cash difference (C minus S) = Cash Difference (D)			5,281		
	Value per Point (V) (D divided by P)			$0.028		
	Return					
		From:	To:			
	Return	SYD	SIN	1,636	50,400	308
	Return	MEL	LAX	1,978	83,800	305
	Return	SYD	HNL	2,332	52,000	236
	Total Sample - Domestic Return Economy			5,946	186,200	849
	Cash difference (C minus S) = Cash Difference (D)			5097		
	Value per Point (V) (D divided by P)			$0.027		
	# Enter into shaded cells only					

VALUATION STRATEGY

Treat points like foreign currencies. Convert your points to a cash equivalent, expressed in a familiar currency, per point. Use this valuation when:

• Evaluating offers of points from credit card companies and suppliers.

• Deciding whether to book a flight by redeeming points or paying cash instead.

4.2 REDEMPTION STRATEGY

You don't have to be rich to travel well.

EUGENE FODOR,
Travel writer and founder of Fodor Travel Guides

Why Read This Chapter?

You will learn to get at least two or three times the value from your points than the average frequent flyer. This will result in more free flights.

It's What You Do With Them

My dad was a World War II veteran. Starting at age 18, he served four years in the Australian Army. Two and a half of those years were spent in the jungles of Papua New Guinea, Borneo, and other Pacific islands, wondering where the next shot would come from.

Meanwhile, my mum was raised in the Australian country town of Cootamundra during the Great Depression. Her blacksmith father was the only one in the family who ate meat. It was expensive, but the family felt he needed it to fuel his heavy labour.

Many years later, I was to be named after Mum's brother Bruce, my favourite among an impressive group of uncles. Uncle Bruce did heavy labour after school in the Blacksmith's workshop. In return, he was given the privilege of having the dripping fat from the grill applied to his school sandwiches.

My parents rose from that less-than-easy background. With my uncle's help, my dad built the house where my family grew up. They did so with their own hands. Mum and Dad did not pay anyone to do things they could do themselves.

They found a cheap block in what was then known as "the bush," now a southern suburb of Sydney. Dad brought home building materials on the daily commuter train, and Uncle Bruce provided skills he had learned while training as a carpenter. At similar times, they built a house for Mum and an identical one for my auntie. They accomplished it on weekends and after hours, funding it with their day jobs.

They built a life from nothing, and I was raised in a lovely home. After many years, Dad bought his first new car. My uncle, his best mate, bought one, too. They had been working a double-length week since leaving the Army.

Many years later, it was time for me to leave school. In a case of perfect timing, the new Australian prime minister, Gough Whitlam, ushered in a brief period of enlightenment in the history of financing Australian education. When I took my final school exams, university fees had already been scrapped. That idea didn't last long. I soon found myself paying fees, but when I left school, it was free, and everyone wanted in. Luckily, I just scraped through with the required marks. But what do you reckon the chances were of Dad and Mum going soft and giving me time off while waiting for university to start?

The next day, I was taken to the small printing works my loving dad now owned. Before he bought it, he had worked in it since he left the army with undiagnosed PTSD. He got me busy wrapping parcels by a procedure worthy of a Boeing factory. Tighter! Harder! Faster! He soon got reminded that the son he loved was better with his head than his hands. He spread the newspaper before me at lunchtime and said, "Get a job."

I picked one that required no experience and phoned them. Dad drove me to the interview in the city the same day. I started the next day. I was unsure of the job's details. Bewildered, I found myself in an accounting office. I liked the numbers and the short skirts around the office. I decided to study finance instead of chemistry.

Having been raised by parents who started with nothing but were now doing well, my dad taught me his wisdom, which he often repeated: *"It's not just the dollars you earn. It's what you do with them."*

When I took that job, the wily old accountant I worked for took a shine to me and imparted his life advice. *"It's not just the dollars you earn. It's what you do with them."*

But not being the sharpest tool in the shed regarding life skills, I blew plenty of dough before that lesson sank in.

Okay. Thanks for the family history, Shorty, but what's the bloody point?

I am trying to stress this: It's not just the points you earn; it's what you do with them.

People often earn many points and use them on the first available flight. They adopt an attitude of, *"Who cares? I got them for nothing anyway."* But points do not come in unlimited quantities. Getting good value for points is as essential as getting good value for your English pounds, US dollars, or Guatemalan quetzals.

Redemption

Before discussing the redemption of points for flights, let me explain the meaning we attribute to a single word. *Redemption*.

When I was seven, my Sunday school moved from the lady next door to the local church. I have early memories of a man in black robes yelling from the pulpit about fire, brimstone, death, and redemption—scary stuff at seven.

The *Oxford English Dictionary* defines redemption as *the act of being saved from sin, error, or evil*. An example of usage is, *"You will be subject to eternal damnation if you do not achieve redemption."* I have big hopes for the impact of this guide. But helping you with the afterlife is above my pay grade. I am not talking about that kind of redemption.

The dictionary lists a second meaning: *gaining possession of something in exchange for payment*. An example of usage is: *"She obtained food during the war through the redemption of food ration stamps."* In this guide, we use the term *redemption* in the latter context.

Maximising Redemption Value

Maximising your redemption value per point is a significant priority. However, avoiding running out of points is also a major priority. You must balance these priorities.

If we solely wanted to redeem our points for the best cash equivalent value, we would use all our points for Business Class fares. However, we may quickly run out of points and be forced to pay cash for other flights.

Use your points for Business Class only when you have a compelling reason. You may be wasting your points on Business Class if you do not need the flatbed seat. The fact that you can get a higher redemption value by using your points on Business Class should not change your decision.

You either need a Business Class flight, or you don't. Even though you will get a higher redemption value on Business Class than Economy Class, you will use more points for Business. You should often preserve the points by flying Economy, just as you may preserve your cash, even when faced with a bargain.

We prefer to limit our Business Class flights to those that are necessary. That way, we can still get most of our other fares for free. But whatever ticket we buy, we want to get good value.

My mum used to say, *"Doug, it's on special at that price. We should buy it."* My dad used to reply, *"If we buy enough of those specials, Mary, we could go broke trying to save money."* Similarly, your points account can be depleted while you receive great value on Business Class.

It's like saying we can get you a 20% discount on a Mazda but a 35% discount on a Lamborghini. Or a 20% discount on a Guess accessory but a 35% discount on a Louis Vuitton accessory. You could go broke saving money. Similarly, you can achieve a higher redemption value per point by flying Business Class than by flying Economy Class. However, you can run your point account to a zero balance by redeeming them for multiple Business Class flights.

The values in this guide are the minimum values you should expect from your points. You can achieve these values quite easily. If you plan your trips well in advance, you can secure flights that achieve at least these redemption values for your points.

On the other hand, it is easy to use up your points on flights that are worth much less. Do not do that! If you *cannot* save the values listed here for each point used, then keep them for later use. The only exception would be if the points are about to expire and if you can do nothing to stall that expiry.

Note that the values are as of 2025. If you are reading this in a later year, please adjust for inflation.

The steps to ensuring you are achieving an adequate redemption value are:

- Step 1: Assess the best value flight for cash.
- Step 2: Assess the best value flight for points. Consider any supplementary payment required when using points.

- **Step 3**: Ascertain which of the five categories applies to the flight being considered. (e.g. International Business One-Way, Domestic Economy etc.)
- **Step 4**: Deduct the supplementary payment from the cash fare to get the net cash amount. Divide the net cash amount by the points you must use. This will give you the Proposed Redemption Value per point.
- **Step 5**: Compare the Proposed Redemption Value per point to the Target Redemption Values in this guide. Use cash if the Proposed Redemption Value per point is less than our Target Redemption Value for that fare type. Keep your points for an occasion when you can get better value.

Tell Him He's Dreaming

Some of you are thinking, *"You must be dreaming, Shorty. Your point valuations are too high."* If that is where you are, you have been redeeming poorly. For example, people commonly tell me their rule of thumb is one cent per Qantas point. Our rate is a minimum of 1.9 cents for Domestic Economy fares. It averages about 2.5 cents over the various fare types. Therefore, we receive two or three times the benefit from our points compared to many people.

It is just as easy to waste your points as it is to waste your dollars, pounds, or euros. If you are not careful, you can burn many points with a small amount of flying. Be careful to avoid poor redemptions. Ensure you always redeem close to or above our Target Redemption Values.

Our valuations of points are based on booking good-value but commonly available flights. We are as keen to get good value for our points as we are for our cash. This refers to this chapter's fundamental takeaway regarding points: *It's not just how many points you earn. It's what you do with them.*

Perform Your Sanity Check

As a learning exercise, research your Primary Airline by making a few "fake" bookings for cash or points on a couple of your favourite routes. Note the best and worst prices in both cash and points. Then, divide your best cash price by the range of prices expressed in points. Adjust for the supplementary payments. You should see a wide range of answers. Some will resemble our valuations, and some will show very low values per point. It's good to do it yourself occasionally, so you can see how we get our numbers.

You will note that values vary significantly depending on the sample you use. Only you know the routes you fly often. You should include them in your sample when you do your valuations.

Airlines Highlight Bargains

Airlines can see potential empty seats well in advance. Airline predictive models indicate they will likely have seats available on a specific route at a particular time on a specific day. If they do nothing, they will not have people in those seats. Look for these flights that the airlines are trying to backfill.

The airlines prefer to have people redeem points for a seat they may not sell. They know that many points are available for redemption, and it is better for the airline if people use their points on otherwise empty seats.

It will become obvious which flights airlines want to fill. Just browse the flights and note the differences in the points required.

For example, suppose your Primary Airline is American Airlines, and you wish to fly from Los Angeles to Paris. Firstly, consider how you can adjust your trip. If it is the beginning of your annual leave, you may have to leave that day to suit your holiday. However, you may still be able to adjust the departure time. American Airlines presents a neat list of all the fares and strikes through the regular price to clearly show any special prices.

Plan well ahead. Try to obtain unofficial approval from your workplace to take your two-week leave within a specified month. Then, before locking in your leave dates, search for flights over a longer period and consider the options for return flights. With this flexibility, you will find a hole. There will be one or two days when fewer points are required than on the others.

If possible, lock in your exact leave dates after you have found the best flight option. Some jobs don't offer flexibility around leave dates, such as if you are a general working for Vladimir. School and partner commitments impose further restrictions. However, half of the working population can adjust their travel dates.

Many airlines make it easy for you to find the flights they are trying to fill. They want you to see and book them, so they consciously price them low. We are not talking about finding pricing mistakes.

Malaysian Airlines calls their bargain points flights *Enrich Saver*. A recent review of a flight from Kuala Lumpur to London revealed that the standard Business Class points cost 443,100 points. However, on the same day, you could get an *Enrich Saver* Business Class flight for just 85,700 points. The flight time didn't suit my body clock, but who cares when you're flying Business Class and have a flatbed?

United Airlines refers to its bargain flights as *Saver Awards*.

Qantas labels them *Classic Rewards*. Qantas Frequent Flyer allows you to select a filter to view only these flights. If you display all flights, the Classic Rewards flights are labelled. Most flights I book with Qantas are Classic Rewards flights because they use far fewer points.

EXAMPLE

Redemption Strategy

Using the Valuations to Maximise Value

Suppose you have a significant point balance with American Airlines and wish to buy a Return ticket from Los Angeles to London.

Suppose the choices are as follows:

- The lowest cash price for an Economy Return ticket is A$1,350.
- The alternative is to pay 54,000 points plus a supplementary payment of $170.

The cash saved is $1,180, the fare price minus the supplementary payment that would be paid in addition to the points.

Given that 54,000 points are used to save a net $1,180, the saving per point is $0.022. When used for Return International Economy fares, our valuation of American Airlines points is A$0.018.

As this saving is higher than the value of the points, the booking should be made on points.

CASH SAVED WITH POINTS				
Cash Fare (If no points were used)	Supplementary Fee (If points are used)	Cash Saved (If points are used) C-S	Points Required	Savings per Point (also called Redemption Vaule) D div by P
C	S	D	P	V
$1,350	$170	$1,180	54,000	**$0.022**

Use the Valuations to Maximise Value (Example 1)

If you are travelling One-Way in Business Class and the fare is priced at 50,000 Swiss Airlines points (Award Miles), the cash price of the fare should be approximately $3,450. When buying this fare class, we can redeem Swiss points for 6.9 cents per point (50,000 x 0.069 = $3,450).

On the other hand, if you use 50,000 points for a One-Way Economy Class fare, you should get a Swiss flight worth $1,250 (50,000 x A$0.025). Swiss Award Miles typically redeem for less on this fare type.

Suppose you are likely to need to travel on a Swiss Airlines One-Way Business Class fare before the points expire. In that case, you should hang onto your points until then rather than using them on a typical One-Way Economy Class Domestic flight.

Using the Valuations to Maximise Value (Example 2)

We will use my Primary Airline in another example. We have assigned the following Target Redemption Values to one Qantas Frequent Flyer Point:

- A Return Domestic Economy Class value of 1.9 cents (A$0.019)
- A Return International Economy Class value of 2.7 cents (A$0.027)

That is, we try to avoid redeeming our Qantas points for any Return International Economy Class flight unless we save at least 2.7 cents per point.

However, we happily redeem our points for any value greater than 1.9 cents when booking a Return Domestic Economy Class fare.

This may seem contradictory at first. However, remember that the values listed here are the Targeted Redemption Values in each circumstance. We know that one day, we will get 2.7 cents of value when we redeem points for Business Class. However, we also know that if we flew Business Class exclusively to maximise redemption value, we would use up our points faster than we would like to.

Avoid Redeeming Your Points Below Our Recommended Values

If I have not stressed enough the importance of redeeming for a high value, try these numbers for size. As I wrote the first draft of this section, I added some fares to our database.

My fake booking with Qantas was made six months before the theoretical travel date. A Return *Business Class* ticket SYD-LAX-SYD was priced at 2,832,015 Qantas Frequent Flyer points. The airline offered Return *Economy Class* seats on the same flying hardware for 83,800 points plus a $212 supplement.

The points required for the Economy Class fares were a little expensive. We can do better than that. But how crazy was that Business Class fare? Our target Redemption Value for 2,832,015 points, at $0.027 per point, is $76,464!

In this example, we expect to pay no more than 300,000 Qantas points for the Business Class fare, which is often available. On the day in question, Qantas must have worked out they would fill the flight for cash and didn't want any freeloaders that day. They discouraged point flyers by charging almost 10 times the usual amount. By comparison, the Qantas Business Class Round-the-World ticket charge starts at 318,000 points.

We occasionally travel in Business Class when suitable bargains present themselves. But does anyone ever actually redeem their points as badly as the above Business Class example? Most people have never even seen that many points in their accounts at one time. While this is an extreme example, it illustrates that no strategy will save you if you use your points without care.

I recently heard a story about a famous actor who had made millions but was now broke. He had made bad financial choices. It's not what he earned; it's also about what he did with it. This also applies to your points.

Be cautious with your points, just like you are with your cash. Rather than treating your points like free stuff, treat them like valuable foreign currency.

Avoiding Poor Redemptions Associated with Certain Fare Types

As stated in an example above, when flying Qantas, our Target Redemption Value per point for Domestic Return Economy fares is only 1.9 cents (A$0.019). That is because that is the value we can easily find and expect to get when booking that fare type. The comparative Target Redemption Value is 2.7 cents for International Return Economy fares.

The expected redemption value of our points on Domestic Economy fares is relatively low compared to other uses. Therefore, we try to avoid using our points for domestic flights. That's when we use our Secondary or Tertiary airlines, starting with those points that may be in danger of expiring. Or, as a last resort, we may even pay cash if we can't get an excellent points bargain.

It's not just how many points you earn. It's what you do with them.

TRAVEL STORY

Redemption Strategy

Grab Opportunities to Achieve a High Redemption Value per Point

We had a long trip in Europe, followed by a wedding in Brazil on the way home to Sydney. Since we had to travel to Brazil for the wedding, we planned an extension of our trip to Sao Paulo, near where the wedding would be held.

After a Brazilian wedding to remember, we visited the old Spanish town of Paraty. It is spectacular at night and is a UNESCO World Heritage listed site. We visited Isla Grande, an unspoiled island with stunning beaches, excellent hiking trails, wild monkeys, and various other wildlife. Again, World Heritage listed. And then, of course, we made the obligatory and memorable visit to Christ the Redeemer, Sugar Loaf Mountain, and the beaches of Rio de Janeiro.

When planning our flights to Brazil, we stayed flexible when deciding where to spend our last six days in Europe. The departure from Europe was to be around 19th September. We did not lock into a departure point or date until we looked at flight options. Of course, our objective was to achieve either a super-low price or an economical use of points.

We determined that Qantas offered great point deals on British Airways-operated flights out of a few European cities, including the coastal city of Marseille. We could then use Qantas points to travel between Marseille and São Paulo (via London), flying with the Oneworld carrier British Airways. Because we were using points, we had to book through the Qantas site.

An Economy Class ticket per person would cost 45,000 points plus 207 euros. This compares well to an alternative cash cost of 864 euros, providing a redemption value of $0.022. That was lower than our target of $0.028 per point for One-Way International Economy flights, but it was not too bad.

However, the timing of the flights was unfavourable, departing at 6:14 p.m., flying for two hours, followed by a three-hour layover in London. Then, an 11-hour flight to Sao Paulo. We would have to break the journey in London if we were going to make it a pleasant flight. That would have resulted in an unwanted delay plus accommodation costs.

A Business Class Classic Rewards fare was also available for 104,500 points plus € 271 per person on the same flight. The alternative cash cost would have been $8,784 (€ 5,856) for each One-Way ticket. That valued the 104,000 points at A$0.084 each. It exceeded our targeted redemption value of $0.022 for One-Way International Business Class. It was way better value than if we had used them on Economy, as it was a long overnight flight. We would get good value out of those flatbed seats and avoid all the costs of breaking our flight in London. What a deal!

Avoid Redeeming Your Points Below Your Target Valuations

We bought some last-minute flights to Thailand from Sydney.

The flight cost approximately $1,160, so I should have paid that. Instead, I used 129,000 Qantas points, which redeemed them at less than one cent each. Yet our targeted redemption value for Return International Economy flights is $0.027 per point, so we should target flights worth about $3,000 for that many points.

With some planning, getting a return flight for 21,500 points each way is very easy. This would provide a redemption value of $0.027 per point. Or I could have saved the points for even better opportunities.

So why did I redeem our points for less than one cent instead of using cash? My brain faded. I should have paid cash and retained the points for a time when I could get better value.

My behaviour on that occasion is the behaviour I encourage you to avoid.

That week, we had a million dollars' worth of fun, and some unforgettable memories were formed. The trip was a fantastic idea, but we should have paid cash.

The other moral of this story is that you will make mistakes, but it's okay to learn from them and have fun. When flights are free, it's easier to accept booking errors.

EXAMPLE
Redemption Strategy

Increasing Redemption Value per Point by Remaining Flexible—Qantas

Here are some actual figures we noticed recently.

Flight A: Thursday, a Classic Rewards flight for 66,000 points plus $442 cash or $2,864 for the cash-only fare. Using points would provide a redemption value of 3.6 cents per point, which is good.

Flight B: Friday, 354,000 points with no cash supplement or $4,041 cash.

Our theoretical flyer could have paid 354,000 points for a flight that would have cost 66,000 points plus $442 if they had left just one day before!

In summary, the choices were between a Thursday flight for $2,092 worth of cash and points (66,000 x 2.5 cents plus $442) or the same flight on Friday for $8,850 worth of points (354,000 x 2.5 cents).

Stay Flexible.

Stay Flexible on Timing to Achieve High Redemption Values with Upgrades

American Airlines does not always put a flag on its low-cost flights. However, they present all the options for any date as a neat list.

When writing, you could pay 100,000 points, which we value at $4,000, for a Business Class flight from LAX to JFK (booking six months ahead) with a six-hour duration, leaving at 4:30 p.m. or 6:30 p.m. Alternatively, for 26,500 points, which we value at $1,060 worth of points, you could opt for an eight-hour flight leaving at 5:30 p.m., with the extra time being due to a stop.

Adding two hours to your trip time would save 73,500 points. At our weighted average target redemption value of A$0.040 per point, that represents a saving of A$2,940.

If I were running low on points, I would probably have considered a third option: the early morning flight in Economy Class for just 6,000 points, valued at $240. But I am a points scab.

In summary, the choices were a six-hour flight at 4:30 p.m. or 6:30 p.m. for $4,000 worth of points, an eight-hour flight at 5:30 p.m. for $1,060 worth of points or an early morning flight for $240 worth of points.

Stay flexible.

TRAVEL STORY

Redemption Strategy

Achieve High Redemption Values by Using Flights That Airlines Highlight as Points Bargains

Most airlines have a box to tick when you are searching for flights, saying something like "My dates are flexible." Tick it! Most airlines will help you find a bargain.

For example, the United Airways site provides a calendar for the whole month, with the lowest-cost flight for the day appearing in a box. This works whether you want prices quoted in cash or points. United put in the average points charge with a line through it to make it even more apparent. They display the discounted amount below it and label it "Saver Award".

One April, we were searching for a flight from Los Angeles to Paris in mid-July. We prefer to book further in advance, but things happen. The cheapest flight was available daily for 70,000 points, except on

USING POINTS & MILES TO MAXIMISE SAVINGS

Wednesdays when it was 36,000 points. The *average* cost in points was initially highlighted as 70,000 but was clearly crossed out.

If we had locked ourselves into flying on Tuesday, the best price would have been 120,000 points. The difference of 84,000 (120,000 less 36,000) is worth A$2,940 using our target redemption value of $0.035 per point for One-Way Economy International flights.

Yet, somebody will book the 120,000-point flight. They could then say, "Hey, I'm a guru. I got the flight for nothing."

Play the game well. You will be awarded more flights for your points.

REDEMPTION STRATEGY

It's not just the points you earn; it's what you do with them. Before using points, multiply the required points by the Target Redemption Value per point for the relevant fare type. Add any supplementary cash payment to arrive at the points price.

Compare the points price to the cash price. If the points price is higher, consider retaining your points. Make an exception if the points are about to expire and you cannot delay that expiry.

When making decisions about acquiring points, use the Weighted Average Value unless you know the specific fare type for which you will use them.

⑤

Finalising Bookings: Luxury & Safety

OUR TASK IS TO SAFELY transport you from point A to point B at the lowest cost without causing discomfort or inconvenience.

Previous sections outlined how to obtain free or cheap flights.

This section will focus on the finer points to consider that can make your trip more pleasant.

This section will outline:

- *Body-Clock Strategy*—choose the flight time to optimise cost and comfort.
- *Upgrade Strategy*—use the best methods for a free or cheap upgrade.
- *Pack Light Strategy*—pack to reduce cost and inconvenience.
- *Seating Strategy*—get the best available economy seat at no cost.
- *Lounge Strategy*—access lounges for free on most flights and, when you can't, know when to pay.
- *Safety Strategy*—identify which airlines you should avoid.

After reading this section, you will know how to make free or low-cost flights more comfortable while remaining safe.

5.1 BODY-CLOCK STRATEGY

Don't count every hour in the day.
Make every hour in the day count.

Why Read This Chapter?

You will learn how to select your flight time to make your flight more pleasant.

Timing for Comfort

You may enjoy sleeping while upright in an airline seat. If so, you are part of a small club. I call that club the Masochist Club. Most people will have a better trip if they fly when they are usually awake, considering the time zone at their departure point.

Trying to sleep upright in a cramped seat is the most significant contributor to an unpleasant flight. That is, unless you are flying on an airline that has lost most of its safety stars. Then, the most significant contributor to an unpleasant flight may be landing in the sea. We will cover our safety strategy later.

If flying Economy Class, try to fly at a time when you would naturally be awake.

This advice contradicts some budget travel guides that recommend flying overnight to save the cost of a hotel room. Ugh. That is like saving the price of a meal by starving yourself. We advocate travelling in luxury on a budget. But we would never put the budget ahead of a pleasant trip.

Consider your arrival time. Any arrival time is safe if you go from the airport terminal to a hotel with a 24-hour reception. However, if you are arriving in a city with security issues and must find an Airbnb or a Home Exchange, you may not want to arrive late at night.

Within your preferred departure and arrival windows, explore the available flight times.

For most flights, we use the *Body Clock Strategy*. We will not move to an uncomfortable time of day to save 20%. But to save 80%, I am prepared to hang upside down in the baggage compartment and sleep like a bat. However, assuming the price effect is insignificant, we have some self-imposed time slot restrictions. Everyone's acceptable range of time slots will differ.

Look at it this way. People pay a lot extra for a Business Class seat. They enjoy the better wine and eating off a china plate. But people spend the money primarily because they can lie flat during sleep.

Do not gloss over the flight time issue when you book a flight. Consider what it will be like to board the flight when the date arrives. If it is a 10-hour flight, you may have two alternatives:

- Accommodation Saving Method: Board at 9 p.m., watch a movie, eat food until 11 p.m., and then try to sleep while sitting up. Maybe sleep off and on for five hours. You will feel like crap by the time your body thinks it is 6 a.m. Emerge from the plane at a random local time, depending on the local time zone, when your body thinks it is about 7 a.m. Face the day with very little sleep. Your day will not be delightful. You will burn out early. Whatever you save on accommodation is not a bargain because your first day will be unpleasant and unproductive.

- The *Body Clock Strategy*: Board at 10 a.m. Have a coffee and read a book for an hour or two. Have lunch and watch a movie until about 2 p.m. Close your eyes briefly without needing proper sleep. Resume your book for an hour or two. Watch a bit of trash TV. Have an afternoon snack. Do something productive on your laptop. Do something unproductive on your laptop. Emerge from your flight when your body thinks it's 6 p.m. Make your way to your accommodation. The local time will be different, and there is no escape from jet lag. We all must face the issue of jet lag. However, you won't have to strap yourself into a seat and try to sleep in an unshowered, upright position. It is easier to handle the effects of jet lag in a comfortable bed than in an airline seat. Do not worry if your day starts at a weird time for a while. Things will normalise eventually.

The *Body Clock Strategy* can negate the need for a Business Class flight. We only book Business Class when we cannot avoid flying at a time when we would usually be sleeping

FLY FOR FREE

TRAVEL STORY
Body Clock Strategy

Fly at Times That Suit Your Body Clock

We love Hawaii. The four main islands are diverse. Oahu features the city of Honolulu, which boasts beautiful beaches nearby and is home to the fascinating World War II Pearl Harbour historical site.

On the other hand, the island of Kauai is the least built-up. We have hiked along the World Heritage-listed Na Pali Coast twice and rate it as one of the best single-day hikes in the world.

When heading to Hawaii from Sydney, many great experiences await; you don't want to waste a day or two recovering from jet lag after arriving.

You could board a flight to Hawaii at 8:00 a.m. and arrive 10 hours later, when your body thinks it is 6:00 p.m. and is not ready to sleep.

You may have watched a movie while eating, had a drink and a little afternoon doze, read something, or watched TV.

Alternatively, you could board at 8 p.m. After four or five hours, you will be exhausted and need to sleep. The best case for most people will be four or five hours of uncomfortable, restless sleep, usually interrupted.

Either way, you will arrive at an unusual hour due to the time difference. There is no way around time differences. However, your choice of flight time will determine whether you sort out the jetlag effects in a comfortable hotel room, on the streets at your destination, or in that modern torture chamber known as bedtime in Economy Class.

FINALISING BOOKINGS: LUXURY & SAFETY

> **BODY CLOCK STRATEGY**
>
> When flying Economy Class, avoid flight departure times that result in sitting upright in a seat at a time when you would prefer to shower and lie in bed. Plan on adjusting to jetlag in a hotel room, not a plane seat.

5.2 UPGRADE STRATEGY

You live. You learn. You upgrade.

Why Read This Chapter?

We all like upgrades. But pay? Not us. Pray? Too unreliable. You will learn how to secure Business Class upgrades frequently.

When to Pay for an Upgrade

Free upgrades are nice but unpredictable. Before you lock in a stopover between two long Economy Class flights, check the points required for a Business Class upgrade. If you prefer to reach your destination quickly without enduring the discomfort of sitting upright in an economy seat for an extended period, this would be an excellent time to upgrade to a Business Class seat.

We only need an upgrade if it's a long trip and we must sleep. Consider your body clock.

The price of a Business Class return flight from Sydney to London could be prohibitive. But four flights are involved: two on the way there and two on the way back. It may be just one of the outward-bound legs where we need a business-class fare. We find it easier to endure the long homeward trip because we know we can sleep in our beds when we get home.

The benefit of an upgrade will accrue on the flight that occurs when your body wants to sleep. Just because you have one flight on which you know you will use the flatbed is not a good reason to spend cash or points on all four flights.

Airlines will require two separate bookings to combine an Economy Class leg with a Business Class leg. However, separating the bookings will also allow you to search for them separately, optimising the cost of both. If necessary, use two different airlines.

Separating the bookings of the flight legs so that you can book some for cash and some on points may compromise your ability to use the *Return Strategy*; therefore, you should consider this. If you split the journey into two bookings, we recommend combining them with the *Stopover Strategy*. If you cannot do that, you should allow a long layover, as discussed in the *Layover Strategy* chapter (refer to Advanced Strategies for the *Stopover* and *Layover* Strategies).

We discussed our *Body Clock Strategy* elsewhere. The only thing better than that is to get a Business Class flight.

A 12-hour Economy flight leaving at 9 p.m. is unacceptable for us, as it does not align with our *Body Clock Strategy*. However, a Business Class flight leaving at that time is another story. By the time the flight is in the air and dinner is served, the natural time to sleep has arrived. A good night's sleep is assured if we have a flat bed. We will arrive relatively fresh.

Cost of Business vs. Economy

We analysed over 400 flights by 17 airlines. We included only the cheapest options on the days examined.

Our study showed that, on average, the cash price of International Business Class fares is 4.0 times that of Economy Class fares.

However, our study also showed that, on average, fares paid with points for Business Class cost 2.9 times more than those required for Economy Class. The normal premium for a Business Class seat over an Economy seat is a much lower percentage if you pay with points rather than cash.

BUSINESS FARES AS A MULTIPLE OF ECONOMY FARES, ON AVERAGE

Category	Multiple of Economy Class Fare
If paying cash	4.0x
If redeeming points	2.9x

Full-price cash Business Class fares are too expensive for most of us. I have only travelled in a seat that cost four times the price of the Economy option when a business mission justified the cost. Sure, we could sometimes find the money on holidays, but we would prefer to spend it on essentials, such as Formula One tickets or hiking up a mountain.

The Cost of Upgrades—Points

The base cost of a Business Class fare is relatively lower when paying with points. This often makes a discounted points fare an excellent option.

Finding a bargain Business Class flight on points is much easier than finding a bargain when paying cash. You can often pick up a good-value Business Class flight on the ugly leg if you pay with points.

When paying cash, only 7% of Business Class fares in our database were less than 2.0 times the Economy Class fare or less. Almost none were less than 1.6 times the Economy fare.

However, 30% of points fares are offered below 2.0 times the points required for Economy, and 19% at a rate below 1.6 times.

	BUSINESS CLASS: CASH VS POINTS	
	Percentage of Business Class Fares:	
Payment Method	costing less than 2.0 Times the Economy Price	costing less than 1.6 Times the Economy Price
Cash Fares	7%	3%
Point Fares	30%	19%

The discounted points fares are excellent value. We usually take them if the flight is longer than five or six hours, or when we expect to get very tired during a flight and will need to sleep. Use them to avoid those awful flights that require you to sleep while seated.

FINALISING BOOKINGS: LUXURY & SAFETY

High Number of Bargain Upgrades When Redeeming Points

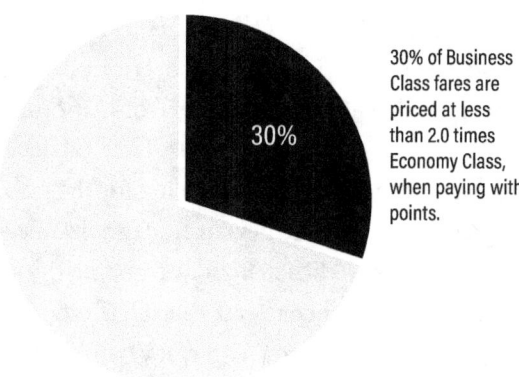

We cannot justify the expense of a cash booking for Business Class at everyday prices. However, it is easy to justify booking the 30% well-priced Business Class points fares. Being flexible with dates can substantially increase this percentage.

We recommend against paying more than 2.0 times the points required for Economy.

Cheaper Options than Business

Another option is to pay the extra fee for some additional legroom. This is usually only a couple of hundred dollars per person. Think of the savings compared to a Business Class seat. The extra legroom will look cheap.

Consider buying a blow-up foot pillow. If you have got the right seat, no one will mind. Check Seatguru.com (refer to next chapter) to ensure you are not getting a seat near where people congregate for the toilet. Consider paying for an exit row. Be discreet with the pillow, as a hostess might ask you to remove it. Put a blanket over it and your feet. This strategy works best if you have a window seat. Combining the extra legroom and the foot pillow can help you stretch out.

I used to do it, but I now take one of the other options. The downside is that carrying the blow-up foot pillow conflicts with my passion for travelling light. But if your habit is to check in a bag, you can easily make room in your carry-on for the blow-up pillow.

Alternative Approaches

Everyone wants to know how to get a discretionary upgrade for free. Searching for bargain priced points flights works more often than any other method.

Some people say you must start by dressing for the part. They say the staff will not upgrade you if you are in your tracky daks. If you're okay with wearing a suit for your next 20 beach holidays, hoping the staff will assess you as worthy on one of those occasions, then go for it.

If you are convinced that the lady with crazy hair is right about getting upgrades when she lights her candles under a pyramid, why not try it?

However, please note that unpaid upgrade awards are always at the discretion of airline staff.

Undoubtedly, a high status level helps. However, we live in an era of flexible pricing models and large data sets. Rarely do airline revenue departments fail to find a way to get a paying customer's bottom into Business Class seats. They will progressively discount the ticket price if there is an empty seat as the flight date approaches. If there are empty seats, they will most likely be at the back of the Airbus.

A mistake by the airline on an outward flight can help you secure an upgrade on the return flight. Qatar lost our bag on the way to Croatia and upgraded us to Business Class on the way home. I struggled to figure out how to engineer a lost bag on the next trip. Ultimately, I decided against leaving a banknote peeking out of the bag and putting a message on the bag saying, "Mr. Baggage Handler, please steal this bag and return it to the address on the label for a reward."

When our extra-legroom seat was double-booked on an Emirates flight, a staff member attempted to upgrade us to Business Class, but the flight was too full. Damn!

All the methods that do not involve paying cash or points have one thing in common. They are not methods.

We prefer to lock in upgrades with points when bargains present themselves, but not with cash.

The foolproof way is to use some points and book a Business Class fare on the 19% of occasions when the premium is less than 60% over the points required for Economy Class. If you want a better than 19% chance of locating one of those bargains, you can considerably improve your odds by being flexible about your flight date.

We do not recommend using extra points to fly Business Class on domestic flights. All companies for which I served as CFO had a policy banning Business Class domestic travel. Business Class for a domestic flight does not present good value because you either do not get a flatbed seat or won't use it.

Some airlines allow you to bid for an upgrade as the flight time approaches. This can work, but is unpredictable. You won't know the outcome until close to flight time. If we need a Business Class flight, we book it. If we don't, we keep our cash or points. However, sometimes a low-ball bid can be adequate. If you are in a gambling mood, have a shot at it. But it is not part of our budget strategy. We want to help you get home on your budget so you can prepare for your next trip.

UPGRADE STRATEGY

Use the Body Clock Strategy as much as possible. However, consider booking Business Class with points when you need to make an overnight flight. Do not use points for Business Class any other time. Ensure points for Business Class are redeemed close to the Target Redemption Value. Additionally, ensure that the Business Class points cost is no more than 2.0 times that of Economy Class, aiming for a ratio of 1.6 times. If you can't redeem close to those values, find an alternative solution.

5.3   PACK LIGHT STRATEGY

> **Passenger:** *"Can you send my bag to a different destination than the one on my ticket?"*
>
> **Check-in Attendant:** *"No, we can't do that, sir."*
>
> **Passenger:** *"Why not? You did it on the last trip."*

Why Read This Chapter?

You will learn how to further reduce the cost of your airfares and make your air travel more convenient. Commuting after you leave the airport will also become cheaper and more manageable.

Benefits of Packing Light

On some trips, the financial cost of carrying more baggage than you need may be subtle. But on most long trips, the price will dent your budget. Travelling light has a few benefits. The quantifiable cash cost is just one.

Eliminating a checked bag can result in significant cost savings. Avoiding checked baggage is the definition of travelling light, but reducing your checked bag from 30 kg to 29 kg by removing the second pair of gum boots is not.

Checked-in baggage is costly for airlines. Fuel usage is heavily related to the plane's weight at take-off. If the average person weighs 80 kg and their average check-in bag plus carry-on weighs 27 kg, then 25% of the passenger-related load is comprised of baggage.

It requires machinery and labour to check your bag, get it to the plane, and load it. More equipment and labour will be needed to unload and move it to the baggage carousel at your destination. Upon landing, passengers can read the signs and locate the baggage carousel. The dumb bags cannot work that stuff out for themselves. The process of tracking a bag is more complex than tracking a passenger. Although I'll admit, the consequences of losing a passenger are much worse than those of losing a bag.

Imagine if airlines treated passengers like they treat our bags. A dedicated desk, known as the Lost Passenger Desk, would be established. *"What was the size and shape of the missing passenger, sir? When we find them, we'll send them to your hotel."*

Many years ago, airlines included the cost of bags in the fare. Eventually, all parties realised passengers made better decisions if their fares were more closely related to airline costs. Why should the person who has no check-in baggage subsidise those who do? If Auntie Flo wants to take five jackets, shouldn't that be at her expense? Airlines and passengers have become aware of this cross-subsidy. Most airlines in most countries are now charging for each bag.

Less weight will also make your trip more pleasant. Don't put that triple cheeseburger down. I'm referring to the weight of your suitcase. The less stuff you have, the easier it will be to unpack, repack, and stay organised. If you must sit on your bag to close it, you will be in organisational trouble during your trip.

The first prize is for avoiding checked-in bags. If you can do this, there are many benefits:

- You will spend no time at baggage carousels moving towards unidentified black lumps and telling yourself to buy a hot pink bag next time.
- You will have less stressful connections. Particularly the ones where you must change airlines during your layover. You will no longer need to collect and recheck a bag when moving from an international terminal to a domestic one. You won't have to wait at the baggage carousel when your flight connection becomes uncomfortably short due to a flight delay.
- You also cannot lose anything if you do not commit to giving your baggage to the airline to look after.

Lost Bags

For international flights, 12 bags were mishandled per 1,000 passengers for the year ended December 2023 *(SITA's 2024 annual insights report)*. Some passengers will have had no bags, and some will have had two, but if we assume there was one checked bag per passenger, 1.2% of bags were mishandled. Suppose you are on a long trip involving 20 flights. That means there is a 24% chance an airline will lose or delay your bag on one of your flights. And if you are travelling as a couple, the odds go to 48%.

This does not reflect the professionalism of the airline industry, which has improved considerably from a mishandling rate of three times that in 2007.

Instead, it reflects on the difficulty of the task. When hundreds of passengers embark on a journey, their numerous bags embark on a different journey. If only your bag could tell you a story. And then, you must meet up at a set time and place after your bag's journey ends.

We met a Canadian lady in Grand Bahama who wore similar clothing daily. The airline had not lost her bag. They knew where it was; it was just that it was having a separate trip from hers. The airline had assured her it would be safely delivered soon. She was only away for one week, so when they found the bag, sending it to her home made more sense. It was not recorded as a *lost* bag. It was classified as a *mishandled* one because they'd found it.

If you take your baggage onto the plane, you will never have to experience walking around a Moroccan 45-degree day in your flight tracky daks because your favourite airline lost your bag again.

Freedom of Movement

If you carry a large amount of luggage, you will incur costs and experience inconveniences long after leaving the airport.

The reason it is called *luggage* is that you must *lug* it. Who enjoys lugging?

The less weight you have, the faster you will get around. Keep eating those fries. I was talking about luggage again.

If two people arrive at the car hire place with two large pieces of luggage and two carry-ons, they cannot hire a Fiat Bambino. A tiny car is very suitable, even preferable, for small islands in places such as Spain, Greece, and Croatia. However, those small cars will not accommodate bulk luggage. You may have to pay to upgrade the vehicle to make your bags comfy.

How to Avoid Checked Baggage

On some long-haul flights, you are allowed to take two carry-on bags, each weighing up to 7 kg. On shorter flights, the theoretical restriction is usually one 7 kg wheelie bag and a personal item.

I travel with a 7 kg wheelie bag and a small backpack. The backpack is small but weighs 7 kg because it holds my electronics. I may be challenged one day, but not yet. I have travelled around the world many times and have never been asked to check my backpack.

If you travel with Ryanair or another low-cost budget airline, this may not work, but you can pay to check in a bag on those rare occasions. Almost all the time, you will get 14 kg of luggage into the plane's cabin at no charge. And what's the worst thing that can happen? On one flight, one day, you may be asked to check in your backpack or wheelie bag. But that is better than checking a bag every time. And if they do ask you to check it in, they will have no facilities or time to charge you for it at the boarding gate. It is likely to be checked in for free.

On our Primary Airline, a personal item is defined as *a small backpack, handbag, camera, or small amount of reading material*. The guidelines for personal items vary from airline to airline, but generally, it will qualify if you can fit it under the seat in front of you. Not that you will put it under the seat in front of you. They may ask you to do that as you board, but just put it in the overhead bin anyway. I have rarely had to take it down.

Place your backpack in the overhead locker top first. When they open the overhead, people should see the fat bottom of the pack. The bigger it looks, the better, because if the plane is full, the staff will quickly look through the overhead compartments to find some small bags they can ask passengers to stow under the seat in front. If the check-in staff tagged your pack, indicating it should go under the seat, ensure the tag is not easily visible.

Ensure your wheelie carry-on bag is the correct size, as an oversized one may be rejected. However, the size limits on the "personal item" are promptly ignored by everybody. Look at your next boarding queue. Every queue includes many people carrying a regulation wheelie suitcase and a backpack that exceeds the vague sizing guidelines. If you do not overdo it, no one will say anything. Any daypack will do. Whatever you do, though, do not ask the staff. They may be obligated to say no. Forgiveness is easier to get than permission.

My TripIt app has recorded all my flights over the last two years. I flew 420,000 kilometres, which equates to 10 times around the world. I never checked in a bag. Nor was I asked to take my day pack from the overhead locker and place it at my feet.

Don't Load Up While Travelling

Try not to buy much stuff while you're away. Like that Sahara Desert snow globe. And the spectacular spoon minder. Resist the temptation to buy crap that will go in the back of your cupboard. Your kids will only put it in the skip bin when they pack up your house one day.

Follow the trekker's mantra. *Take only photographs. Leave only footprints.* The less stuff you have, the further you can walk. With a huge bag, you will find yourself asking for infuriatingly short taxi rides—the type of taxi rides that make Argentinian cab drivers use their particular words about gringos.

Couples Can Compromise

You may compromise if you are a couple.

I travel with very little luggage.

At this point, Lynda says, *"But you don't have hair."* Good point. Or she says, *"If you want me to look like THIS, then I must carry THIS"*—another good point.

I conclude that packing is easier for bald males than hairy females.

We usually take one medium-sized check-in bag because Lynda does need hair products and a few other conveniences. Because we have the bag, we throw in a few other well-considered things that help us economise while on the road, like a Thermos and a small cooler bag. However, by cutting back to just one checked bag between us, we still save a considerable amount on baggage charges. We can fit one small check-in bag, two carry-ons, and my small backpack into a compact car.

Taking one smallish checked-in bag between you and your partner is probably a reasonable compromise. However, it will be comforting to some of you that two bald people with no fashion sense can skip all the checked bags.

TRAVEL STORY
Pack Light Strategy
Caribbean Baggage

Our long-haul flights to the Caribbean from Australia included a baggage allowance in the fare. After arriving in the Caribbean, we had 11 flights over the course of eight weeks. While this may sound onerous, many of these flights were only 30 minutes or so. The Caribbean has limited ferry services, so the flights were necessary for the trip.

Each flight involved an average baggage charge of A$60 per checked-in bag. If a couple can avoid checked baggage on a similar trip, they would save $1,320 in baggage charges (2 x $60 x 11). Consider that before packing those brown boots, in case you don't feel like wearing the black ones one night. And the luxury head pillow instead of the blow-up one. And that big tube of fantastic stuff that is essential to life as you know it. Take a smaller tube.

We checked in one bag between us and saved $660 compared to checking in one bag each.

Packing Guidelines

Reducing your luggage by 10 kg on your first attempt may be too hard. Work towards it by creating space in your bag on one trip and checking in a smaller case on the next trip. Eventually, you may be able to shrink it to the two pieces of luggage you are allowed to carry on for most flights. The target is to reduce your luggage to 14 kg, the free carry-on limit, spread between a regulation-size carry-on and a small daypack.

Many of you will not carry much more than that now, but have not reconfigured your baggage. If you take a check-in bag, you may be tempted to throw in a few extra things you don't need.

Of course, you may occasionally need to make exceptions. I have made exceptions where a business suit was required. I also made an exception when a business conference in Iceland required a Viking fancy dress. It's not that I am implying that Vikings wear fancy dresses. And not that anything would be wrong with that. Shrink your baggage where you can.

Go through every single item, no matter how light or small, and ask yourself, *Is there any possible way I can make this lighter or smaller?* Can you manage with a smaller tube of toothpaste, considering the length of your trip? Can you leave out the cotton buds? Can you carry five pairs of socks instead of seven? Ask yourself, *Can I take a lighter diving bell helmet?* and so on.

- *If in doubt, leave it out.*
- *Nothing new: Do not take anything new, particularly shoes.* Everything you take must be tried and proven. Wear it at home often before deciding to pack it. Otherwise, you might be tempted to take the old comfortable one, just in case the new one doesn't fit well.
- *Do not take spares, except for medical reasons:* If you find yourself packing something "just in case," leave it out. What about taking an extra one in case you lose the first one or it breaks? Following that logic to its conclusion, you will take an extra luggage set. But a spare pair of prescription glasses is a good idea. I wrap mine in a few layers of cling wrap to protect them and put them in with my toiletries. A case for spare glasses is unnecessary because they will probably never be used anyway.
- *Do not travel with gadgets you don't regularly use at home.* Consider the number of hours you will be away and the number of hours you will use your gadgets.
  You may be flying for 40 hours over the course of a four-month trip. Four months equals 2,880 hours (120 days x 24 hours). If you

don't have your big noise-cancelling earphones and must use the ones supplied by the airline, you can still watch the movies. Does the marginal benefit of those headphones for 40 hours of flying (1.4% of your trip) justify carrying them for the other 2,840 hours? On the other hand, you may be travelling for a short two-day trip and taking eight-hour flights each way to get there. You may need to sleep to go to work on your return. Then, the big noise-cancelling earphones may be worthwhile. The 16 hours you will use the earphones in 48 hours is 33% of your trip.

- *Do not pack for more than seven days:* If you are away for three days, pack for three days. If you are away for six days, pack for six days. If you are away for one week, pack for one week. However, if you are away for three weeks, pack as if you are going away for one week. If you are away for three months, pack as if you are going away for one week. A one-week supply of clothes leaves plenty of time to wash. If you are away for three weeks, don't pack 21 pairs of undies plus two, just in case.

- *Don't take something just in case.* Don't think, *What else should I take, just in case I need it?* and put it in. Instead, think, *Am I sure I will use this?* If not, remove it. The whole world has shops.

- *Take clothing that can be mixed and matched:* If you must pack for your Instagram followers, avoid taking the aqua blue mohair headband that only goes with that pearl grey activewear. Your luggage will multiply. I leave my aqua blue mohair headband at home.

- *Wear materials that you can rinse in a basin and dry quickly:* I mean, dry the clothes quickly, not the basin. Some items require a short wear-wash-dry-wear cycle, such as underwear and T-shirts. Ensure that some items are made of material you can wash in a hand basin when you cannot access one of those infernal washing contraptions. If you travel to a warm location, avoid packing denim jeans, as they are bulky, heavy, and take a long time to dry. Consider purchasing full-length travel pants from outdoor shops. You can wash them in a basin and dry them quickly. They occupy one-third of the space.

- *Do not take your home favourites:* If you are packing something because it's your favourite at home, do not pack it in your suitcase unless you need it. At home, in the cool part of the year, I like my track pants and the remains of two small lambs in the form of my favourite UGH boots. Leave it all out. Make do with socks on your feet, multi-purpose lightweight travel pants, a t-shirt, and a fleece. Do not pack that coat made of Mongolian grizzly with the big tree on the front just because you wear it at home.

- *Shrink every item:* Size matters. Please review all items in your proposed luggage and determine how to shrink them. If you must take those hair products, determine how much you will use during your trip and find a container that allows you to take only the necessary amount.

- *Buy consumables while away:* Do not take large quantities of anything that can be purchased elsewhere (which is almost everything, by the way). Do not pack two months' consumables if you go away for two months. You should visit grocery stores regularly to get your top-ups. Your country does not have a patent on toothpaste. The whole world sells it.

- *Avoid travelling with valuable items:* Electronics are generally expensive, heavy, and attractive to steal. You should only take the ones you cannot do without. Take cheap jewellery. If all your jewellery is expensive, then that's your fault. It would have been better if you had a partner like me. Cheap.

- *e-Reader (e.g., Kindle):* Try giving up paper books when travelling. I love paper books, but they stay at home. I like to take my guidebooks, but I take the e-version. Not all guidebooks are available as e-books, so I thoroughly review those before leaving and scan the necessary pages. Paper is one more enemy of travelling light. Take none.

- *Don't accumulate papers as you travel:* Photograph receipts, brochures, and souvenir tickets and dispose of the paper.

- *Computer:* I use my computer to work on the road, so I try to find ever lighter-weight ones. Next time you buy one, consider purchasing the slimmest and lightest that will do the job. My computer is very slim. She's a beauty. She is the only valuable item I travel with, apart from Lynda. I put her in the room safe, hide her, or take her with me. The computer, I mean, not Lynda. I ensure that anything important is backed up. It would be best to assume your equipment will get stolen one day. Hope for the best and plan for the worst.

- *Phone*: Get one with the best built-in camera available. It will save you from having to carry a separate camera. I love photography, but I also love travelling light.

PACK LIGHT STRATEGY

Limit checked-in bags to a maximum of one per couple. Never pack for more than seven days. Avoid packing valuables and paper. Additionally, consider bringing a phone with a high-quality camera. If in doubt, leave it out.

5.4 SEATING STRATEGY

> **Passenger:** *"Steward, can I change my seat because of that crying baby?"*
>
> **Steward:** *"Not when it's your baby, sir."*

Why Read This Chapter?

When travelling Business Class, it is hard to get a poor seat. However, when travelling in Economy, the differences between similarly priced seats can be substantial. This chapter teaches you how to secure the best Economy Class seat on any plane.

Features of the Best Seat

Okay, you've got yourself a free flight or a great deal. That's good enough. Right? Hell no! You want the best seat available.

While differences between most Business Class seats will be subtle, the differences between Economy Class seats can be huge.

Select your seat early to ensure your preferred window or aisle. Try to do this when you book your flight.

Most people are aware of the differences between window and aisle seats. The window seat is near the window, and the aisle seat is near the aisle. Pretty straightforward? It may surprise you that some seats labelled as window seats do not have a window. I am serious. There are at least two in many commercial airliners. Due to the construction of planes, a few window seats have a blank wall where the window would usually be. They build them this way for some stupid reason, like needing to bolt the wings on. Please do what you must do, Boeing, but airlines should not call them *Window* seats. Perhaps they should call them *Wall of Disappointment* seats.

Then there is the piggy seat. The airlines don't call them that. They try not to call them anything, as most people wish they didn't exist. But they call them middle seats if they must name them.

The band of people who enjoy being piggy in the middle is tiny. Piggy in the middle can be good for a child sitting between two parents. And I know some young men pray they get a member of the Swedish Bikini Team on each side of them, but that's unlikely.

Seat selection goes way beyond choosing an aisle or a window. You do not want to be seated next to the bathrooms.

Even if you didn't get the seat closest to the bathroom, you do not want the one where people congregate in front of you during the peak bathroom hour. I do not enjoy having one of those guys near me who talks loudly to his mate. I do not want to hear about the price of taxis in Western Iran or his opinion on the odds of China invading a country I am already done with. Stay away from seating near bathrooms.

Try to get ahead of the bit that looks like a wing. Because it *is* a wing. The engines are typically mounted under the wings and produce significant noise. You will hear more noise when in the seats behind those engines than if seated ahead of them. That is why First Class is always at the front. You will want to get as far forward as possible, all other things being equal. At least get ahead of the wing.

However, don't get too close to the bulkhead. The bulkhead is the feature that acts like a wall, keeping people like me from entering Business Class without paying. It also holds bits of the plane together, so let's not be too picky. However, the bulkhead is also where many airlines allow people with babies up to six months old to sleep in a bassinet. They hook onto the bulkhead. The bassinets hook on, not the babies.

Don't get me wrong. I love babies. I love them when they are part of my family. I love babies in my house and other people's houses. Lynda and I currently pray for more babies in the form of more grandchildren. No pressure, kids! However, when on a flight for seven hours with seven more remaining, I prefer not to sit close to a random baby.

I have fathered several babies. I get that it's a significant experience for a baby to fly, which can sometimes make the flight a significant experience for a parent. I've been there and done that. It is natural for babies to cry. It has nothing to do with their upbringing or character. Sometimes, they cry because of ear pain caused by changes in air pressure.

Babies are all different, just like people. Come to think of it, they *are* people. Just tiny ones that poop a lot and cry at 3:00 a.m.! Some people change their babies less often than others, and that's their privilege. Some smells, however, do not blend well with the bouquet of a Chardonnay. Bulkheads. Be warned!

Using SeatGuru

There are other complications, meaning you will need help choosing your seat.

For example, many seats look the same on a seating diagram. However, one may have a transformer for the entertainment system under the seat in front. That takes away some of your footroom. And let's face it. A slight reduction in footroom doesn't matter much if you are in someone's car for only 30 minutes. However, on a 14-hour flight, losing a bit of footroom is a significant issue. It is pathetic how those few centimetres can assume some importance, mainly after many hours have passed in *Economy Class*.

Thankfully, help is available through a website dedicated to finding the best seat on any given plane. The site www.seatguru.com tracks the aircraft used on each route daily. They do not just keep track of the plane type but the actual aircraft. Clever stuff, hey? And don't worry, Scrooge. It's free.

Enter the flight number and departure date. The SeatGuru system will show you a seat map of the very same plane you'll be flying on. Seats colour-coded red are bad and should be avoided. The best seats are green. If possible, try to get the green seats. Avoid the red ones at all costs. There's often a charge for the green seats, but there's never a discount for the red ones.

Red often signifies bad smells, noisy kitchens, or the flash of a bathroom light as the door opens and closes every time a passenger needs the facilities.

There is also that noise those airline toilets make. Is all that fuss necessary? I think the Boeing guy, who was taken off the instrument design and allocated to the toilet design, created those huge sucking noises as a cry for attention.

The seats that are left white on the seat diagram are fine. Just avoid the red ones. The green seats are often worth it on a long flight, even with an extra charge.

The *www.seatguru.com* site is fantastic and worth using to find the best seats. Book early and select your seat when the airline allows you to.

In summary, here are the tips for avoiding bad seats:

FINALISING BOOKINGS: LUXURY & SAFETY

- Go to the SeatGuru map. Avoid anything red.
- Take a green one if it is available and free of charge.
- Assuming you do not get a green one, my advice is to ignore the five rows following the bulkhead. If you cannot get a green seat, there is no reason to lob into the baby zone unless you have a baby or are a baby. No. I mean, a real baby. Not an adult who behaves like a baby. Also, ignore the three rows closest to the rear bulkhead, as you do not want to be near the toilet or kitchen. SeatGuru will only colour the worst of these seats red.
- Then choose from the remaining white seats, considering your preference for aisle, window, and piggy-in-the-middle.
- Within the above restrictions, get as far forward as you can.

Choices for Each Seating Configuration

Often, if you are on a long flight, the seating configuration in Economy will be 3-4-3. That is three on the left, four down the middle, and three on the right.

The obvious considerations are:

- In the window seat, no one will ever disturb you.
- The aisle passenger must consider that the window passenger and piggy-in-the-middle occasionally want to get up. A well-trained window person often gets up if Piggy has already disturbed you. But there's no guarantee of that.
- Piggy gets both. They get to disturb the aisle, and they get to be disturbed by the window.

The key to the diagrams below is as follows:

- Each square represents a seat.
- Black means the seat you are sitting in.
- White means an empty seat.
- Grey means a seat in which another passenger is seated.

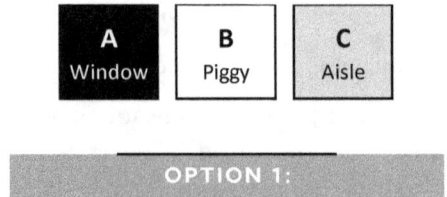

OPTION 1:

Base Case—two passengers next to each other with a low likelihood of being disturbed

If two of you travel together, taking the aisle seat in a bank of four and the one next to it in the same bank of four is a good option. You can get up at any time without disturbing anyone else. The other two will always follow the most accessible route out the other side, even if they are not together.

This is one of the two options that Lynda and I prefer. We will take it if Lynda thinks she will get some sleep, as she will never be asked to get up. I always need an aisle seat. I get claustrophobic if I'm unable to get up and down regularly. Yes, I am precious. Okay?

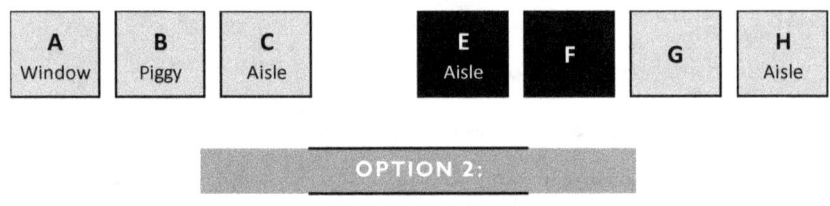

OPTION 2:

Two aisle seats

The other option that works for us, particularly if Lynda doesn't think she will sleep, is for us both to take aisle seats. We allocate aisle seats in the same row but with the aisle in between. We can still pass each other things, watch the same movie if we want, or quickly get up together for a leg stretch. We will both have people wanting to get out, but if we are not sleeping, then that does not matter.

This option has another advantage. About half the time, if the plane has empty seats, an empty one will be beside you. If the plane has spare seats, airline staff or passengers will avoid choosing the piggy seat for another single passenger.

If you are alone in the aisle seat on a bank of four, the staff will likely try to leave the seat next to you empty.

FINALISING BOOKINGS: LUXURY & SAFETY

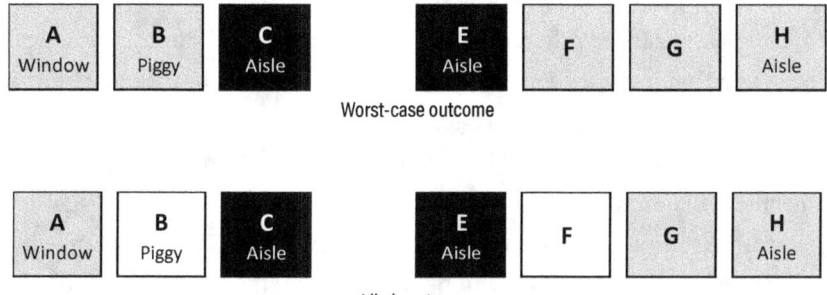

Worst-case outcome

Likely outcome

Occasionally, you may be lucky enough to be on a flight with many empty seats. In that case, you are well placed to secure enough seats for napping, lying down, etc.

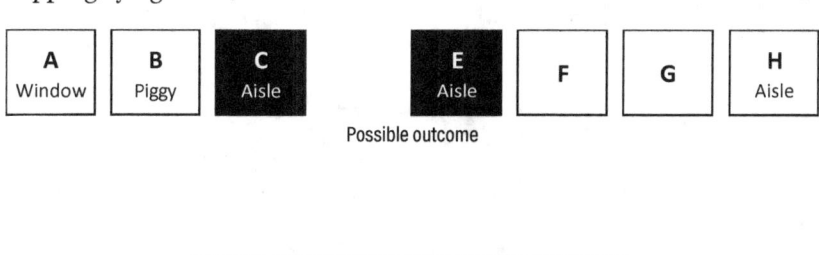

Possible outcome

OPTION 3:

Aim to capture a bank of three with an empty seat between you

If you or your travel partner likes the window seat, you should capture the extremities on the bank of three. It increases the chances of an empty seat between you. If that doesn't work out because the plane is chock-full, the passenger stuck in the middle will always swap. If not, talk across them a lot, and they will surrender.

This may not be how your airline prefers to load its passengers.

When I tried to allocate seats this way when making a recent Qantas booking, I started by allocating myself an aisle seat. Then, I allocated Lynda a window seat, leaving the middle seat blank. The Qantas software automatically moved me back to the piggy seat so Lynda and I would be seated together.

If you encounter this issue when booking with your chosen airline, a workaround is available. Make two separate bookings. Then, the seats will stay allocated as you choose. That's not so bad. We often must make two bookings anyway. Some airlines do not allow us to make a single booking for two passengers on different fare types. Frequently, we want the fare type for Lynda that includes a check-in bag, but we want a cheaper one for me that does not allow a check-in bag.

If you have made two bookings to secure your preferred seat allocations, the check-in counter staff may ask if you would like to be seated together. Just say, *"No thanks. We like our window and aisle seats."* If you end up with someone between you, that will be quickly sorted out on the plane. But you will likely secure an empty seat beside you.

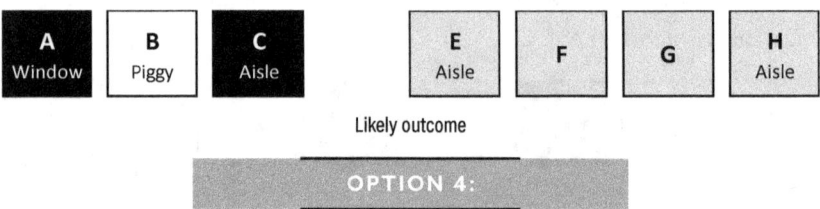

Likely outcome

OPTION 4:

If the seat configuration is 2-3-2, allocate your seat early enough to secure one of those pairs.

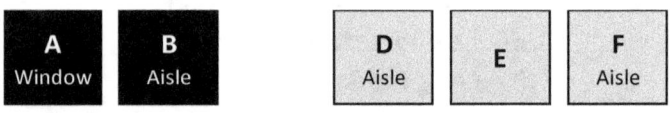

The pair of two

SEATING STRATEGY

Avoid seats in the five rows following the front bulkhead, the three rows in front of the rear bulkhead, and any seat flagged as red by www.seatguru.com. Within these constraints, sit as far forward as you can.

5.5 LOUNGE STRATEGY

Luxury must be comfortable. Otherwise, it's not luxury.

COCO CHANEL

Why Read This Chapter?

You will learn how to make waiting for flights more pleasant while reducing costs.

Lounge Benefits

The Budget Luxury Travel method is not only about cost. We want to enjoy our trips and never factor suffering into our travels. Remember, any idiot can be uncomfortable.

We usually try to use a lounge when waiting more than 60 minutes for flights. I have averaged at least 50 flights yearly for business and a dozen for vacations for most of the last 30 years. For the last few years, we have retired from full-time employment. This has allowed us more time for leisure travel. We have continued to take an average of 50 flights annually. At least half of the time, we have had free access to lounges. Let us suppose we have saved an average of $100 per time. That's a significant saving, and a lot of discomfort avoided.

Nothing of our travel budget is saved in the end. But avoiding spending money at airports means we can afford to spend more at our destinations. We can only afford our extensive journeys if we stick to our budget.

However, lounges have only a little bit to do with saving money. Complimentary lounge access is more about comfort and keeping the L in TALT. Tight-Arse <u>Luxury</u> Travel.

Lounges are excellent places to sit. With exceptions, there are usually not many people. Lounges are unlike public areas, where swarms of passengers clamour for the hard, cold plastic bucket chairs. The noises of public address systems, roller bags, beeping trolleys, food outlets, and many other passengers surround you.

It is common to see tourists wearing standard-format souvenir T-shirts that say something like *I Love Paris* with a heart and an Eiffel Tower. If I were to buy one of those, it would say *I Hate Airports* with a skull and crossbones and a picture of a plane with a line through it. However, as long as we need planes to travel worldwide, we will need airports.

Like everyone else, I have often been stuck in crowded public areas. We know what it's like. Sometimes, if I'm alone, the highlight is walking to the bathroom. It gives me a reason to get out of my bucket chair.

The public toilet area is sometimes okay and sometimes not. I often like to splash my face between flights. Typically, there are no paper towels. Trying to direct the hot air from the hand dryer onto my face never works well.

By contrast, lounges have sparkling-clean bathrooms. There are clean hand towels, and the basin will be clean. Better still, I can shower there—no, not in the basin—in the shower.

But besides the comfort, warmth, washing facilities, and relative quiet, it also has financial benefits. Free stuff, right? *"Now he's talkin'!"* says Uncle Scrooge. I'm with you, Scrooge.

TRAVEL STORY
Lounge Strategy

A Long Wait in Paris—How Much You Can Save

While writing this travel story, Lynda and I sat in the Paris American Airlines Business Class lounge. We were waiting for a Qatar Business Class flight to Doha. We expected a two-hour layover before boarding our flight to Phuket, Thailand.

We were provided free access to the associated Business Class lounge because we had redeemed points for a Qatar Business Class flight. Qatar and American Airlines are part of the Oneworld alliance, so the Qatar Business Class ticket got us access to the American Airlines Business Lounge.

FINALISING BOOKINGS: LUXURY & SAFETY

We were at the end of a three-month trip around Europe. The weather had been good—all except for a heat wave in Madrid that would have melted sensitive body parts off a brass matador. We were tired after a long trip, so we decided to get to the airport early. We were in the lounge by noon for our 4 p.m. flight.

I did not keep track of Lynda's consumption while we were in the lounge.

However, let's discuss my consumption.

I had:

- A hot "bistro-style" lunch. Not too much, because I didn't want to fill up entirely, as I was looking forward to a Qatar Business flight dinner later. I am a master of moderation when future excesses are imminent.
- A crème brulée. I was in Paris, after all.
- A pistachio-flavoured brulée. Nice one, American Airlines.
- A coffee.
- One champagne. French, of course.
- One gin and tonic.

Then I heard the rattling of ice cubes in another. . . Whoops. There was a lot of free-poured spirit in my double gin and tonic. Okay. Quadruple. Don't judge me. I was on holiday.

What would the bill be for one person in the outside world, say, at a café in Paris or my hometown of Sydney?

• Small hot lunch	$ 30
• Small crème brulée (Yes doctor—small)	$ 15
• Small pistachio crème brulée	$ 15
• Coffee	$ 5
• Two glasses of champagne	$ 40
• Three brutally "double" G&Ts	$ 45
The total bill in the free world	$150

Lynda doesn't eat much, so she skipped the brulée despite my gluttony coaching. But, of course, she had a meal. And neither of us is bashful about drinking high-quality wine. Or, come to think of it, low-quality wine. So, I reckon Lynda's bill in the free world would have been about $100. So that's around $250 for the two of us for the afternoon.

But we were not in the free world. We were in the retail twilight zone between the real world and the world that zips around in a titanium tube, watching television at 30,000 feet.

Prices are high in the rarefied atmosphere of the waiting room for titanium tube entry. Prices in airport captivity are well known to be double those of the free world. So, I reckon a couple of hours of free lounge food and drinks could be much more than my $250 valuation. Of course, if we were out with the passenger swarm, we would have bought cheap crap. However, it is challenging for a couple to spend a few hungry and thirsty hours in any airport without spending at least $100.

Plus, we had hours of comfort. We planned to do it all again during our two-hour layover in Doha, increasing the payoff.

Gaining Access

Primary Airline

We have covered the reasons for selecting one airline as your Primary Airline. If you have flown with a particular airline frequently, you may qualify for complimentary lounge access.

The required status credits can only be acquired by flying. The correct status provides unlimited access if you have a boarding pass with the right airline or one of its partners. It also gives your travelling partner access.

The catch is, with rare exceptions, status credits only accrue if you have paid for the flight in cash.

Frequent Flyer Access

You may not have flown enough paid flights to earn the status credits required for unlimited lounge access for a year, but airlines often provide limited passes if you have gained some status credits in the preceding 12 months.

With many airlines, if you achieve the status level below that required to gain ongoing lounge access, you usually get a couple of passes for the following membership year. It's not much, but it's a start.

Business Class Tickets

With a Business Class ticket, you can almost always access a Business Class lounge no matter who you fly with, even if you paid for the ticket with points.

Lounge Passes with Certain Credit Cards

Many credit cards provide lounge access. Check your fine print. Amex is the one that most commonly provides this benefit, as do many airline-branded credit cards. The variety of terms is too voluminous to list here. Check your credit card website.

If you cannot get complimentary lounge access any other way, it may be worth changing your credit card provider. If you do, ensure you get sign-on bonus points and a low annual fee.

Third-Party "For profit" Lounges

Many major airports now have these lounges. They are operated by firms for profit rather than being part of a loyalty program. Many are branded with Plaza Premium, Primeclass Lounge, Pearl Lounge, or Maharba Lounge. You can pay to enter these lounges. Yes. I said *pay*, Scrooge.

Priority Pass

Anyone can join Priority Pass for a one-year standard membership of US$99. Then, you pay US$32 per visit per person. Prestige membership is US$429 and includes unlimited visits. The member's guest will incur a US$32 charge per visit regardless of the membership type.

There are ways some people can avoid the standard membership joining fee. Membership is given away in various ways. Google *Priority Pass membership* and see what comes up on the day.

I am a Platinum member of Interval International, the organisation we use to trade our timeshare for other people's timeshare. Interval International Platinum offers access to Priority Pass Standard Membership without requiring a joining fee. For more details, refer to our sister publication, *Stay for Free*, which provides free and low-cost luxury accommodation information. However, please note that you cannot be a member of Interval International unless you own a timeshare.

Priority Pass offers access to over 1,300 lounges worldwide. We carry Priority Pass as a backup option. If we are at an airport and need a shower or must wait more than an hour, we will consider paying a third-party provider or utilising Priority Pass access. The Priority Pass provides many options. You will usually find one with complete services. The Priority Pass app confirms the facilities of each lounge.

These lounges are worth considering, particularly if you consider the cost of buying a meal in an airport. Dinner and a drink will generally cost as much as the Priority Pass lounge access. Some of the paid lounges are small and can become crowded, while others are spacious. Airline lounges are often the best option, but any lounge is better than none.

If you are only at the airport for 30 minutes and want a cheeseburger and Coke, it won't be worth paying a lounge entry fee. However, if you have just flown 14 hours from Sydney to Dubai and are about to connect with a flight to Europe, paying for a lounge with all the facilities, including clean showers, is worth it.

Lounge Access Ratio

The best way to access a lounge is for free. This can be achieved by having adequate status credits with one airline, which will likely be your Primary Airline. Let's examine which airlines offer the most attractive system for gaining free access.

We have determined the value of flights that must be purchased for cash to earn enough status credits to gain lounge access. We refer to that amount as the Lounge Access Ratio.

We have calculated the Lounge Access Ratio for many airlines using the same sample of flights we used to determine the value of points.

For example, suppose the dollar cash cost of flights in our sample was $20,000 and earned 1,200 status points. If 600 status points were required to gain lounge access, the Lounge Access Ratio would be 10,000:1. A $10,000 spent on flights in a membership year is needed to earn enough status credits to qualify for one year of lounge access. The lower the ratio, the better. We have rounded the costs off to the nearest A$100.

FINALISING BOOKINGS: LUXURY & SAFETY

LOUNGE ACCESS RATIOS	
Airline	**Ratio**
Air Canada	18,500:1
Air Europa	9,300:1
Air France	20,400:1
Air New Zealand	19,700:1
American Airlines	Paid Access
British Airways	14,000:1
Cathay Pacific	14,000:1
Delta Air Lines	Paid Access
Etihad Airways	21,400:1
Emirates	20,900:1
Lufthansa	7,700:1
Malaysia Airlines	11,700:1
Qantas	16,600:1
Qatar Airways	25,800:1
Singapore Airlines	15,400:1
Swiss	8,400:1
Thai Airways	28,900:1
United Airlines	Paid Access
Virgin Australia	10,500:1

As you can see, paying for enough flights to gain Lounge Access can be expensive with some airlines. But this is not about buying lots of flights to gain access. It is about ensuring you stay aware of your entitlements if you purchase many flights. You can often tweak your approach to gain access without spending extra.

For example, when you are ready, review the *Couples Strategy* discussed under the Advanced Strategies section. If you travel as a couple, you can use the *Couples Strategy* to cut the above ratios in half after you have mastered the strategies up to this point.

FLY FOR FREE

TRAVEL STORY
Lounge Strategy

Qantas Club Lounges

Given our drive towards free flights, we often do not qualify simply because our longest flights are free, so they usually do not attract status credits. Buying Qantas flights to gain lounge access would require spending $16,600 annually. An alternative for us is to pay $540 for one year of access to a selection of lounges. This applies to all Qantas lounges and a limited range of lounges operated by Qantas partners. Membership gained through status points will be more effective for many people, as it provides reciprocal rights to enter all Oneworld lounges when flying with Oneworld member airlines.

Europe is one of our favourite destinations. Singapore and Dubai are frequent stops on our way there. We also commute frequently through London to visit family in England. The Qantas Club membership includes access to lounges in those locations. In our circumstances, paying for a Qantas Club membership would be worthwhile if we did not have access to a complimentary lounge.

We are also members of the Qantas Points Club, a scheme that benefits those who have earned many points through credit card and retail activities. Membership in Qantas Points Club allows us to earn status credits on QF flights paid for with points, albeit at reduced rates.

No Lounge? Then What?

Work out how you will get fed and watered while at airports. Plan this out as you put together your detailed budget and itinerary.

In some airports, you will have free access to lounges. In others, you will have access but must decide whether to pay. Consider whether you need additional lounge facilities, such as showers, which may influence your decision.

Most of us struggle with making decisions when tired, which is all too common on the day of a flight. Consider the best option during the planning phases. Note it on your itinerary so you go into automatic mode.

Decide whether to:

- Eat in the airport's commercial area.
- Pay your way into a lounge.
- Or buy food outside the airport and take it to the airport with you.

LOUNGE STRATEGY

Follow the Airline Selection Strategy. If you are not flying Business Class and do not have sufficient status with the relevant airline to gain lounge access, consider the following options. First, check if your status provides limited passes or if your credit card provides access. Second, consider purchasing a Priority Pass. Third, if you need a shower or must wait more than one hour, consider paying for access to a private lounge.

5.6 SAFETY STRATEGY

> **Pilot:** *"The bad news is, we have lost engine one. The excellent news is engine two is no longer on fire."*
>
> MADAGASCAR *(the movie)*

Why Read This Chapter?

There is a poor correlation between the price of an airline ticket and the safety of the associated flight. Buying an expensive ticket may mean getting a higher-quality whisky, but it does not necessarily indicate the airline is safe. Flying with an airline that offers cheap seats does not make the airline unsafe. Just because you have heard of an airline does not make it safer than one you have not heard of.

This chapter will teach you how to identify airlines you should avoid based on independently compiled safety data.

Zero Tolerance for Poor Safety

I might be a tight-arse, but... hang on... let me rephrase that. I *am* a tight-arse. However, I do not want to be a *dead* tight-arse. We have imposed one constraint on our money-saving travel techniques. We will not fly with airlines that have a poor safety rating.

We lack extensive knowledge about airline safety, and we have no technical expertise in this area. However, we take safety seriously and can share our precautions.

There is often considerable folklore surrounding the safety of a particular airline. We like objective criteria, and we keep it simple.

Safety Ratings

Before we fly on an airline, we check their safety rating at www.airlineratings.com.

To view an airline's rating on this site, click Airline Safety on the home page. The airlines are listed alphabetically, and the column on the right-hand side provides each airline's safety rating.

This safety rating system is not bulletproof but provides a helpful filter. We take notice of it. Their rating system works by awarding airlines seven stars and then deducting stars if an airline fails specific criteria. A rating of seven stars falls short of saying that the airline is remarkably safe. But it is the filter we use because we have not found a better one. We are grateful to the organisation that provides this free service.

Criteria for the Ratings

What are the criteria for losing stars?

Criterion—Fatality Free (Three Stars): A quote from the website: *"Three stars are deleted from the rating if the airline has had any fatalities to passengers or crew due to an accident in the prior ten years."*

"If deaths occurred through acts of terrorism, hijacking, or pilot suicide, they have not been included. Nor if the death is not attributable to the airline (faulty manufactured part)."

"If an airline suffered a fatal accident through no fault of its own, such as a runway incursion on the active runway (an accident where an unauthorised aircraft, vehicle or person is on a runway), this has also not been included."

The organisation is ignoring things that it appears the airline cannot control. This criterion is quite forgiving. For example, if someone dies from *fuel tanker in head syndrome*, the incident is likely to be categorised as a runway incursion. The accident would not affect the airline's rating. Given that the ratings are not overly harsh, any loss of stars for this criterion means we will avoid flying on the airline.

Criterion—Incident Rating (Three Stars): From airlineratings.com: *"Has the airline suffered numerous pilot-related incidents? If yes, then one or more stars are deducted."*

Criterion—Audits (One Star): *"Has the airline and its country of origin passed all the major audits? We look at the IOSA audit, ICAO country audit, EU and FAA bans."*

We do not feel good about an airline if it fails any of these audits. Maybe we could forgive them if we understood why they failed. However, we cannot get into that level of detail, and even if we had the time, we would not have understood the reasons for failure.

Imagine if we did dig deeper. What if we discovered, for example, that the wing wobbler went into the what's-a-name pipe without the proper oil? Or the cyber scope was not working correctly. Or that the airline did not meet International Safety Standard number 1484. Would we be better equipped to make a value judgement? We cannot possibly delve into such audits.

Similarly, we do not have time to be outraged about *King Wots-a-Name Airways'* unfair treatment. We cannot determine whether *She'll Be Right Air* has been fairly treated. Any collective body that knows more about airline safety than we do is qualified enough, which isn't saying much. Even the International Society of Flying Rubber Chickens knows more about airline safety than we want to learn.

Overall

All the above criteria sound so important that we cannot think why we would want to fly with an airline that has lost a single star.

If the airline does not receive seven stars out of seven from airlineratings.com, then we will do everything possible to avoid it.

Occasionally, we make educated, balanced decisions that lead to a compromise. But since we discovered this site, we have never flown on any airline with less than six stars.

We encourage you to surf the Internet and form your own opinion on safety matters, as we are not qualified to make any recommendations in this area.

We are merely sharing with you what we check before booking our flights.

TRAVEL STORY
Safety Strategy

Flight into Bulgaria

We have only needed to fly on a six-star airline once. This was a safety-related decision. We could only reach our destination in Bulgaria by plane, as our route lacked adequate bus or train infrastructure.

Only two airlines were servicing our route. The seven-star one got us in late at night. Given our limited knowledge of security in Sofia, we did not want to wander the streets late at night searching for our informally arranged Home Exchange accommodation. We decided to take the six-star airline that landed in the middle of the day.

It was a balanced safety decision, and the only time we have consciously booked an airline with fewer than seven stars.

SAFETY STRATEGY

Put safety ahead of economising. Check whether an airline has seven stars under the www.airlineratings.com criteria and include that information in your decisions.

6

Step-By-Step Implementation Plan

WE HAVE PRESENTED YOU WITH a great deal of detail. In this section, we will provide you with a step-by-step plan for:

- Earning points and miles.
- Managing points and miles.
- Finding the best value cash flights.
- Using points and miles to maximise savings.
- Finalising bookings.

No new strategies are introduced in this part.

After reading this section, you will understand the order in which strategies should be considered when planning and booking your trips.

More strategies are presented after this section. These are not essential in the early stages. Execute this plan first. After you have mastered the basics, return to the Advanced Strategies in the final section.

6.1 EARNING POINTS & MILES

Step 1: Selection Strategy

Focus your point-earning activities on one Primary Airline. Ensure your Primary Airline offers numerous point-earning opportunities with credit card companies and retailers. Ideally, your Primary Airline should have broad geographic coverage, be a member of one of the big three alliances and be financially strong.

Select a Secondary Airline to widen the number of retailers and credit card companies from whom you can earn points.

Add Tertiary Airlines to ensure you have at least one airline in your portfolio that belongs to each of the Oneworld, Star Alliance, and Sky-Team alliances. Add other airlines if they have a "no expiry" policy for their points. Consider the Budget Luxury Traveller Star ratings when making your selection.

Step 2: Credit Card Strategy

Before proceeding, please consult your financial advisor, as everyone's financial circumstances are unique. Subject to advice regarding your unique financial circumstances, sign up for one credit card with sign-on bonus points, a discounted annual fee for the first year, and a companion card if you have a partner.

You should cancel the card after spending the qualifying amount and checking that the sign-on bonus and points for usage have been received. A possible exception is if you need the card to implement the Payment Strategy. If you already have a credit card, reduce your limit on that existing card to ensure that your overall credit card limit does not increase.
See your financial advisor regarding whether you should repeat the Credit Card Strategy and, if so, how long you should wait between applications.

Step 3: Payment Strategy

Pay for almost everything using a credit card that attracts points. Avoid excessive transaction fees on large one-off purchases. Your partner should use a companion card.

Step 4: Retail Strategy

Consult the websites for your Primary and Secondary airlines and compile a Retail Partners Register. Take note of the organisations you do business with that can provide you with points. Activate a link, download an app, or click through your loyalty accounts to earn points from retailers. Before making a purchase, check if there is a way to arrange for the retailer to provide points and be prepared with the relevant app or card.

STEP-BY-STEP IMPLEMENTATION PLAN

6.2 MANAGING POINTS AND MILES

Step 1: Checking Strategy

- Check credit card sign-on bonuses have been received.
- Check that you are getting monthly credits from the credit card supplier.
- Ensure your points have been credited from new or changed set-ups with retailers.
- Check that points have been credited from large retail transactions
- Keep your boarding passes and mark them off against your points accounts.

Step 2: Expiry Strategy

Opt to join loyalty programs that have a No-Expiry policy. If you use an airline with a loyalty program with an Activity-Based expiration policy, determine how you intend to keep your account active. Deprioritise any airline with an Issue-Based expiry policy, particularly one that requires using points less than 36 months from their earned date.

Step 3: Point Transfers Strategy

If your airline loyalty program has an Activity-Based expiry policy, automate the conversion of retailer rewards to frequent flyer points. If the loyalty program is Issue-Based, consider accumulating points in your retailer's program or credit card program and transferring them only when required for a specific flight booking.

6.3 FIND THE BEST VALUE CASH FLIGHTS

Step 1: Search Strategy

Identify at least two booking sites or search engines you prefer.

Use one of these to identify the cheapest cash flight you can work with and the most direct flight at a reasonable cost. Price the flights for cash for a few days on either side of your chosen date.

Record the options. Use at least one more search engine to try and identify a better deal. Then, check the airline's cash price directly on the airline's site.

Step 2: Budget Airline Strategy

Check which budget airlines operate within the region you plan to fly. If these airlines do not appear in your searches, they may have opted out of the search services to save money and lower fares. Check prices directly on the airline's website.

Ensure price comparisons include the extras, such as baggage, seat allocation, and meals, to the extent you need them.

Step 3: Return Strategy

Engineer your itinerary to allow a choice between Return and One-Way fares when finalising bookings. For every booking, compare a Return ticket to the equivalent pair of One-Way tickets.

If you use a combination of cash and points, try to use the points in the One-Way sections.

Step 4: Cheapest Day Strategy

If possible, base your draft plan on flying on Monday through Thursday. As your itinerary solidifies and you're ready to book, consider as wide a range of dates as practical. Price your flights before committing to an event that forces you to fly on a specific day.

Step 5: Cheapest Time Strategy

Check all time slots for international flights, as there are no consistently cheaper timeslots. Avoid travelling on domestic routes between noon and 2 p.m. six days a week and 11:00 a.m. to 4:00 p.m. on Sundays.

6.4 USING POINTS TO MAXIMISE SAVINGS

Step 1: Find the Best Value Flight for Points

Repeat the *Search Strategy, Return Strategy, and Timing Strategies* described above for fares that can be purchased by redeeming your points.

The search will be much easier than your search for cash flights. It will be a narrower search as you will usually be restricted to one or two airlines with which you have adequate points. However, the outcomes of the searches for cash and points are typically different. They should each be the subject of a separate search.

When selecting the cheapest cash flight, you may have determined that One-Way flights are uneconomical. However, try again with points, as the outcomes of the Return Strategy can be significantly different for points versus cash.

Don't forget to use the timing strategies again.

Step 2: Valuation Strategy

Treat points like foreign currencies. Convert your points to a cash equivalent, expressed per point, in a familiar currency.

Step 3: Redemption Strategy

It's not just the points you earn; it's what you do with them. Before using points, multiply the required points by the Target Redemption Value per point for the relevant fare type. Add any supplementary cash payment to arrive at the points price.

Compare the points price to the cash price. If the points price is higher, consider retaining your points. Make an exception if the points are about to expire or you cannot delay that expiry.

6.5 FINALISING BOOKINGS—LUXURY AND SAFETY

Step 1: Body Clock Strategy

When flying Economy Class, avoid flight departure times that result in sitting upright in a seat at a time when you would prefer to shower and lie in a bed. Plan on adjusting to jet lag in a hotel room, not a plane seat.

Step 2: Upgrade Strategy

Use the Body Clock Strategy as much as possible. However, consider booking Business Class with points when you need to make an overnight flight. Do not use points for Business Class any other time. Ensure points for Business Class are redeemed close to the Target Redemption Value. Also, ensure that the Business Class points cost is no more than 2.0 times that of Economy Class, aiming for a ratio of 1.6 times. Find an alternative solution if you can't redeem close to those values.

Step 3: Pack Light Strategy

Limit checked-in bags to a maximum of one per couple. Never pack for more than seven days. Avoid packing valuables and paper. If in doubt, leave it out.

Step 4: Seating Strategy

Avoid seats in the five rows following the front bulkhead, the three rows in front of the rear bulkhead and any seat flagged as red by www.seatguru.com. Within these constraints, sit as far forward as you can.

Step 5: Lounge Strategy

If you are not flying Business Class and do not have sufficient status with the relevant airline to gain lounge access, consider the following options. First, check if your status provides limited passes or if your credit card provides access. Second, consider purchasing a Priority Pass. Third, if you need a shower or must wait more than one hour, consider paying for access to a private lounge.

Step 6: Safety Strategy

Put safety ahead of economising. Check whether an airline has seven stars under the www.airlineratings.com criteria and include that information in your decisions.

Step 7: Booking Strategy

Book directly with the airline if using an intermediary does not provide a significant benefit.

Book international flights 91-120 days in advance and domestic flights 61-90 days in advance to secure the best pricing while avoiding excess schedule changes that can occur if you book even further ahead.

7

Advanced Strategies

I'll show you this once, and only once.

KAMIKAZE PILOT INSTRUCTOR

Introduction to Advanced Strategies

You may wonder why I've placed a treasure trove of strategies at the back of the book rather than weaving them into the main body of this guide.

Let me illustrate why I made that decision.

I am a career finance executive. You may have an image of a career finance executive standing in their city office, surveying the skyline like a master of the universe, working out how to take home a seven-figure bonus. It may be by buying a zillion shares for $1.13 each at 10:07 a.m. and selling them an hour later for $1.15. You can imagine them sipping red wine on their boat at the end of the day.

Or perhaps, if your tastes extend to 1987 movies, your image may be of Michael Douglas walking the beach in his dressing gown. He calls Charlie Sheen to deliver the line, *"Money never sleeps, pal. Just made $800,000 in Hong Kong gold."*

I was a more *typical* finance executive in the 1980s. I worked for a manufacturer in the middle of an outer suburban industrial area. I wasn't doing any share deals or buying Hong Kong gold. On a good day, I would get to buy a sausage roll from the drive-in food truck. The business produced automotive parts from asbestos in those days—not a red wine in sight.

I had just delivered a hard copy of my presentation. It was prepared on a dot matrix printer, with graphs prepared on a plotter, an outdated contraption. (A plotter was like a robot holding felt-tip pens.) My presentation appeared like something prepared by a junior NASA scientist working out of his garage. It showed we could reduce unit costs by stopping overtime and adding a second shift.

The gnarly old Operations Manager, twice my age, bowled into my cubicle. He dropped my midnight work back on my desk and said, *"See that guy on number 16?"* I looked through the window at a 120-kilogram biker on machine number 16. He had piercings and face tattoos in an era before tattoos became fashionable among Instagram influencers. He explained,

> *"He and his mates will revolt if you take away their overtime pay. And if we go to a second shift, things will go wrong when I am in bed. I'll get calls all night. I'll need time to hire a night foreman. And, before we present this to the CEO, can you do me a favour and add some bits to tell the CEO how well we are doing?"*

Then, as he walked out, he turned and said, *"...and KISS."* I looked up at him quizzically. He explained, *"Keep It Simple, Stupid."*

That's what coaching looked like in the 1980s.

I learned that I needed to avoid overcomplicated explanations.

Nearly forty years later, when I had completed an early draft of this guide, I realised I had prepared something the guy on machine number 16 may find hard to understand. I thought over that Operations Manager's advice again. I said to myself, *"KISS. Keep It Simple, Stupid."*

That led me to relocate some strategies to the back of the book because they are not part of the fast track to get you flying for free. It is not so much that they are challenging. They are just optional.

They are an unnecessary complication when you are first setting yourself up. By moving them to a section that you can later return to, I have made the core plan more straightforward.

We have delivered on the promise in the title without these strategies. We suggest you implement the plan up to this point, return to the guide after achieving your first free flight, and implement the strategies in this final part.

Review them now. However, please don't attempt to implement them until you have worked through the implementation plan in the previous section.

Here is a reminder of what we have covered so far:

- Earning points.
- Managing points.
- Finding the best value cash flights.
- Using points to maximise savings.
- Finalising bookings while maximising luxury and safety.

You can achieve all the above objectives if you read no further.

You should treat the advanced strategies in this part as bonus content.

Flying Strategies

We start with a series of optional strategies to consider when booking flights. As a group, Flying Strategies are designed to maximise your points and, in some circumstances, improve your status—all at no cost.

- Simplicity Strategy
- Fly:Free Ratio Strategy
- Consistency Strategy
- Couples Strategy

Points Purchasing Strategy

Yes, there are times when you should consider buying points. We outline how to decide when to use the *Point Purchasing Strategy*.

Itinerary Strategies

These three strategies overlap. They are effective ways to reduce the cost of your travel and apply whether you are travelling using cash or points.

- Transport Strategy

- Hub Strategy
- Route Strategy

Connection Strategies

These strategies aim to make your flying experience more enjoyable by reducing the stress and discomfort often associated with making flight connections.

- Layover Strategy
- Stopover Strategy

Miscellaneous Strategies

- *Round-the-World Strategy*: Using Round-the-World tickets to find low-priced and free flights on long trips.
- *Retail Strategy*—Gift Cards: This is a valuable extension to *Retail Strategy* that I did not want to introduce too early into your learning curve. It is an opportunistic way to earn sizable batches of points.

ADVANCED STRATEGIES

7.1 FLYING STRATEGIES

I can't make everyone happy. I'm not a plane ticket.

Why Read This Chapter?

There are several strategies to consider before booking a flight. In this chapter, you will learn:

- How to keep things simple and reduce effort (*Simplicity Strategy*).
- Which airlines reward you the most for flying with them (*Fly:Free Ratio Strategy*).
- How to collaborate with your partner to ensure you balance achieving status and earning points (*Couples Strategy*).
- How to maximise loyalty program rewards by achieving consistency between operator, booking site, and loyalty program (*Consistency Strategy*).

Simplicity Strategy

Speaking of keeping things simple, let's cover how to handle the myriad rules associated with loyalty programs. The most complex of these rules governs the number of points you may earn.

Each airline publishes points tables and rules on its website. These rules change frequently.

To calculate your points for a booking, you need some or all of this information:

- The length of the flight.
- The cost of the flight.
- The fare class (Premium Economy, First, etc.).
- The fare code (E, H, B, X, etc.).
- Whether it is operated directly or by a partner.

- If operated by a partner, which partner?
- The booking site.
- Your status with the booked airline.
- Your status with the partner operating the flight.
- The bylaws of each airline's loyalty program related to rewards.

All loyalty programs have their unique set of rules.

Theoretically, you could examine all the data every time you book a flight. This would:

- Take a significant amount of time.
- Be prone to error.
- Slowly drive you mad.

The time spent analysing the complexity is better spent elsewhere. There are many more effective ways to spend your travel planning time.

Following our simplified strategies is more effective regardless of your airline selections. We have developed a set of strategies that make maximising your rewards simple. Consistently follow our strategies every time. That will provide excellent long-term results. Sometimes, you may take a deep dive, but most people struggle to maintain that level of interest. As the lady once said, *"Ain't nobody got time for dat!"*

> ### SIMPLICITY STRATEGY
> Consistently applying a set of simple strategies will provide the best long-term results. Don't spend much time examining loyalty program websites besides those of your Primary and Secondary Airlines. The time saved can be better used in other areas of travel planning.

Fly:Free Ratio Strategy

Most of the points you earn will be from non-flying activities. This is because it is rare to earn points when flying on a free ticket. We fly for free most of the time, and you will be too.

However, there will be occasions when you *must* pay cash for a flight. This could be because your selected airlines may not service the required route. You may often pay cash for a flight because it is priced so low that you would rather keep your points.

Fly:Free Ratios

Some airlines will reward you more for flying than others.

The Fly:Free Ratio measures the number of flights you must take to earn enough points to be awarded a similar flight for free. The ratio is expressed as a number. For example, if the number is 8.0, you can expect to pay for 8.0 flights to earn enough points for a similar flight for free.

Of course, we do not suggest paying for 8.0 flights to get a free one because there are many other ways to earn points. However, we still want to earn a high number of points when we buy a flight. The ratio does expose an essential difference between various loyalty programs.

The lower the number, the better. If an airline has a low ratio compared to others, you must pay for fewer flights to earn a free flight.

For this purpose, the Fly:Free Ratios revealed below assume you have the lowest status. Your Fly:Free Ratio will be better if you have a higher status because a higher status usually attracts a point loading. However, we have put all the loyalty programs on a level playing field for comparison purposes.

If you use the term *Fly:Free Ratio* when talking to an airline executive, they will not know what you are talking about. We invented the term. We could have called it *"The Number of Times You Must Fly to Qualify for a Free Flight"*, but that would have been cumbersome.

Remember, a lower ratio is better because you must fly fewer times to earn enough points for a free one.

The ratio is affected by the type of fare. Domestic and international flights, as well as Economy and Business Class flights, provide different results. Using a consistent mix, we have calculated averages across various fare types for a sample of airlines. The results appear below.

Below is a sample illustrating how the Fly:Free ratio varies among airlines.

Fly:Free Ratios by Airline

FLY:FREE RATIOS	
Airline	Fly:Free Ratio
Air Canada	17
Air Europa	18
Air France	11
Air New Zealand	32
Alaska Airlines	12
American Airlines	10
British Airways	15
Cathay Pacific	13
Delta Air Lines	23
Emirates	22
Etihad Airways	38
Hawaiian Airlines	26
Lufthansa	29
Malaysia Airlines	15
Qantas	11
Qatar Airways	23
Singapore Airlines	11
Southwest Airlines	38
Swiss	21
Thai Airways	18
United Airlines	11
Virgin Australia	11

Fly:Free Ratio Calculation Template

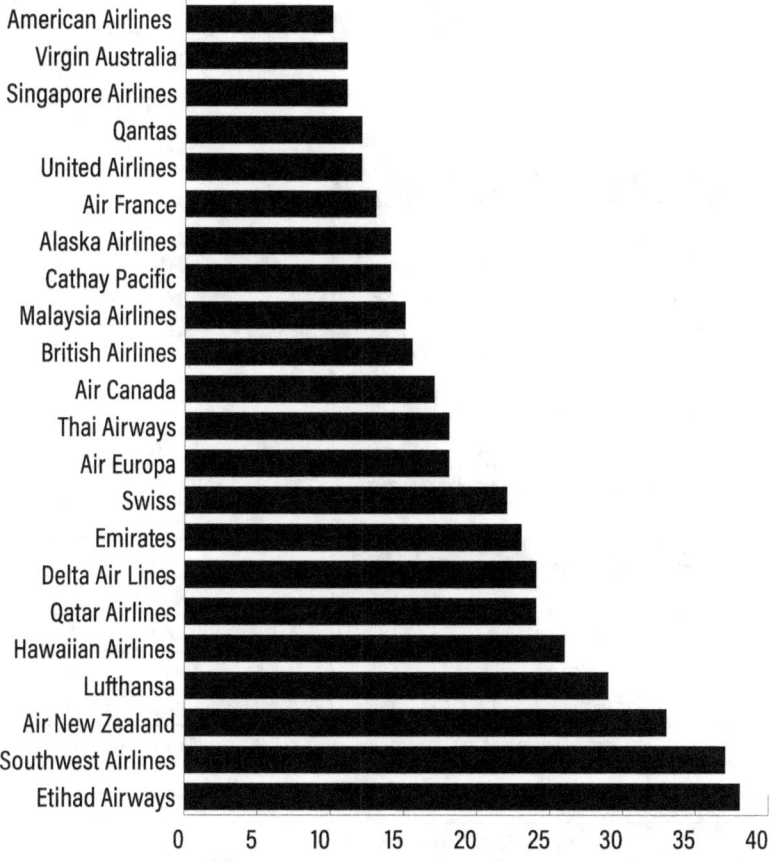

If you would like to calculate the Fly:Free Ratio for another airline, a template and instructions are provided in the Free Stuff.

The template we can send you looks like this. Enter data in the shaded boxes.

FLY:FREE RATIO CALCULATION TEMPLATE						
Sample Airline						
International Economy						
				Points Awarded	Points Required	Fly Free Ratio
				A	P	F
				Points	Points	
One-Way						
		From:	To:			
28-Feb	One-Way	JFK	LHR	3,296	19,000	6
7-Mar	One-Way	LHR	JFK	3,296	19,000	6
28-Feb	One-Way	LAX	CDG	6,704	27,500	4
7-Mar	One-Way	CDG	LAX	6,704	43,500	6
28-Feb	One-Way	JFK	TYO	1,554	35,000	23
7-Mar	One-Way	TYO	JFK	1,554	35,000	23
Total Sample - Domestic One-Way Economy				23,108	179,000	8
Return						
		From:	To:			
	Return	JFK	LHR	6,592	46,000	7
	Return	LAX	CDG	13,408	46,000	3
	Return	JFK	TYO	3,108	70,000	23
Total Sample - Domestic Return Economy				23,108	162,000	7
			Total Sample	46,216	341,000	7
		Fly:Free Ratio (P divided by A)		7.4		
# Enter into shaded cells only						

With no status and no other points, you must fly approximately 7.4 times, on average, with the above sample airline to get a free International Economy Class flight.

You can ignore these ratios when choosing your Primary and Secondary Airlines. Most of the points you earn for those airlines will come from the *Credit Card Strategy*, *Payment Strategy*, and *Retail Strategy*.

However, your Tertiary Airline points will be earned through flying, so consider the Fly:Free Ratio when selecting which Tertiary Airlines to support.

In principle, you should fly with the airline with the lowest Fly:Free Ratio, all other things being equal. But it will be rare for all other things to be equal.

> **FLY:FREE RATIO STRATEGY**
>
> Points from flying will never be as crucial as non-flying activities. However, you should maximise points from cash flights. The Fly:Free Ratio rates how generous airlines are with awarding points for flying. It is factored into the Budget Luxury Travel loyalty program ratings. Allow those ratings to influence your choice of Tertiary Airlines.

Consistency Strategy

Most major airlines have partners, and many flights have a codeshare arrangement. Each partner will have its unique flight code for the same flight, meaning you can book the same plane through either partner's website. Only the flight number will change. When doing so, you can choose any partner's loyalty program number in that alliance.

There can be many ways to book the same flight. We prefer to book directly with the airline, which eliminates many variables. However, when partners are code-sharing, there are still choices to make.

You can book through one partner's website (e.g. Qantas), and fly with a partner in the same alliance (e.g. British Airways). You can nominate either loyalty program number.

Each booking method will earn a different point value. However, we usually get the best points and status outcomes if we book and fly with the same airline and nominate that airline's frequent flyer number.

You will maximise the value of points earned if you follow our *Consistency Strategy*. That involves these steps:

- Ascertain which airline is operating the flight.
- Join that airline's loyalty program.
- Book through that airline's site.
- Quote the loyalty program number for that same airline.

Earning fewer or no points can be expected if you do not follow the *Consistency Strategy*.

The adverse effect of the *Consistency Strategy* can be that it may force you to earn rewards with an airline other than your Primary or Secondary Airline. However, if you think you can avoid the expiry of the points, the *Consistency Strategy* is best.

Many travellers will assume that because two airlines are part of the same alliance, they will receive the same value in points regardless of how they book. This is incorrect. The outcome of a codeshare flight will differ depending on how you book and the loyalty program you specify.

If you are paying cash for a codeshare flight, you will earn the highest value in points if you:

- Find out who operates the flight you want to travel on. It is the one thing you cannot change.
- Book it through the operator's website, pay the operator the cash, and use the operator's frequent flyer loyalty program number.

EXAMPLE 1

Consistency Strategy

Be Consistent when Flying on a Code-share Flight

Qantas and British Airways—Sydney to London

In this example, Qantas and British Airways operate the Sydney (SYD) to London (LHR) flight on alternate days.

Suppose Qantas operates a flight from Sydney to London and is code-sharing with British Airways. The next day, British Airways takes its turn to operate the flight and code-shares with Qantas. Let's look

ADVANCED STRATEGIES

at the three ways you could book a Flexible Economy ticket and see the outcomes.

	CONSISTENT VS INCONSISTENT BOOKINGS (EXAMPLE 1)								
Option	Site Used to Book	Operating Airline	Member Number Quoted	Points		Point Value		Status Credits	% required for lounge access
				Type	No.	Calculation	Value		
A	--- Qantas ---			Points	21,700	21,700 x $0.025	$543	140	23%
B	Qantas	British	Qantas	Points	10,500	10,500 x $0.025	$263	70	10%
C	--- British ---			Avios	10,586	10,586 x $0.029	$307	120	20%

OPTION A:
This option is for a codeshare flight operated by Qantas. Option A is to book on the Qantas site and quote your Qantas Frequent Flyer number. We refer to this as *consistency*, as the booking site, the operating airline, and the member number are all associated with one airline.

OPTION B:
This option is for a codeshare flight operated by British Airways. Option B is to book on the Qantas site and quote your Qantas Frequent Flyer number. We call this *inconsistent*.

OPTION C:
This option is for a codeshare flight operated by British Airways. Option C is to book on the British Airways site and quote the British Airways Executive Club member number. This is another *consistent* option.

CONCLUSION:
Note the consistent options have the better loyalty program earnings:

    A. **Qantas** booking site. **Qantas** member no. **Qantas** *operated* flight.

    C. **British** booking site. **British** member no. **British Airways** *operated* flight.

Note the inconsistency in the option with the poorest earnings:

    B. Qantas booking site. Qantas member no. British Airways operated flight.

EXAMPLE 2

Consistency Strategy

Be Consistent when Flying on a Code-share Flight

Qantas and Emirates—Sydney to Dubai

Qantas is part of Oneworld, but Emirates is not. However, the two airlines have a separate alliance. Suppose Qantas operates a flight from Sydney (SYD) to London (DXB) and is code-sharing with Emirates. Qantas may operate the flight one day, and Emirates may operate the flight the next day. Let's examine the two ways to book an Economy ticket and compare the outcomes.

CONSISTENT VS INCONSISTENT BOOKINGS (EXAMPLE 2)									
				Points		Point Value			% of credits required for lounge access
Option	Site Used to Book	Operating Airline	Member Number Quoted	Type	No.	Calculation	Value	Status Credits	
X	--- Qantas ---			Points	6,750	6,750 x $0.025	$169	60	10%
Y	Qantas	Emirates	Qantas	Points	3,700	3,500 x $0.025	$88	-	0%

OPTION X:

This is a codeshare flight operated by Qantas, which was booked on the Qantas website. The Qantas Frequent Flyer number would be quoted.

OPTION Y:

This is a codeshare flight operated by Emirates, which was booked on the Qantas site. The Qantas Frequent Flyer number would be quoted.

CONCLUSION:

Note the *consistency* for the option with the better earnings:

> X. Booking on Qantas site. Qantas operated flight. Qantas member number

The *inconsistent* booking will earn you less:

> Y. Booking on Qantas site. Emirates operated flight. Qantas member number

EXAMPLE 3
Consistency Strategy

Be Consistent when Flying on a Code-share Flight

Virgin Australia vs. Partners

In this example, Virgin flies one route and codeshares with six partners. Each partner airline operates the flight on different days. But in every case, we could book it through Virgin, pay cash to Virgin, and quote the Virgin Australia Velocity member number.

Virgin Australia awards five points per Australian dollar spent on Virgin Australia domestic flights and that will earn the most points.

When flying Economy on partner airlines, you will be awarded the following Virgin Australia Velocity Points. All these will earn a lower value in points than if you booked through Virgin Australia and flew on a Virgin Australia operated plane.

- Group 1: Flights operated by United, Virgin Atlantic, Etihad, Qatar 0.25 points per mile.
- Group 2: Flights operated by Singapore Airlines: 0.5 points per mile.
- Group 3: Flights operated by Air Canada: <u>nil</u> points.

Again, the *Consistency Strategy* achieves the best reward outcome. If you are booking with an airline and paying cash, try and fly on a plane operated by that airline, not its partner.

FLY FOR FREE

TRAVEL STORY

Consistency Strategy and Simplicity Strategy

Don't Try to Read All the Details on Loyalty Program Websites

Hawaiian Airlines vs. Partners

This story will illustrate how complex loyalty program rules can become.

Let's suppose you occasionally fly to Hawaii with Hawaiian Airlines, but American Airlines is your Primary Airline.

That implies that when you fly with Hawaiian, you should enter an American Airlines loyalty program membership number. The Hawaiian site does allow that. The value of points earned will be significantly lower using that method. Instead, you should join the Hawaiian loyalty program and enter your Hawaiian member number.

You may think, "I will look up the rules and decide each time." Although you may attempt it occasionally, you will soon become weary of it.

As an example of complex rules, the following are direct quotes from the Hawaiian Airlines site.

- *You can earn JetBlue Miles when flying Hawaiian Airlines. But when travelling Economy, you will get anywhere between 12.5% to 50% of the miles you would get if you used your Hawaiian Airlines Frequent Flyer Number, depending on which of the following booking classes you fly: F, S, P, A, Y, W, Q, V, B, S, N, M, I, H, G. You will get nil if your booking class was D, R, E, U, T, Z, O.*

The site provides more details, including a schedule that shows which percentages apply to each booking class. Good luck with that! It also says:

- *You won't earn AAdvantage® miles on flights operated by*

Hawaiian Airlines between the U.S. Mainland and Hawaii or on flights marketed by Hawaiian Airlines (booked as an HA flight number).

Believe it or not, we have simplified what is stated on the Hawaiian Airlines website by omitting much of the detail they provide.

If a person has American Airlines as one of their favourite airlines, they may diligently add their American Airlines AAdvantage number, thinking they will get 100% of the miles. The fact that American Airlines appears in the Frequent Flyer drop-down box on the Hawaiian Airlines site may provide some comfort. You may think you are earning points, but often, due to the complexities, no points will be earned.

If you follow the *Consistency Strategy*, you will achieve the best outcome.

CONSISTENCY STRATEGY

Ascertain which airline is operating the flight, join that airline's loyalty program, book directly on that airline's website, and quote the loyalty program number for that airline. Only make an exception if:

- You are chasing status and wish to quote your Primary Airline loyalty program number.

- You think the points with the operating airline will expire before you can use them.

Couples Strategy

Do you have a partner with whom you regularly travel? This section will demonstrate how you can collaborate to achieve a better outcome for both parties. If you want more value from your partner, now's your chance!

If you have a lot of points, you can use them to cover fares for yourself and your partner. When the points are exhausted, you will be required to pay cash. This seems logical, but there is a more effective option for couples.

Note that, with rare exceptions, you will only earn status credits on paid flights.

When you travel as a couple, both partners will benefit from each other's status. All lounges permit one guest to accompany one member. Two people travelling together can join the priority check-in line and the priority boarding line, even if only one partner has status.

To ensure you both receive the benefits associated with status, one partner can pay cash for their flights until the desired status level is achieved. The other partner can be on the same flight but fly for free on points. Be sure to find a flight with a good points price and a reasonable cash price before making the two separate bookings.

One partner can follow strategies that maximise status until they have earned the level that provides lounge access, which also brings other significant benefits. The other partner could forget about status and focus on flying for free.

EXAMPLE
Couples Strategy

How a Couple Can Both Benefit from Status, Rather than Neither, at No Additional Cost

Four Return Economy Flights for a Couple, Sydney to London

Suppose you and your partner plan to take four return flights together in one year. Your flights will likely go to different destinations, but we've used the same destination in our example for simplicity.

To further simplify this example, let us also assume that all the return

ADVANCED STRATEGIES

flights from Sydney to London cost the same. In this example, each Return ticket will cost either 130,000 Qantas points or $2,000.

You have two options.

OPTION A:

- You and your partner fly for free on the first two journeys. Make two bookings using points. Make the second two journeys using cash.

OPTION B:

- When booking each of the four journeys, make separate bookings for yourself and your partner. Pay cash for all four of one partner's bookings. Pay for all four of the other partner's bookings using points.

OUTCOMES

Cash flights will attract 190 Status Credits (plus Points) per return flight. Flights paid for in exchange for points will not attract either Status credits or points.

Under option A, each partner earns 380 Status Credits (2 cash flights at 190 credits per flight).

Under option B, your partner earns no Status Credits, however, you earn Status Credits on all four flights, totalling 760 Status Credits. That is enough Status Credits to gain gold status with Qantas. Gold status will be applied for the remainder of the year and the entire following year.

COUPLES STRATEGY EXAMPLE									
	Partner 1			Partner 2			Total		
	Cash	Points	Status Credits	Cash	Points	Status Credits	Cash	Points	Status Credits
Option A									
Flight 1	2,000		190	2,000		190	4,000		380
Flight 2	2,000		190	2,000		190	4,000		380
Flight 3		130,000			130,000			260,000	
Flight 4		130,000			130,000			260,000	
Total	4,000	260,000	380	4,000	260,000	380	8,000	520,000	760
Option B									
Flight 1	2,000		190		130,000		2,000	130,000	190
Flight 2	2,000		190		130,000		2,000	130,000	190
Flight 3	2,000		190		130,000		2,000	130,000	190
Flight 4	2,000		190		130,000		2,000	130,000	190
Total	8,000		760		520,000		8,000	520,000	760

The total cost of option A and option B will be the same: $8,000 and 520,000 points. Under both options, 760 Status Credits will be earned.

However, under option A, the Status Credits are split between you and your partner, and neither earns a helpful quantity. Under option B, the Status Credits are focused on a single partner, allowing both to enjoy the benefits.

Under option B, you can access the lounges at no cost. You can sign your partner into the lounge and grant them access to priority baggage handling, priority check-in, and priority boarding queues.

Note that under both options:

- The cash paid is the same.
- The points redeemed are the same.
- The points earned are the same.
- The status credits earned are the same.

By focusing all the cash-paid flights on one partner, as in Scenario B, both partners benefit from the Gold membership you obtain. Under Scenario A, neither partner gets any Gold status benefits.

ADVANCED STRATEGIES

If two partners were to achieve Gold status, most of the partner's status level benefits would be redundant. Providing the couple travels together, a partner without status would only miss the 75%-point loading. But that only applies to paid flights, and most of our flights will be free.

The partner without status will get access to the lounge, priority check-in and priority boarding. Rarely would anyone need two additional baggage allowances. For example, Gold members of Qantas can take three additional 32 kg bags in addition to the standard 32 kg. Unless you and your partner plan on taking more than 160 kg of checked-in bags, one partner's achievement of Gold status is enough.

COUPLES STRATEGY

One partner should consider prioritising status credits over points if a couple requires status.

If you are flying on your Primary Airline, one partner can pay cash for airfares until the targeted status level is achieved. The other partner can redeem points and fly for free. You will both benefit from having one partner with high status.

7.2 POINTS PURCHASING STRATEGY

Once the travel bug bites, there is no known antidote, and I know I will be happily infected until the end of my life.

MICHAEL PALIN

Why Read This Chapter?

You will learn when it is worthwhile to purchase loyalty points and how to do so. If you can buy the points required for a flight for less than the cash cost of the flight, why pay cash?

Purchase Points?

Check if purchasing enough points for your proposed flight is cheaper than paying cash.

Generally, the points sold by loyalty programs are not a bargain at full retail. However, most programs occasionally offer points at special prices for a limited period, and it is not uncommon for them to provide prices with significant discounts. It is worth reviewing these discount offers, which can be as high as 50% when they become available.

The list below provides examples of selling prices at full retail at the time of publication. Updates are available on the airline websites. Not all airlines offer to sell points.

The five circumstances under which it is worth buying points are as follows:

<u>General Use</u>: If the price of the points is below our weighted average value, buying them while they are on special may be worthwhile. We recommend buying at a minimum discount of 30% from the weighted average if the purchase is for unknown future use. Given the unknown future use, we allow this 30% buffer as a margin for error.

<u>Fare Type</u>: If you know that your habit is to fly only on a particular fare type (e.g. International Economy Return), then ensure the proposed purchase is at a significant discount from our valuation for that fare type.

Remember that the value of points changes according to how you intend to use them. Given that you know what type of fare you require, you can afford to make a lower allowance as a margin for error. We suggest 20% is enough in this circumstance.

<u>Specific Fare</u>: The points may cost less than the cash fare you are considering. A points purchase is low risk, provided you have checked that the fare you need is available for points.

<u>Generating Activity</u>: You may have points in a loyalty scheme that are about to expire, and you need to generate account activity to reset the expiry date on all the points in the account. You can buy the minimum parcel of points for a small amount, which will count as an activity.

<u>Top-Up</u>: You may have almost all the points required for a long flight but are just a few thousand short. You can top up for a small cost and take that flight almost for free.

Compare Cost to Valuation

We have compared the offer prices at the time of publication to our valuations. You will observe that most are not bargains. However, it is also easy to see that if the points are offered at a substantial discount, as they are from time to time, deals will be available. The key is to compare the value of the points to the current purchase price.

POINTS PRICES AT FULL RETAIL

Airline	Loyalty Program	Name of Point	Offer Price Per Point		Weighted Average Value of Points A$0.000
			Airline's Quoted Currency	Price per Point A$0.000	
Air Canada	Aeroplan	Points	CAD 0.025	0.028	0.028
Air France	Flying Blue	Miles	USD 0.017	0.025	0.022
Alaska Airlines	Mileage Plan	Miles	USD 0.028	0.042	0.024
American Airlines	AAdvantage	Miles	USD 0.024	0.036	0.024
British Airways	Executive Club	Avios	GBP 0.018	0.033	0.029
Delta Air Lines	Sky Miles	Miles	USD 0.035	0.052	0.015
Emirates	Skywards	Miles	AUD 0.048	0.048	0.026
Hawaiian Airlines	Hawaiian Miles	Miles	USD 0.018	0.027	0.018
Malaysia Airlines	Enrich	Points	MYR 0.060	0.020	0.042
Qatar Airways	Privilege Club	Avios	USD 0.023	0.034	0.058
Thai Airways	Royal Orchid	Miles	USD 0.035	0.052	0.024
United Airlines	Mileage Plus	Miles	USD 0.038	0.057	0.027
Virgin Australia	Velocity	Points	AUD 0.023	0.023	0.020

EXAMPLE
Points Purchasing Strategy

Before Booking a Specific Flight, Check the Current Price of Points

Qatar Airways—Sydney to Doha

Qatar is an undiscovered destination for many. Attractions include an excellent Museum of Islamic Art, a traditional market, and a Falcon Souk, where local Qataris buy Falcons trained to hunt. This practice is on the UNESCO World Cultural Heritage List.

The Sheikh has constructed a museum to display his extensive collection, which includes 600 cars, antique furniture, and other items.

ADVANCED STRATEGIES

A sunset Dhow trip is an unforgettable experience, but try to visit in the cooler months, November to February. You can organise a private 4WD tour to the inland sea, Khor Al Adaid.

At the time of writing, Qatar offered points for $0.034 per point, while our weighted average valuation is $0.055 per point. If we redeemed Qatar points (Avios) for an International Economy return fare, it would not be worth buying points, as we value them at $0.031 if used for that purpose. However, points may be worth buying if you intend to redeem them for an International Business One-Way fare, as this type of fare is costly with Qatar Airways. But ensure the required flight is available for points.

When using Qatar Avios for an International Business One-Way fare, we would save approximately $0.195 per point.

As a more tangible example, a One-Way Business Class flight from Doha to Sydney currently costs $2,148, or 35,000 Avios (points). Why would we pay cash if we can buy the points for $1,190 (35,000 x $0.034)?

Qatar requires a single Avios (point) to be earned before you can purchase additional Avios.

We often travel to Qatar to visit our daughter and son-in-law, who recently moved there for a few years for career reasons. Qatar Airways is the leading airline connecting Sydney and Doha. Buying points may make sense.

One feature of buying points is that you pay a flat rate, regardless of how you use them; however, their value will depend on their intended end use.

Before purchasing points for a specific flight, ensure that the flight you want is available for the number of points you expect to use. Sometimes, a flight available for cash is unavailable for points.

TRAVEL STORY
Points Purchasing Strategy

Consider Buying Points When They Are On Special

We enjoyed travelling between the Caribbean countries of the Bahamas, the Cayman Islands, St. Kitts and Nevis, St. Martin, and Antigua. American Airlines services this area well, and we plan to travel to other countries in this area.

American Airlines was selling points at a 35% discount off its regular pricing at the time of writing.

When we considered the option of paying points for a flight, we found that it cost 35% less to buy the points and book the flight with them than to pay the cash price. Consider purchasing the points when you see such deals.

POINTS PURCHASING STRATEGY

Compare the latest selling prices of points before booking a flight for cash. Purchase points if:

- *General Use: They are on sale for at least 30% below the weighted average value of the points.*
- *Fare Type: They sell for 20% below the Targeted Redemption Value for the specific fare type you expect to fly soon.*

ADVANCED STRATEGIES

- *Specific Fare: You have identified a specific flight, and buying the points is cheaper than paying cash. But first, check that a points flight is available.*

- *General Activity: You wish to create some activity on your account to avoid the expiration of existing points.*

- *Top-Up: You need a small top-up of your points balance to book a free flight.*

7.3 ITINERARY STRATEGIES

I phoned my doctor. I told him I broke my leg in two places.
He said, "Stop going to those two places."

Why Read This Chapter?

This guide is about getting a free flight or a cheap flight. It takes a couple of things for granted. It assumes you need a flight because you have determined the best route to your destination and the most suitable mode of transport. But do you need a flight? The answer is not always obvious.

In this chapter, you will learn the following:

- To ask yourself, "Do I need a flight?" (*Transport Strategy*)
- The benefit of flying between hubs (*Hub Strategy*)
- Why the apparent route is not always the best (*Route Strategy*)

The strategies presented in this chapter involve identifying different options for your travel itinerary. The wider your options, the better your chances of finding a free flight or reducing the cost of your journey.

Transport Strategy

Do you need a flight? Flying is not always the most efficient mode of transportation. For shorter journeys, buses and trains are often more cost-effective than planes and frequently take no longer than a flight.

Consider the time you spend in the airport and the travel time between the airport and your accommodation. Typically, you will leave your accommodation in a central part of the city to go to an airport well outside the city.

On the other hand, train stations and bus terminals are almost always in the middle of the departure and arrival cities. The train or bus will pick you up from the centre of town and deliver you to the centre of the destination city.

This is particularly worth noting when planning European travel. Fast trains are often more suitable for medium distances, and buses can be a good option for shorter distances.

The Route

You should arrive at an airport two hours before a domestic flight and three hours before an international flight. The baggage check processes need to be more rigorous at airports than at bus and train terminals. The words, *"What was that loud bang?"* are much more worrying on a plane than on a bus.

When catching a bus, the check-in process takes about 15 minutes for the entire bus. Bags are rarely required to be securely screened. If you are conservative like us, you can afford to arrive at the bus station 30 minutes before departure. When you reach the other end, collecting your bag will take only five minutes.

Overall, catching a bus or train versus a plane will typically save you:

- 30 minutes on the journey to a centrally located bus departure terminal rather than a less conveniently located airport.
- 150 minutes due to the need to arrive only 30 minutes before a bus or train departure, versus three hours before flight time.
- 30 minutes on arrival due to the more complicated disembarking and baggage collection process at the airport, as compared to bus or train terminals.
- 30 minutes due to a typically centrally located arrival terminal for a bus or train, compared to arriving at an airport well outside the city.

The benefits of the fast plane can be eroded to the point that it is hard to justify the higher cost.

Google Flights can highlight flight costs to alternate airports when searching. It is often worth considering taking a cheaper flight to an alternative airport and completing your journey by train or bus.

FLY FOR FREE

TRAVEL STORY

Transport Strategy

Before Booking Flights, Explore Alternative Transportation, especially if the Distances are under 1,000 km

Lynda and I planned a trip to Eastern Europe. We enjoyed spending time near the ocean and visiting the Albanian Riviera.

This stretch of the Northern Mediterranean coastline is one of the last to be discovered by tourists. We decided on Himare as our seaside base location. It has enough civilisation to have beautiful accommodation, but is less busy than the more famous Dalmatian coast to the north.

The Adriatic coastline is beautiful, as is the drive through the granite mountains on the way back to Tirana, the capital.

We thoroughly enjoyed Albania. When we departed, we had to make our way to Marseille. We had also accepted the offer of another home exchange, where we could use a house for free. We investigated travel options from Tirana to Marseille.

Marseille surrounds a port where hundreds of moored yachts provide a spectacular display on a summer night. Like most marina areas worldwide, the port is well-catered with restaurants and bars. We also enjoyed the town's area from Cours-Julien to the Vieux-Port and the recently restored fortress at the mouth of the harbour.

Marseille is only a short bus ride to Cassis, the starting point for one of Europe's most beautiful hikes through the Calanques. The hike winds through valleys with stunning granite cliffs, past turquoise waters and pebble beaches worthy of a National Geographic feature.

The cheapest flight from Tirana (Albania) to Marseille included a long layover in Vienna. Two tickets would have put a $998 dent in our budget.

ADVANCED STRATEGIES

However, Google Flights drew our attention to low-cost flights from Tirana to Nice. We explored options for travel between Nice and Marseille and found that FlixBus offers frequent services for just A$13 per person.

We booked the bus trip six months in advance, allowing us to choose any seat. We decided on the Panoramic Seat option. This pair of seats is located upstairs at the front, offering panoramic view windows. The upgrade cost was A$6 each. It provided an excellent price contrast to an upgrade on a plane. The plane to Nice and the bus to Marseille cost A$530 for the two of us, rather than $998 for the flight from Tirana to Marseille with the long layover.

Combining a plane and a bus sounds less direct, but it took more than four hours less door-to-door and was approximately half the price. We also benefited from the experience of looking out the front of the bus. While most of the view was of freeway traffic, it was still more fun than exploring the back of a plane seat.

The bus dropped us in the centre of Marseille, just a short Uber ride from our accommodation. This saved us the cost of a transfer from Marseille airport.

In summary, flying all the way would have taken 10 hours and 40 minutes and cost $1,059, including the commute from Marseille airport. Flying part of the way and completing the journey by bus took six hours and cost $530.

TRANSPORT STRATEGY EXAMPLE

BASE CASE - Fly from Tirana to Marseille

	DURATION Hrs:Mins	COST FOR TWO A$
Flight from Tirana to Vienna	1:35	998
Layover in Vienna airport	6:00	
Flight from Vienna to Marseille	2:00	
Exit flight, collect bag, exit airport	0:30	
Uber from Marseille Airport to City	0:35	61
Total Base Case	10:40	1,059

ALTERNATE ROUTE - Fly from Tirana to Nice Take Bus from Nice to Marseille		
	DURATION Hrs:Mins	**COST FOR TWO** A$
Flight from Tirana to Nice Airport	2:05	492
Exit flight and wait for bus	1:10	
Bus: Nice Airport to Marseille City	0:05	
Exit bus, collect bag, exit terminal	2:40	38
Total Alternate Case	6:00	530

TRAVEL STORY

Transport Strategy

Explore a Stopover Location to Make Alternate Transport Options Viable

Many people have seen Prague, but Lynda and I didn't get there until 2023. By then, it had shaken off the shackles of the communist era and was a vibrant city. It has retained its old-world charm, particularly in the centre of town. The magnificent traditional sights around the Charles Bridge, Prague Castle, and the medieval Old Town Square should not be missed. Modern craft breweries and a lively nighttime atmosphere now supplement these traditional sites.

Not only is the Prague city centre World Heritage listed, but it is only one hour by train to two other World Heritage areas: Cesky Krumlov and Kutna Hora. Allow one day each at these locations when you are in the Prague area. Cesky Krumlov is one of the most beautiful small cities we have visited, and Kutna Hora is another lovely historic small city that we particularly enjoyed. We drove to both places, but a train from Prague would have been better. Both these cities are best explored on foot.

Our free accommodation in Prague was arranged through Home Exchange, and we used it as a base to explore other areas of the Czech

Republic by renting a car for day trips. That included a trip to Telc, another World Heritage town.

Prague was hard to leave, but we were excited because we had another free week of accommodation in a beautiful apartment in the centre of Budapest, Hungary. When planning the trip, we investigated flight options. Our extensive itinerary meant a Return ticket would not work, so we priced a One-Way ticket from Prague to Budapest.

The points flights were expensive and time-consuming, as most flights went via Vienna and required an overnight stop. The cheapest and only direct flight was with the low-cost carrier Ryan Air. The price was $260 for two, including Lynda's checked-in bag. But flying can become a drag.

Instead, we decided it would be better to see what was between Prague and Budapest, so we caught the bus to Brno at $18 each. We stayed two nights and saw this wonderful town. We will never forget wandering the city, watching the local population while sipping Aperol Spritzers in the afternoon, and eating street food in the beautiful city centre at night.

Then we caught a FlixBus for $50 each from Brno to Budapest.

Flixbus's general guideline is to arrive 15 minutes before the scheduled departure. Boarding took 10 minutes for the whole group. Security checks were not required, and there were no baggage charges. The bus departed and arrived at the central bus stations in each town.

We travelled by bus between Prague and Budapest for six hours and 40 minutes over two days. The flight was only one hour and 10 minutes, so the travel component took five hours and 30 minutes longer. However, commuting to and from the airport at each end of the flight would have taken time and required waiting for an Uber. We could walk to and from the bus stations. Also, we would have had to endure the recommended three-hour period at the airport before the flight.

When you allow for these other factors, the difference in travel time is negligible. All you see in a plane is the back of the seat in front. While buses choose freeways rather than scenic routes, you still see much more out of the bus window than out of a plane window.

By enjoying a two-night stay in Brno, we discovered a beautiful part of the Czech Republic that we would have missed if we had chosen air travel over ground transport. Consider slowing down your trip to fit in an interesting diversion.

> **TRANSPORT STRATEGY**
>
> Before booking a flight, consider other modes of transport, such as buses and trains. Calculate the cost and end-to-end time for both options. Combine this strategy with the Route Strategy. Consider flying to a city near your destination and completing your journey by bus or train.

Hub Strategy

We all think we are a bit special when we go flying. Some think they are special when they don their Gucci shoes and Armani jacket. I think I am special when wearing a clean pair of shorts. But we must not kid ourselves. Airlines are logistics businesses. To the airline logistics guys, neither of us is special. We are just human parcels being delivered.

We humans are a bit more complicated than regular parcels. Standard parcels wrapped in brown paper and tied with string do not require feeding or provision of facilities. Transporting humans is complicated because they must travel on the same plane as another parcel, a bag, and be reunited at their destination.

Delivering bags and their custodial humans is more complicated than delivering regular parcels. However, all logistics businesses rely on similar microeconomics.

What Are Hubs?

I have served as Chief Financial Officer for several logistics companies. They all have major distribution hubs. The goods are moved in volume between hubs. More volume equals lower transport cost per unit. Then, smaller, less efficient deliveries are sent out from the hubs. Airlines also have hubs.

Hubs are airports with significant facilities for everything from refuelling to large-scale baggage handling. They are equipped to handle the largest planes and thousands of people.

Large planes are required for long-distance flights and generally fly between Hub airports.

To illustrate the efficiency of flights between hub airports, we chose a large sample of fares from our database. Those flights were operated by 19 airlines, all on different routes of different lengths. As expected, the longer the flight, the lower the cost per kilometre. However, our analysis revealed a significant cost difference for flights longer than 500 kilometres versus those shorter than 500.

On average, flights up to 500 km cost passengers 74 cents per kilometre, four or five times the cost per kilometre for flights over 1,000 km.

FARE PRICE PER KILOMETRE	
Cost per Kilometre	
Flight Distance	Fare Price per Km A$
Up to 500km	$0.74
501km to 1,000 km	$0.29
1,001km to 10,000km	$0.20
Over 10,000km	$0.13

Optimising the economics of moving parcels remains the same regardless of their contents. If the parcels are people, it does not matter. Optimising microeconomics relies on the same principles, whether the parcels are Christmas gifts in boxes or hungry humans. Airlines operate more efficiently over long distances, using large planes. Such planes usually fly between the hub airports, which are their main distribution centres for deliveries of people.

The hubs see many human parcels flown in and out. You will often have a layover between departure points and arrival destinations, and these stops are almost always at hub airports.

Flights under 500 km should be avoided. For distances of less than 500 km, consider trains and buses.

This general principle of using air travel between hubs and avoiding flights less than 500 km works—until you reach Southeast Asia! The competition between budget airlines in that region is so intense that flying even short distances can be viable.

Flying from Hubs to Secondary Airports Is High Cost

The airlines use their large planes between hubs to achieve economies of scale. The number of passengers moved between the hubs is enormous. In any business with high volume, there are volume-related savings, commonly referred to as *Economies of Scale*. The planes are larger, and the cost is less per kilometre. This translates into savings for you.

Many parcels, including people, are delivered to secondary locations from the hubs. These movements are usually in smaller, less efficient planes over shorter distances.

Any airline that did not operate a hub-based distribution system for its cargo would be unable to compete.

Other forms of transport should always be considered when not travelling between hubs.

Of course, some small planes, such as Lear Jets, fly rapidly between airports, large and small. They are expensive and are operated by companies such as Execujet or Netjet. Unless your name starts with Warren and ends with Buffett, you should focus on the hub-to-hub routes. Hi, Warren. I love your work. Email me if you need a chief financial officer. . . or an in-flight bartender.

Potential Departure or Destination Hubs

Determine the hub airports near your point of departure and your point of arrival. When searching for flights, include the nearest hubs. This will provide a broader range of possible fares. You may find that flying hub-to-hub and using ground transport to your destination costs considerably less than flying point-to-point.

Hubs will always include the largest city in the relevant country. However, they will often include less obvious ones. For example, it will come as no surprise to most people that hub cities in Spain include the capital, Madrid, and the popular tourist destination and sizable commercial city of Barcelona. However, if you have not been to Spain before, you may not be familiar with Malaga, yet it is a significant hub serving southern Spain.

To determine the hubs:

- Google *flight map images [insert airline]* and look at where the air route lines are all coming together.
- Do an Expedia search between your starting and ending locations. Ignore the prices briefly and note where the listed airlines are stopping. Each airline will have a superhub, and many will have a few smaller hubs.

Some hubs are obvious. Singapore Airlines has a superhub in Singapore, and Austrian Airlines has a superhub in Vienna. Similarly, most international flights by Italian airlines fly via Rome or Milan. Many hubs will be less intuitive in large countries such as the USA.

EXAMPLE
Hub Strategy

Look at Ground Transport Options for Journeys Under 1000 km

Here are some examples of the difference in Economy Class return fares per kilometre. We chose a random date two months out. You will find exceptions where budget airlines have chosen to dominate a popular short route. However, the examples below are typical of the scale of difference in cost per kilometre between long and short routes.

FARE COSTS PER KM - LONG VS SHORT			
LONGER JOURNEYS			
- between Hubs	Fare A$	Distance Kilometres	Cost per Km Cents (A$)
Singapore - London	1,877	21,690	8.7
London - Sao Paulo	1,606	28,406	5.7
Los Angeles - New York	1,032	7,878	13.1

SHORTER JOURNEYS			
- between Smaller Airports	Fare A$	Distance Kilometres	Cost per Km Cents (A$)
Newcastle - Canberra	244	371	65.8
Bucharest - Sofia	147	301	48.8
Flagstaff - San Diego	625	575	108.7

> **HUB STRATEGY**
> Fly between hubs to reduce end-to-end travel costs. Consider using ground transport between your departure point and a hub airport or between a hub airport and your destination.

Route Strategy

The obvious route is not always the best.

The longer you fly, the longer the flight crew must be paid, the more wear and tear on the plane, and the more fuel required. There is no denying that the shortest distance between two points is a straight line. So, logically, flying in a straight line between your departure and arrival locations should provide the cheapest fare, right?

Wrong.

Experiment with different routes, recognising that the shortest route is not always the cheapest. It's best to leave your intuition behind when searching for the most affordable flight.

The economics of running an airline can yield surprising outcomes. It can often be cheaper to travel the long way around. Airline direct costs, such as labour and fuel, influence airfare prices, but many other costs are not immediately apparent. For example:

- An airline may know they will fill a plane on a direct route but expect to have empty seats on a longer indirect route. They may prefer to sell you one of the otherwise empty seats at a low price. This may apply even if the distance travelled is much longer. There is no future for an airline that flies empty seats.

- Airlines must consider where they want their planes to end up. They may wish to use a route to relocate their aircraft, but they may have to offer low prices to fill the plane.

TRAVEL STORY
Route Strategy

Examine a Wide Range of Routes and Do Not Assume the Shortest Route is the Cheapest

The area known as British North Borneo before World War II now comprises the Malaysian states of Sarawak and Sabah. Before the war, the British had prohibited headhunting in this area. However, during the war, they declared it "game-on" under the condition that only Japanese heads were targeted.

I can't imagine how terrifying it must have been for a conscripted, spectacled, 60 kg Japanese accountant to be thrust into a jungle, knowing 120 kg muscle-bound head-hunters were lying in wait with purpose-made swords, looking for a trophy.

I heard a lot about North Borneo when I was growing up. My dad fought there. Dad was an anti-tank gunner. Since there were no Japanese tanks available to shoot at in Borneo, his regiment got a lot of odd jobs.

One of those jobs was to escort a medic to the chief of a Dayak head-hunting tribe deep in the jungle. I don't know what was wrong with the chief. Maybe he had a back strain from too much head-lopping. Whatever his medical complaint, the chief was thankful for being treated and gave the soldiers gifts. These included the 1943 Dayak head-hunter sword, which the chief gave to Dad.

We wanted to retrace some of Dad's steps and explore this area on the way to Europe. This included exploring Kuching in Sarawak, visiting Brunei, and climbing Mount Kinabalu near Kota Kinabalu (KK) in Sabah.

Lynda and I were excited to book the heavily regulated Kota Kinabalu climb, as only 130 climbers are allowed daily. We wanted to be two of the only four climbers who could book one of the two private ensuite cabins halfway up the mountain. We had a booking for July 6th, so that date on our itinerary could not be changed.

Kuching is at the western end of the Borneo north coast, Brunei is in the middle of that north coast, and Kota Kinabalu is at the eastern end of the same coast. Due to various factors, we needed to start our exploration of North Borneo from Kuching at the western end.

Travelling in a straight line, Kuching-Brunei-KK seemed the obvious route. It is the shortest distance across the north coast, west to east. We planned to make this logical progression across the top of the island.

Borneo doesn't look that big on a world map, as it is next to the vast continent of Australia. But that is an optical illusion. Borneo is the third-largest non-continental island in the world, after Greenland and New Guinea.

Flying was the only viable option, given the long distances and our timeframes.

After spending three nights in Kuching, we planned to spend three more nights in Brunei before heading to Kota Kinabalu (KK), the pickup point for the Mount Kinabalu climb.

The total flight cost for the logical and shortest route, Kuching-Brunei-KK, was $2,894 for two. We had already committed to the mountain climb, and those flights would have worked, but we didn't like the price.

The experimentation went into overdrive. The solution was to:

- Take a seemingly illogical and much longer path from Kuching, flying over the top of Brunei, to Kota Kinabalu. This Kuching to KK flight cost $210 for the two of us.
- Then we could retrace the previous flight path, travelling west from KK to Brunei, for $224.

The price for the shortest and most logical route was $2,894, but the longer, less logical route was $434.

THE SHORTEST ROUTE IS NOT ALWAYS CHEAPER — EXAMPLE

BORNEO - ALTERNATE ROUTES

Obvious, Straight Line Route

	Distance Kilometres	Fare A$
Kuching to Brunei	949	1,464
Brunei to KK	257	1,430
Total	1,206	2,894

BACK TRACKING ROUTE

	Distance Kilometres	Fare A$
Kuching to KK	1,141	210
KK to Brunei	257	224
Total	1,398	434

By taking the longer, indirect route, we saved $2,460 on flights, an 85% saving.

Note that if we had given our original schedule to a travel agent or flight booking agent, we would have ended up with a bill for $2,894. By booking things ourselves, we could make personal decisions on the run that an agent could never do for us. We flexed our route to suit the much cheaper flights.

ROUTE STRATEGY

Be flexible with the route, and do not assume that the shortest distance between two points is the cheapest. Experiment with the order of the airports you are flying between. Consider nearby airports and supplement your travel with other forms of transportation.

ADVANCED STRATEGIES

TRAVEL STORY
Route and Transport Strategies

Include Ground Transport to Open Up a Wider Variety of Route Options

We needed to travel from Vienna to visit our son's family near Birmingham. The price of a British Airways One-Way Economy flight to Birmingham was £189 each (approximately A$682 for two).

Two alternate flights were:

- Manchester: £118   (A$440 for two)
- London: £58   (A$210 for two)

The cost of a train from London Heathrow to a bus terminal at Euston Street, plus the bus trip to Birmingham, was $62 each. We decided to fly to London and take the bus at a total cost of $334 for two.

The direct flight would have been more convenient, but it was over twice the price. Decisions often involve a trade-off between time and money. A working couple, a family of five, a retiree and a young backpacker will make different decisions. Just make sure you are aware of your options.

Our changes to the route resulted in a 51% reduction in costs.

| 7.4 | CONNECTION STRATEGIES |

> *Luxury, to me, is not owning a lot of stuff.*
> *Luxury, to me, is feeling unrushed.*
>
> TIMOTHY FERRISS, Author of The 4-Hour Workweek

Why Read This Chapter?

You will learn some ways to:

- Take the stress out of making flight connections (*Layover Strategy*).
- Break up long journeys to make them more pleasant (*Stopover Strategy*).

Layover Strategy

Avoid Tight Connections

Face that the day is a write-off if you board a flight. You may arrive in time to see a tourist site or have a nice dinner. You will probably at least wander the streets a little. But it will not be a productive day. Your day is done.

There is no benefit in rushing and exposing yourself to time pressures.

The time to make your flight as painless as possible is when you prepare your trip planning spreadsheet and make bookings.

The things that will determine the ease of your flying day are:

- The number of hours in airline seats.
- The number of hours in airports.
- Your flight times.

You won't make a lot of difference to your comfort by changing the emphasis from your right butt cheek to the left five hours into that ten-hour flight. Buying a fluffy neck pillow at the airport won't change things much.

When planning, it can be tempting to make your layover very short to reach your destination early. However, short layovers can add significant stress with little or no benefit. When you arrive at your destination, tired from flying, you probably won't do much anyway.

When booking connecting flights, allow for the first plane to be delayed. A one-hour layover is too tight. Getting a replacement flight on short notice can be challenging and expensive if you miss your connecting flight.

Planning Is Not Enough

The European Union has legislated to allow airlines to overbook by 10%. They can sell 110 tickets for a plane that has only 100 seats. What numbskull came up with that dumb idea? It can lead to a mess they try to figure out on the day. Airlines operating within the US operate similarly.

They say it makes the airline industry more profitable. Of course, it does. When there is a *no-show*, the airline can clean up by selling the seat twice.

If a single airline were to engage in this practice of overbooking, it would likely lose business. However, because the airlines have banded together and lobbied various governing bodies as an industry, they all engage in this practice, and the public has no way of escaping it.

If this idea is such a good one, why don't we start selling the same stadium seats to multiple people? Let's double-book restaurant tables while we are at it. I would much rather get bumped from a restaurant table because of a double booking than be stuck at an airport in a foreign city because of a double booking.

And besides, why do we want to make airlines more profitable anyway? Richard Branson is a friendly billionaire, but increasing his wealth is not my objective. Sorry, Dick.

Lynda and I wasted a day of our holiday in the Canary Islands because Air Europa overbooked our flight. They felt they had done the right thing by sending us to a "C" grade hotel for a night with a meal voucher. Free canteen food—just what we wanted. Did that compensate for forfeiting one night in Tenerife? Certainly not.

Call me old-fashioned, but if I buy something, it's mine. Please don't sell it twice. We have enough reasons to worry about missing a connection.

They say that the benefits trickle down from the wealthy owners to the poor suckers in Economy Class. However, an Oxfam study revealed that we live in a world where, if the eight wealthiest people on the planet pooled their assets, they would own the same amount as if the poorest half of the world's population pooled theirs. So, I think the trickle-down theory is in trouble. Refer to www.oxfam.org/en/press-releases/just-8-men-own-same-wealth-half-world.

When you arrive for your flight:

- You may get bumped off that flight.
- You may arrive late.
- Your connecting flight time may have been changed to an earlier time.
- It may take a while for your bag to come off the first flight, delaying your transit to the next flight.

Allowing extra layover time can help alleviate much of the stress.

Same Airline for Short Layovers

For connecting flights, use a single booking with a single airline where possible. The airline must get you to the destination on your ticket. That means they must organise a replacement flight if the first plane is too late for your connection.

However, everything changes if you book the first leg with one airline and the second with a different airline. If the two flights are with different airlines, and the first flight is late, that becomes your problem.

The airline guarantees that you will arrive at your destination but does not guarantee the exact timing. Once you arrive at your ticketed destination, the airline's obligation has been discharged. Arriving too late for your connecting flight is always a risk. If the connecting flight is on a separate booking with a different airline, you must pay for a new flight. Fares purchased at short notice will usually be exorbitantly priced.

A delay of the first flight could cost you a bomb.

Do not read that last sentence out loud if you are reading this at an airport.

However, suppose you have a single ticket to your destination, and the airline has chosen to break it into two flights for logistical reasons, such as flying via a hub. In that case, any missed connections are their problem. Obtaining a replacement flight will be at the airline's expense.

But there may be more to consider than the money. The airline may fly out of your layover location infrequently. A delay may mean missing something, such as a boat or a wedding. If your arrival time at the final destination is critical, ensure you allow plenty of time between connecting flights. How long? We recommend at least two hours, but we are more comfortable with three.

We go further and avoid boarding two flights on the same day. However, not everyone has time for that, and sometimes we don't.

EXAMPLE
Layover Strategy

Make Your Connections the Airlines' Problem and Keep Them Working For You

Imagine you are travelling from Sydney to Paris via Dubai. If the first long-haul flight from Sydney to Dubai was late, you could miss your connection to Paris.

If both flights are with British Airways (BA) on a single booking, BA will prioritise you on the next available flight. Two connecting flights booked under a single ticket with the same airline will ensure that you do not have to pay for the replacement of the second flight. In this case, BA would prioritise your place on the first available flight to Paris over people on standby.

But if you made two separate bookings with two airlines and missed your connection, you would probably have to pay for a replacement flight for the second leg. The replacement flight is likely to be at exorbitant last-minute prices.

FLY FOR FREE

TRAVEL STORY
Layover Strategy

Allow More Time For Transit Stops if You Are Combining International and Domestic Flights

San Francisco is an excellent city for walking. And then there are the trolley cars. There is the historic trolley car (tram) made famous by those old black-and-white movies, such as *A Streetcar Named Desire*, although that movie was set in New Orleans. However, there are also magnificently restored ones from the 1960s, 1970s, and 1980s, sourced from all over the US, that form the backbone of public transportation. It's like an outdoor working museum for tram buffs.

San Francisco is one of the loveliest large American cities. It has the Golden Gate Bridge and Alcatraz. It's also the gateway to wine country and Yosemite.

After spending a week next to one of the Dominican Republic's excellent white-sand beaches at Punta Cana, we wanted to visit San Francisco on our way to Hawaii.

American Airlines offered a great deal, including two flights connecting through Charlotte, North Carolina. When planning that transit, I made a rookie mistake. I got sucked into thinking a one-hour layover would be okay. It was on the same booking with the same airline, so I assumed they would check the bags all the way through. I thought we had to go through the transit area to catch the second flight.

However, I had forgotten that we would have to clear customs when we landed in Charlotte, USA. We came from the Dominican Republic and planned to stay in San Francisco for a few days. However, we did not have the option of delaying immigration clearance until we reached San Francisco. I didn't think of that when booking.

Consider your transfers and ensure you have factored in the bags if the layover time is tight. We collected the bag, cleared a long customs queue, checked the bag back in again through the domestic terminal and ran for that flight. We made it with only seconds to spare, which was very stressful. Tight connections are a terrible idea.

EXAMPLE
Layover Strategy

Make Your Connections the Airline's Problem

Say you wanted to fly from Sydney to London. Let's consider what would happen if you used Qantas for the first leg from Sydney to Singapore and Swiss Air for the second leg to London.

If the Qantas flight were late, causing you to miss your connection, Qantas (or any other airline) would likely claim that they delivered you to Singapore, and you received what you paid for.

In this example, the Swiss Air people would say your late flight with Qantas has nothing to do with them. For Swiss Air, your no-show meant they had to fly an empty seat to London, and you would have to buy another flight at last-minute prices.

However, if you had made a single booking with either one of those airlines and the first flight was late:

- There would often be many other people on the first flight with the same problem. The airline might delay the connecting flight to help everyone catch it. This would be in the airline's interest, as they would not want to be obligated to provide free replacement fares for many people.

- The connecting flight might be forced to leave without you, but that would become the airline's problem. They must keep their commitment and ensure you arrive at your ticketed destination. You might still experience a delay. However, the airline would find a solution and cover the costs.

TRAVEL STORY
Layover Strategy

The Single Booking Advantage. Keep the Airlines Working For You

Once, when we travelled from Paris to Sydney, we met with friends in Phuket. Lynda and I were invited to spend time at their beautiful resort, as they had a spare room. Other long-serving friends have their permanent home nearby, so calling in on our way back to Sydney was a no-brainer.

Phuket is an excellent destination for anyone. It is renowned for its beautiful beaches. Patong Beach is worth checking out, but there are better beaches like Kamala Beach. The town along and behind Patong Beach is renowned for its excellent restaurants and vibrant bars. The street food is terrific.

The Phi Phi Islands are an excellent place to visit, provided you can overlook many tourists. In flat water on a sunny day, it's still worth the trip. The offshore sea caves near James Bond Island also make a great day tour. After being delivered to the area by a large boat, you can enter a cave lying back in a rowboat, floating under a low cave roof. When you come out to the other side of the caves, there is an open sky again, along with pristine jungle-lined cliffs teeming with monkeys.

Wat Mongkol Nimit is also worth a visit. The Big Buddha is a must-see destination in the southern part of the island, particularly for its commanding views over the island and the ocean. The Sunday night markets in Thalang Road, Phuket town, are also worth visiting.

Phuket is a great base. You can cross to the mainland via a bridge for day trips to Krabi to see the limestone karst formations on land and sea or to visit the resorts at Khao Lak.

We had a layover in Doha on our way to Thailand. On this occasion, we did not want to use the *Stopover Strategy* outlined elsewhere for two reasons. First, we wanted to spend all the days with our friends in Thailand. Second, we found a bargain points flight travelling in Business Class. We could not book that flight if we wanted to break the trip in two.

After four months of travel, we looked forward to a Qatar Business Class flight, which was paid for using Qantas Frequent Flyer points. The flights were great except for one catch. After a boarding delay, our first flight sat on the tarmac in Paris for a long time. The delay was due to an air traffic controller's strike. Our flight was scheduled to arrive in Doha two hours and 40 minutes before the connecting flight to Phuket. Qatar operated both flights, and they were part of the same booking.

It was not Qatar Airways' fault that our first flight was late. But we expected the boarding gate to be closed when we arrived in Doha.

Because both flights were all on the one ticket, two things happened:

- Firstly, the crew in Doha, flying the connecting flight to Phuket, got all the other passengers on board and settled them. Qatar extended the boarding time by approximately 10 minutes to accommodate connecting passengers from our delayed flight.
- Secondly, the Qatar ground staff were informed and mobilised a Qatar representative. She was waiting specifically for us as we came up the Doha air bridge from the first flight.

The airline representative walked and ran with us to the next gate. It was a long walk with sprints in between, and we used every minute of the extended boarding time. She was in constant phone contact with the gate to ensure they knew we were on our way.

Most people need a few minutes to orient themselves in an unfamiliar airport, check the boards, and figure out where to go. The Qatar representative was ready to save us those vital minutes.

We moved so quickly that we were out of breath by the time we got to the connecting flight. The boarding passes were initially rejected due to the standard boarding cut-off times. The staff at the gate had to override the standard computer settings so the light would turn green when the boarding passes were scanned.

Without the concerted effort of the airline staff, we would have been stranded. We probably would have missed a day in Thailand with our friends. Instead, we would have spent the time in the airport or a nearby hotel.

If the connecting flight had been with a different airline, the stay would have been at our own expense. Then, we would have had to pay for a new ticket from Doha to Phuket. The replacement ticket would have been at last-minute prices. To stay on budget, we would have been stuck with Economy Class even though the ticket we paid for (with points) was Business Class.

Qatar would not have had a representative to meet us if we had travelled with a different airline on the second leg. They would have no record to indicate that we had a connecting flight.

Also, an unrelated airline would not have delayed the normal boarding process for the connecting flight.

> **LAYOVER STRATEGY**
>
> Allow extra layover time if your bags cannot be checked through your layover destination. Those circumstances are likely if you move between international and domestic flights. If you must have two connecting flights with a short layover, book them with a single airline under a single booking number.

Stopover Strategy

If you have the time, consider using the *Stopover Strategy*. Fly into your transit stop one day and fly out on a different day.

Your flight will be more pleasant because:

- You will have less stress.

- You will sleep in a proper bed and be refreshed for your second flight.
- You may see something new at your transit stop, depending on your spare time.

Try splitting a single booking into two if you can leave at least one night between the two flights. With that much time between flights, the risks of missing connections are almost non-existent. Splitting the booking usually incurs a small cost but can provide an excellent return on investment.

Splitting a journey into two bookings often opens fare-saving opportunities. For example, we sometimes fly from Sydney to Europe via Singapore. For half the price of Singapore Airlines, we can fly on a short daytime flight with Scoot, the same company's budget airline. On the longer leg from Singapore to Europe, we usually find a flight on points with a full-service Oneworld airline, often in Business Class.

If Lynda and I need to take two flights to our destination, we try to turn that into an opportunity to see something in the layover city. Layovers sitting in airports are boring, uncomfortable, and tiring. If your first flight is late, making the connection can be stressful.

It is often worth adding a day in the layover city, even if that means one less day at your destination. Getting off a flight, going to a hotel, and touring the town that night or the next day is more pleasant. Then, you can use the *Body Clock Strategy* (covered elsewhere) on both legs of the journey. You will arrive feeling relatively fresh. The final journey will not be exhausting. Additionally, you won't have to worry about what happens if your first flight is delayed.

The alternative of pressing on will give you more time at your destination, but you will arrive tired and need recovery time. Going straight through will not give you as much quality time at your destination as it may appear on your trip-planning spreadsheet.

Consider these options.

<u>Option 1</u>: Transit Hotel: Check into a hotel <u>within</u> the airport transit area.

Many large airports have hotels inside. They are not expensive, and you can usually book them in four-hour intervals. You can shower, sleep in a real bed, get up, and go to your gate. There will be no baggage collection. The hotel is just like another gate, entirely contained within the airport. Just make sure you have a change of clothes and some toiletries in your carry-on.

Option 2: *Airport Hotel: Check into a hotel <u>near</u> the airport.*

Collect your bags and proceed to the airport exit. Consider staying at a hotel within walking distance or a short cab ride away. Almost all commercial airports have hotels nearby. After showering and getting a good sleep, return for the next flight and recheck your bags. Disregard local time in your transit city. Your body won't be there long enough to adjust to it. Time your next flight to suit your body clock. When booking, consider when your jet-lagged body would want to sleep.

Option 3: *Stopover: Spend one to two days at your transit stop.*

For this option, consider staying at a hotel in the transit city to allow you to explore the area. This may mean two nights' accommodation with a clear day in between. Even if you have been to that city often, walk in your favourite area or discover something new. No matter how many times you have been there, most places will have something to offer in the surrounding area.

If your trip is, say, 21 nights, it has cost you nothing. Either way, you will still be paying for 21 nights' accommodation. It's just about where you spend them and how good you feel.

Option 4: *Side Trip: Take a side trip from your transit stop.*

If you have more time, consider taking a side trip. For example, if we travel from our hometown of Sydney to Europe via Singapore, we can include a side trip to Vietnam, Laos, Malaysia, Cambodia, or many other places.

If you travel via the Middle East, you could spend time in one of the countries you have not seen. We recently decided to explore a few lesser-known areas of the United Arab Emirates outside the more famous cities of Dubai and Abu Dhabi. Fujairah and Sharjah provided unique experiences, and we look forward to further stopovers in the other Emirates each time we pass through Dubai.

If you're travelling to the East Coast of the USA via the Pacific, con-

ADVANCED STRATEGIES

sider taking a side trip to Yosemite or a West Coast city. The possibilities are endless.

Ask yourself how important it is to leave on a fixed date and reach your destination by the chosen date. For a holiday, the journey is as important as the destination.

The longer your overall trip, the more viable the side trip option becomes.

> **STOPOVER STRATEGY**
>
> Recognise that travelling all night results in unproductive travel the following day. Depending on the time you can spare, check into a hotel within the airport for a few hours, stay overnight next to the airport, spend two or three nights in the layover city, or spend more than a few nights on a side trip.

7.5 MISCELLANEOUS STRATEGIES

I haven't been everywhere. But it's on my list.

Why Read This Chapter?

You will learn two more strategies that will come into play rarely, but when they do, they can be very effective:

- Firstly, we will cover the *Round-the-World Strategy*. This can be a great use of either your points or your cash when planning a long trip across multiple continents.

- Secondly, we will review an extension of the *Retail Strategy* regarding using gift cards. This can provide occasional significant boosts to your points balance.

Round-the-World Strategy

Round-the-World tickets can often offer a great way to achieve fantastic value. But they are only worthwhile if you can be away long enough to use all the stops. Large airline alliances offer this type of ticket.

So, how do you get access to those tickets? Go to your Primary Airline's website. For example, our Primary Airline is Qantas. All roads for Round-the-World tickets lead you to one of the Round-the-World booking tools, one for each alliance. Individual airlines cannot get the coverage to offer such tickets.

When we go to the Qantas website and click on the Qantas *Round-the-World* option, we are taken to the Oneworld Alliance *Round-the-World* booking tool.

The Oneworld policy allows up to 16 stops if you pay cash. The deal may be favourable if you have the time to see most destinations. Various restrictions will become apparent when you use the tool, but they are very reasonable. The main one, for example, is that you progress in one direction around the world. That is to be expected. Otherwise, it would be called a

Go-in-Random-Directions ticket rather than a *Round-the-World* ticket. You can backtrack a little within a region, as defined by Oneworld.

- You can enter many cities. However, stick with the larger ones, which we call hub cities (*Hub Strategy*). If you choose smaller airports, it may take multiple flights to get there and back. You could use two legs (flights) to divert to a smaller place and then return to the hub city. The ticket only allows a specified number of flights, so don't waste them.
- Stick with the hubs, and if you want to divert to a smaller city, book a separate Return ticket to get back on track.
- Try to stay on the main routes so you do not use too many of your allowed legs to get somewhere. A map will display your flight path as you go. Try not to make your route look like a spider's web.

For example, you are only allowed four flights per continent for the One-World cash ticket. Try searching on Expedia or Skyscanner to see which airlines fly the route you're after. Take notice of which cities are serviced by your alliance (Oneworld, Star Alliance, SkyTeam).

A carefully constructed Round-the-World flight can give you tremendous value for cash and even better value for points.

For example, you can book a Round-the-World Business Class flight for 318,000 Qantas points per person or 132,400 for Economy. The point-based flight allows only five stops. The cash fare allows 16 stops. Choose cities on different continents to extract the most value when paying with points. Once on a continent, you can pay for buses, trains, or short flights.

> **ROUND-THE-WORLD STRATEGY**
>
> When booking a lengthy trip, consider purchasing a Round-the-World ticket, especially if you have points with your Primary Airline.

Gift Cards—Extension of Retail Strategy

Keep an eye on offers related to gift cards. They can present some great opportunities. Gift cards often provide ongoing discounts, such as a $100 card for $95.

Secondly, retailers often provide additional store points for specific products or limited periods.

Thirdly, retailers usually allow you to credit the value of a gift card to an online account. Buying online at retailers affiliated with your airline will earn you more points. The overall discount can be substantial when the discounts are stacked and combined with the benefits of the points.

EXAMPLE
Retail Strategy

Earn Extraordinary Numbers of Points from Special Gift Card Offers

While writing this section, I received an email alerting me to a deal on Apple Gift Cards at a local retail chain (Big W). This was a repeat of the same special deal that had been run several times before. I took more notice on this occasion, as Lynda and I intended to buy ourselves Apple watches.

The deal was:

- Buy gift cards for 10% cash back.
- Earn 20 times the usual number of store points.

Purchases from Big W usually earn Woolworths Everyday Rewards at a rate of one point per dollar spent. These can be traded at a rate of two store points for one Qantas point. On this occasion we earned 20 Rewards per dollar spent.

ADVANCED STRATEGIES

Buying $1,000 worth of Apple Gift Cards earned 20,000 store Rewards, which could be converted into 10,000 Qantas Frequent Flyer Points. This was in addition to the cashback referred to above. Big W provided a 10% credit on our store rewards card, which could be used to purchase everyday items from their store.

Given that Qantas Points are worth $0.025 (2.5 cents), the $1,000 purchase attracted $250 worth of Qantas Points. Additionally, we received a $100 store credit (10%). That represents a 35% discount on our watches when purchased from Apple.

We followed Apple's instructions to redeem the gift cards for credit to our Apple account. We then used our *Retail Strategy* and logged into the Apple website to buy the equipment online. Apple then paid us one Qantas Point for every dollar spent, representing an additional 2.5% discount, bringing the total discount to 37.5%.

As the benefits discussed were provided in points and store credit, the Apple invoice showed a gross retail payment of $1,000. The Apple store invoice included a $91 tax. This tax is the Goods and Services Tax (GST) in Australia. It's like VAT (value-added tax) in many countries, including the UK, or a state sales tax in the United States.

Like many countries, the Australian authorities allow the value-added tax (GST) to be claimed back after clearing immigration. You must present the goods to the airport TRS (Tourist Refund Scheme) office and provide an invoice dated within 60 days of departure. They will credit your credit card with the tax value. Don't let the term "Tourist" fool you. Aussie citizens qualify, too.

The whole thing is a bizarre waste of government resources. Why would a government pay for an office, computer systems and full-time staff to give correctly collected government money to people who take their trinkets on holiday? Or to citizens of a foreign country, so they can receive a discount that our citizens do not qualify for when staying at home?

However, we use it to our advantage. The refund represented another 9.1% discount, bringing the total discount on our Apple Watches to 46.6%.

FLY FOR FREE

Effectively, we bought $1,000 worth of watches from Apple for just 53.4% of the regular price. We spent more, but I rounded the amount to $1,000 to make the numbers easier to follow.

———————————————

Conclusion

Travel is glamorous, only in retrospect.

PAUL THEROUX

Why Read This Chapter?

This chapter revisits our initial objectives and provides examples of achieving them.

Objectives Revisited

This guide is part of a comprehensive plan to help you travel the world in luxury for just US$70 per person daily. Achieving that means you could travel for one 30-day month for US$2,100 per person.

The budget covers airfares, accommodation, tours, entry fees, and all forms of local transportation. It excludes day-to-day food. Our recommended accommodation types ensure that your expenditure on food is the same as it would have been if you had stayed at home. You will remain within the budget if you dine out only slightly more often than at home. We recommend restricting your dining out to unique locations or when trying the local cuisine. These are essential parts of travel.

If your day-to-day meals are based on grocery purchases that you must make at home if you did not travel, that is not a travel expense. Those costs would exist whether you travelled or not.

Without our strategies, airfares alone could quickly deplete our budget. This guide is intended to help you keep your airfares (or alternative country-to-country transport costs) to no more than one-third of the budgeted US$70 per person per day.

Another third of your travel budget is reserved for accommodation. For more information, refer to our upcoming guide, *Stay for Free*. If you contact us, we will add you to our mailing list and notify you when that guide becomes available.

The final third of your travel budget is reserved for miscellaneous costs, such as entry fees, side tours, hire cars, local transport and dining at unique locations.

Travel costs vary widely, but most organised tours cost between US$200 and US$400 per person per day, and a daily rate of US$700 per person is not uncommon. A typical 30-day tour, including airfares to reach the starting point and return home, typically costs between US$6,000 and US$10,000 per person. Following the Budget Luxury Travel method, the same trip will cost US$2,100 per person.

Costs often prohibit many people from travelling any more than a short trip every one or two years. To travel more often, paying the prices most people pay can seriously damage travellers' financial plans.

Budget Luxury Travel guides aim to fix that problem. Most people have numerous other financial demands beyond travel. We present methods that enable people to travel widely without compromising other life plans.

Our guides also enable people who may be cash-poor but time-abundant, such as many retirees, to travel extensively over long periods.

Our strategies can help you to realise your travel dreams.

Finally, we wish you well and leave you with one example of the airfare costs and savings associated with one of our recent trips. The example illustrates the power of combining some of the Budget Luxury Travel strategies detailed in this guide. While this example only covers airfares, the savings enable us to keep to our overall budget of US$70 (A$100) per person per day.

We wish you well and hope we have helped you to achieve your travel dreams.

CONCLUSION

TRAVEL STORY

Savings Using the Budget Luxury Travel Method

The tables below outline a fare-by-fare description of a recent trip.

The key takeaways are as follows:

- The total cost of airfares without using the strategies in this guide would have been A$15,491 per person or A$30,982 for a couple.

- If we had placed the bookings in the hands of a travel agent, the costs would have been far greater than the A$30,982 described above. That is not because travel agents do not do a good job. It is because the best travel agents will never be able to make the hundreds of decisions only you can make as you work through the process.

- You can change your mind about the route, the day of travel, the type of transport, the hour of travel, layover strategies, stop-over strategies, airline choice, class of travel and other matters as you go. It is not feasible for a third party to consult with you on all the options for every flight.

- The actual cost after using the strategies in this guide was A$2,873 per person or $5,746 for Lynda and me as a couple.

- The normal retail cost is quoted below for comparison. It was the best available cash cost for each flight after applying the strategies in the "Finding the Best Value Cash Flights" section. Without the strategies in that section, the comparative cost would have been significantly higher.

- The savings, compared to the best available cash flight options, were A$12,618 per person ($15,491 normal cost less our cost of $2,873). That makes the redemption value 3.3

Australian cents per point. This compares favourably to our valuation of 2.5 cents per Qantas point (representing 97% of the points used) and the Singapore Airlines valuation of 3.2 cents per point.

- We have a budget of US$70 or A$100 per person per day to travel the world. Without using the strategies in this guide, the entire budget for the trip, plus additional funds, would have been spent on airfares.

CONCLUSION

	ACTUAL TRIP DATA					SAVINGS FROM POINTS STRATEGIES AND ROUTE STRATEGIES			
Date	From		To		Airline	Type	Our Cost per Person		Normal Retail Cost
							Points	Program	A$	A$
27-Jun	Sydney	SYD	Singapore	SIN	Qantas	One Way	31,500	QFF	90	797
28-Jun	Singapor Kuala Lumpur	SIN KUL	Kuala Lumpur Kuching	KUL KCH	Malaysian	One Way	14,000	QFF	73	164
1-Jul	Kuching	KCH	Kota Kinabalu	BKI	Air Asia	One Way			59	59
2-Jul	Kota Kinabalu	BKI	Sandakan	SDK	Air Asia	Return			91	91
4-Jul	Sandakan	SDK	Kota Kinabalu	BKI	Air Asia					
11-Jul	Kota Kinabalu	BKI	Brunei	BWN	Air Asia	One Way			75	75
14-Jul	Brunei	BWN	Singapore	SIN	Singapore	One Way	8,500	KrisFlyer	13	228
19-Jul	Singapore	SIN	London	LHR	Qantas	One Way	50,300	QFF	317	2,642
	London	LHR	Vienna	VIE	British					
28-Jul	Vienna		Munich		Vienna-Munich by Bus			FlixBus	39	232
3-Aug	Munich	MUC	London	LHR	British	One Way	20,000	QFF	46	295
			Birmingham		London-Birming.by Bus			Megabus	55	
15-Aug	Birmingham	BHX	Amsterdam	AMS	KLM	One Way			245	245
	Amsterdam	AMS	Prague	PRG						
22-Aug	Prague		Brno		Prague-Brno by Bus			Regiojet	36	331
	Brno		Budapest		Brno-Budapest by Bus			FlixBus	29	
30-Aug	Budapest		Belgrade		Budapest-Belg. by Bus			FlixBus	35	406
3-Sep	Belgrade	BEG	Sofia	SOF	Air Serbia	One Way			177	177
8-Sep	Sofia	SOF	Vienna	VIE	Austrian	One Way			142	142
	Vienna	VIE	Tirana	TIA						
13-Sep	Tirana	TIA	Nice	NCE	Wizz Air	One Way			220	449
	Nice		Marseille		Nice-Marseille by Bus			FlixBus	35	
19-Sep	Marseille	MRS	London	LHR	British	One Way	104,500	QFF	120	3,916
	London	LHR	Sao Paulo	GRU		Business				
	Various Bus and Ferry Trips within Brazil									
4-Oct	Rio De Janeiro	GIG	Buenos Aires	AEP	Aerolineas	One Way			191	191
	Various movements, including crossing to Uruguay by ferry and Buses to Montevideo									
22-Oct	Montevideo	MVD	Santiago	SCL	LATAM	One Way			435	453
24-Oct	Santiago	SCL	Mexico City	MEX	LATAM	One Way	30,200	QFF	57	2,503
26-Oct	Mexico City	MEX	Phoenix	PHX	American	One Way	18,000	QFF	109	573
27-Oct	Phoenix	PHX	Lihue	LIH	American	One Way	30,300	QFF	16	515
4-Nov	Lihue	LIH	Honolulu	HNL	Hawaiian	One Way			81	81
4-Nov	Honolulu	HNL	Sydney	SYD	Qantas	One Way	31,500	QFF	87	926
						QFF	330,300			
						KrisFlyer	8,500			
						Points	338,800			
								Total A$	2,873	15,491
								Total US#	1,839	9,914
						Total Savings A$ per person		A$	12,618
								US$	8,076

271

ANALYSIS OF SAVINGS			
		ACTUAL TRIP DATA	NORMAL RETAIL COST
Days on Tour	Days	131	
Transport Cost per Day	US$	14	76
Budget Luxury Travel budget per day per person, Twin share	US$	70	70
Percentage of total travel budget	%	20%	108%
Savings by using alternate transport for short trips	US$	831	
Savings by using frequent flyer points	US$	7,245	
Redemption value per point	US$	0.021	
Redemption value per point	A$	0.033	

Other Budget Luxury Travel Guides

Email us, and we will add you to our list of people to advise when the following Budget Luxury Travel guides are released:

- **Stay for Free:** *Strategies for Free and Low Cost Luxury Holiday Stays*
- **Budget Luxury Travel:** *Luxury Travel on US$70 Per Day*

Free Stuff

Contact us at www.budluxtravel.com to request these free items, which include instructions where applicable.

- Retail Partners Register Template (*Retail Strategy*)
- Example of a completed Retail Partners Register (*Retail Strategy*)
- Point Valuation Template (*Valuation Strategy*)
- Point Valuation Template—Weighted Average (*Valuation Strategy*)
- Latest Schedule of Airline Point Valuations (*Valuation Strategy*)

CONCLUSION

- Flight Research Template (*Search Strategy*)
- Fly:Free Ratio Calculation Template (*Flying Strategies*)

Also, feel free to email us at budluxtravel.com if you have suggestions for improvement or questions you would like researched and answered in the next edition.

Appendices

Appendix A: Key Features of Airline Loyalty Programs

A table follows with the following data for a range of airlines:

- *Airline*—Name of the airline.
- *Loyalty Program Name*—The name of the loyalty program associated with the airline.
- *Equivalent Currency—Points*: What you must earn for free flights. Common names are Miles or Points, but there are others.
- *Equivalent Currency—Status Credits*: What you need to accumulate to earn higher status.
- *Lounge Access Level*:
  - *Name*: The name of the status level required for lounge access.
  - *Entry*: The number of status credits required to reach the lounge access level. We focus on levels up to that point, as we believe the best payoff is achieved at that level. Higher levels are nice, but after the lounge access level, you reach the point of diminishing returns.
- *Point Loading—Level*: At the base membership level, you will accumulate points for flying according to tables published on each airline's website. A growing percentage loading is added to this base as you progress through status levels. This is the required status level to achieve the percentage loading shown in the next column.
- *Point Loading +%*: We only quote the loadings for the lounge

membership level here. For example, at the Platinum status level for Air Canada, you will get 75% additional points on top of the base amount.

- *Expiry policy*: This is the criteria by which an airline determines the dates on which your points will expire.
- *Type*:
    - Some programs have a policy under which points expire after a defined number of months from the date they were issued. The table uses the abbreviation *"Issue"* to refer to these *Issue-Based* Expiry policies.
    - Other programs have a policy under which all points in the account expire after a specified number of months of inactivity on the account. The table uses the abbreviation *"Activity"* to refer to these *Activity-Based* Expiry policies.
    - The remainder have a policy of never allowing points to expire. The table refers to these as *No Expiry*.

- *Period*: This indicates the months from the Issue or the Last Account Activity date.
- *Major Alliance*: There are three large international alliances. The abbreviations in the table are *Star* for Star Alliance, *One* for Oneworld and *Sky* for SkyTeam. A dash indicates they are not part of the big three.

APPENDICES

Airline	Loyalty Program	Equivalent Currency		Lounge Access Level		Point Loading		Expiry Policy		Major Alliance
		Points	Status Credits	Name	Entry	Level	+%	Type	Period	
Air Canada	Aeroplan	Points	SQM or SQS	Elite Gold	50,000	Platinum	75%	Activity	18 mths	Star
Air Europa	Suma	Miles	Level Miles	Gold	32,000	Gold	75%	Activity	18 mths	Sky
Air France	Flying Blue	Miles	Experience Points	Gold	180	Gold	75%	Activity	24 mths	Sky
Air India	Maharaja Club	Points	Tier Points	Gold	30,000	Gold	50%	Issue	36 mths	Star
Air New Zealand	Airpoints	Dollars	Status Points	Gold	900	-	-	Issue	48 mths	Star
Alaska Airlines	Mileage Plan	Miles	Elite Miles	MVP Gold	40,000	MVP Gold	50%	Activity	24 mths	One
All Nippon Airways	Mileage Club	Miles	Premium Points	Platinum	50,000	Platinum	105%	Issue	36 mths	Star
American Airlines	AAdvantage	Miles	Loyalty Points	Purchase Access		Platinum	60%	Activity	18 mths	One
Austrian Airlines	Miles and More	Miles	Qualifying Points	Frequent Flyer	325	-	-	No Expiry	-	Star
British Airways	Executive Club	Avios	Tier Segments	Silver	600	Silver	32%	Activity	36 mths	One
Cathay Pacific	Marco Polo	Asia Miles	Status Points	Silver	300	-	-	Activity	18 mths	One
Delta Air Lines	Sky Miles	Miles	Miles	Purchase Access		Platinum	29%	No Expiry	-	Sky
Emirates	Skywards	Miles	Tier Miles	Gold	50,000	Gold	50%	Issue	36 mths	-
Etihad Airways	Guest	Miles	Tier Miles	Silver	25,000	Silver	25%	Issue	18 mths	-
Garuda Indonesia	Garuda Miles	Miles	Tier Miles	Platinum	30,000	Platinum	25%	Activity	12 mths	Sky
Hawaiian Airlines	Hawaiian Miles	Miles	Segments	Gold	30	-	-	No Expiry	-	-
ITA Airways	Miles and More	Miles	Qualifying Points	Frequent Flyer	325	-	-	No Expiry	-	Sky
Japan Airlines	Mileage Bank	Miles	Fly-On Points	Saphire	50,000	Saphire	50%	Issue	36 mths	One
Korean Airways	Skypass Club	Miles	Points	Morning Calm	80	-	-	Issue	10 years	Sky
KLM	Flying Blue	Miles	Level Miles	Gold	180	Gold	75%	Activity	24 mths	Sky
Lufthansa	Miles and More	Miles	Qualifying Points	Frequent Flyer	325	-	-	No Expiry	-	Star
Malaysia Airlines	Enrich	Points	Elite Points	Gold	60	-	-	Issue	36 mths	One
Qantas	Frequent Flyer	Points	Status Credits	Gold	500	Gold	75%	Activity	18 mths	One

REFERENCE TABLE (CONTINUED) / LOYALTY PROGRAM FEATURES (CONTINUED)

Airline	Loyalty Program	Equivalent Currency		Lounge Access Level		Point Loading		Expiry Policy		Major Alliance
		Points	Status Credits	Name	Entry	Level	+%	Type	Period	
Qatar Airways	Privilege Club	Avios	Q Points	Silver	135	Silver	25%	Activity	36 mths	One
Singapore Airlines	KrisFlyer	Miles	Miles	Gold	50,000	Gold		Issue	36 mths	Star
Southwest Airlines	Rapid Rewards	Points	Tier Qual. Points	Purchase Access		A List	25%	No Expiry	-	-
Swiss	Miles and More	Miles	Qualifying Points	Frequent Flyer	325	-	-	No Expiry	-	Star
Thai Airways	Royal Orchid	Miles	Qualifying Miles	Gold	50,000	Gold	10%	Issue	36 mths	Star
Turkish Airlines	Miles & Smiles	Miles	Status Miles	Elite	40,000	-	-	Issue	36 mths	Star
United Airlines	Mileage Plus	Miles	PQP	Gold	10,000	Gold	60%	No Expiry	-	Star
Vietnam Airlines	Lotus Miles	Miles	Qualifying Miles	Gold	30,000	Gold	50%	Issue	36 mths	Sky
Virgin Australia	Velocity	Points	Status Credits	Gold	500	Gold		Activity	24 mths	-

Appendix B: How We Allocate Stars to Loyalty Programs

The objective criteria for our allocation of stars to loyalty programs are as follows:

Program Stars for Network Alliance Size:

- Oneworld members   ***
- Star Alliance members   ***
- SkyTeam members   **
- Range of independent partners   *
- Few or no partners   -

Program Stars for Expiry Policies (refer to Expiry Strategy chapter):

- No expiry policy   *****
- 36 months of inactivity   ****
- 24 months of inactivity   ***
- 18 months of inactivity   **
- 12 months of inactivity   *

APPENDICES

- 48 months from earning   **
- 36 months from earning   *
- 24 months from earning   -

Program Stars for Ease of Lounge Access (refer to Lounge Access Strategy):
Lounge Access ratios:

- Less than 15,000:1   ***
- From 15,000:1 up to 20,000:1   **
- Over 20,000:1 up to 30,000:1   *
- Over 30,000:1   -
- Must pay for lounge access   -

Program Stars based on Fly:Free Ratios (refer to Flying Strategies):

- 0 to 10..................   *****
- 11 to 15................   ****
- 16 to 20................   ***
- 21 to 25................   **
- 26 to 30................   *
- >30....................   -

Appendix C: Point (Mile) Valuations by Major Currency

	REFERENCE TABLE		A$ AUD POINT (MILE) VALUATIONS				
			Targeted Redemption Value per Point				Weighted Avg Value
	Airline	Loyalty Scheme	One-Way		Return		
			International		Domestic	International	
			Econ.	Bus.	Econ.	Econ.	Bus.	
			A$	A$	A$	A$	A$	A$
	Air Canada	Aeroplan	.036	.042	.020	.016	.031	.028
	Air Europa	Suma	.035	.011	.021	.030	.009	.025
	Air France	Flying Blue	.033	.036	.014	.012	.012	.022
	Air New Zealand	Airpoints	.920	.920	.920	.920	.920	.920
	Alaska Airlines	Mileage Plan	-	-	.024	-	-	.024
	American Airlines	AAdvantage	.036	.024	.028	.018	.010	.024
**	Austrian Airlines	Miles and More	.024	.061	.007	.012	.030	.025
	British Airways	Executive Club	.027	.085	.010	.012	.026	.029
**	Cathay Pacific	Marco Polo	.038	.070	.016	.020	.049	.037
	Delta Air Lines	Sky Miles	.018	.013	.017	.015	.010	.015
**	Emirates	Skywards	.026	.039	.028	.016	.032	.026
**	Etihad Airways	Guest	.023	.015	.013	.013	.017	.015
*	Hawaiian Airlines	Hawaiian Miles	.020	.032	.013	.018	.023	.018
	ITA Airways	Miles and More	.024	.061	.007	.012	.030	.025
**	KLM	Flying Blue	.033	.036	.014	.012	.012	.022
	Lufthansa	Miles and More	.024	.054	.006	.012	.026	.023
	Malaysia Airlines	Enrich	.048	.055	.017	.038	.038	.042
	Qantas	Frequent Flyer	.028	.022	.019	.027	.020	.025
**	Qatar Airways	Privilege Club	.040	.195	.046	.031	-	.058
**	Singapore Airlines	KrisFlyer	.034	.057	.019	.019	.035	.032
	Southwest Airlines	Rapid Rewards	-	-	.019	-	-	.019
**	Swiss	Miles and More	.025	.069	.009	.012	.033	.027
	Thai Airways	Royal Orchid	.024	.033	.010	.021	.031	.024
	United Airlines	Mileage Plus	.035	.039	.017	.021	.020	.027
	Virgin Australia	Velocity	.022	.012	.016	.028	.012	.020

** For small countries (eg Switzerland) domestic definition includes directly neighbouring countries.
* For Hawaiian Airlines international definition includes flights to mainland USA.
Qantas: Includes 2025 devaluation.
Qatar Airlines: It is difficult to redeem points for Business Class - sample size was inadequate for valuation purposes.

APPENDICES

	REFERENCE TABLE		US$ USD				POINT (MILE) VALUATIONS
			Targeted Redemption Value per Point				
	Airline	Loyalty Scheme	One-Way	Return			Weighted Avg Value
			International	Domestic	International		
			Econ.	Bus.	Econ.	Econ.	Bus.	
			USD	USD	USD	USD	USD	USD
	Air Canada	Aeroplan	.024	.028	.013	.011	.021	.019
	Air Europa	Suma	.024	.008	.014	.020	.006	.017
	Air France	Flying Blue	.022	.024	.009	.008	.008	.015
	Air New Zealand	Airpoints	.617	.617	.617	.617	.617	.617
	Alaska Airlines	Mileage Plan	-	-	-	-	-	-
	American Airlines	AAdvantage	.024	.016	.019	.012	.007	.016
**	Austrian Airlines	Miles and More	.016	.041	.005	.008	.020	.017
	British Airways	Executive Club	.018	.057	.007	.008	.017	.020
**	Cathay Pacific	Marco Polo	.025	.047	.010	.013	.033	.025
	Delta Air Lines	Sky Miles	.012	.009	.012	.010	.007	.010
**	Emirates	Skywards	.017	.026	.019	.011	.021	.017
**	Etihad Airways	Guest	.016	.010	.009	.009	.011	.010
*	Hawaiian Airlines	Hawaiian Miles	.013	.022	.009	.012	.015	.012
	ITA Airways	Miles and More	.016	.041	.005	.008	.020	.017
**	KLM	Flying Blue	.022	.024	.009	.008	.008	.015
	Lufthansa	Miles and More	.016	.036	.004	.008	.018	.016
	Malaysia Airlines	Enrich	.032	.037	.011	.026	.025	.028
	Qantas	Frequent Flyer	.019	.014	.013	.018	.014	.017
**	Qatar Airways	Privilege Club	.027	.131	.031	.021	-	.039
**	Singapore Airlines	KrisFlyer	.023	.038	.013	.013	.024	.021
	Southwest Airlines	Rapid Rewards	-	-	-	-	-	-
**	Swiss	Miles and More	.017	.046	.006	.008	.022	.018
	Thai Airways	Royal Orchid	.016	.022	.007	.014	.021	.016
	United Airlines	Mileage Plus	.024	.026	.011	.014	.014	.018
	Virgin Australia	Velocity	.015	.008	.011	.019	.008	.014

** For small countries (eg Switzerland) domestic definition includes directly neighbouring countries.

* For Hawaiian Airlines international definition includes flights to mainland USA.

Qantas: Includes 2025 devaluation.

Qatar Airlines: It is difficult to redeem points for Business Class - sample size was inadequate for valuation purposes.

FLY FOR FREE

REFERENCE TABLE — POUNDS STERLING GBP — POINT (MILE) VALUATIONS

	Airline	Loyalty Scheme	One-Way International		Return Domestic	Return International		Weighted Avg Value
			Econ.	Bus.	Econ.	Econ.	Bus.	
			GBP	GBP	GBP	GBP	GBP	GBP
	Air Canada	Aeroplan	.019	.022	.011	.009	.017	.015
	Air Europa	Suma	.019	.006	.011	.016	.005	.013
	Air France	Flying Blue	.018	.020	.007	.006	.006	.012
	Air New Zealand	Airpoints	.497	.497	.497	.497	.497	.497
	Alaska Airlines	Mileage Plan	-	-	.013	-	-	.013
	American Airlines	AAdvantage	.019	.013	.015	.010	.005	.013
**	Austrian Airlines	Miles and More	.013	.033	.004	.006	.016	.014
	British Airways	Executive Club	.014	.046	.005	.006	.014	.016
**	Cathay Pacific	Marco Polo	.020	.038	.008	.011	.027	.020
	Delta Air Lines	Sky Miles	.010	.007	.009	.008	.005	.008
**	Emirates	Skywards	.014	.021	.015	.008	.017	.014
**	Etihad Airways	Guest	.013	.008	.007	.007	.009	.008
*	Hawaiian Airlines	Hawaiian Miles	.011	.017	.007	.010	.012	.010
	ITA Airways	Miles and More	.013	.033	.004	.006	.016	.014
**	KLM	Flying Blue	.018	.020	.007	.006	.006	.012
	Lufthansa	Miles and More	.013	.029	.003	.006	.014	.013
	Malaysia Airlines	Enrich	.026	.030	.009	.021	.020	.023
	Qantas	Frequent Flyer	.015	.012	.010	.015	.011	.013
**	Qatar Airways	Privilege Club	.021	.105	.025	.017	-	.031
**	Singapore Airlines	KrisFlyer	.019	.031	.010	.010	.019	.017
	Southwest Airlines	Rapid Rewards	-	-	.010	-	-	-
**	Swiss	Miles and More	.013	.037	.005	.006	.018	.015
	Thai Airways	Royal Orchid	.013	.018	.006	.012	.017	.013
	United Airlines	Mileage Plus	.019	.021	.009	.011	.011	.015
	Virgin Australia	Velocity	.012	.007	.009	.015	.007	.011

** For small countries (eg Switzerland) domestic definition includes directly neighbouring countries.
* For Hawaiian Airlines international definition includes flights to mainland USA.
Qantas: Includes 2025 devaluation.
Qatar Airlines: It is difficult to redeem points for Business Class - sample size was inadequate for valuation purposes.

APPENDICES

REFERENCE TABLE — EUROS EUR POINT (MILE) VALUATIONS

	Airline	Loyalty Scheme	Targeted Redemption Value per Point					Weighted Avg Value
			One-Way		Return			
			International		Domestic	International		
			Econ.	Bus.	Econ.	Econ.	Bus.	
			EUR	EUR	EUR	EUR	EUR	EUR
	Air Canada	Aeroplan	.022	.025	.012	.010	.010	.017
	Air Europa	Suma	.021	.007	.013	.018	.006	.015
	Air France	Flying Blue	.020	.022	.008	.007	.007	.014
	Air New Zealand	Airpoints	.564	.564	.564	.564	.564	.564
	Alaska Airlines	Mileage Plan	-	-	.015	-	-	.015
	American Airlines	AAdvantage	.022	.015	.017	.011	.006	.015
**	Austrian Airlines	Miles and More	.015	.038	.004	.007	.018	.015
	British Airways	Executive Club	.016	.052	.006	.007	.016	.018
**	Cathay Pacific	Marco Polo	.023	.043	.010	.012	.030	.023
	Delta Air Lines	Sky Miles	.011	.008	.011	.009	.006	.009
**	Emirates	Skywards	.016	.024	.017	.010	.020	.016
**	Etihad Airways	Guest	.014	.009	.008	.008	.010	.009
*	Hawaiian Airlines	Hawaiian Miles	.012	.020	.008	.011	.014	.011
	ITA Airways	Miles and More	.015	.038	.004	.007	.018	.015
**	KLM	Flying Blue	.020	.022	.008	.007	.007	.014
	Lufthansa	Miles and More	.015	.033	.004	.007	.016	.014
	Malaysia Airlines	Enrich	.030	.034	.010	.024	.023	.026
	Qantas	Frequent Flyer	.017	.013	.012	.017	.012	.015
**	Qatar Airways	Privilege Club	.024	.119	.028	.019	-	.036
**	Singapore Airlines	KrisFlyer	.021	.035	.012	.011	.022	.019
	Southwest Airlines	Rapid Rewards	-	-	.012	-	-	.012
**	Swiss	Miles and More	.015	.042	.005	.007	.020	.017
	Thai Airways	Royal Orchid	.015	.020	.006	.013	.019	.015
	United Airlines	Mileage Plus	.022	.024	.010	.013	.012	.017
	Virgin Australia	Velocity	.014	.008	.010	.017	.008	.013

** For small countries (eg Switzerland) domestic definition includes directly neighbouring countries.

* For Hawaiian Airlines international definition includes flights to mainland USA.

Qantas: Includes 2025 devaluation.
Qatar Airlines: It is difficult to redeem points for Business Class - sample size was inadequate for valuation purposes.

About the Author

Bruce Short is a Certified Practising Accountant and a Fellow of CPA Australia. He holds a Bachelor of Business, a Graduate Diploma in Accounting and Finance, and a Master of Business Administration from the University of Technology, Sydney.

After 12 years of working in accounting positions in various industries, he served as a chief financial officer for over 30 years in a dozen organisations across multiple sectors, advising owners, CEOs, and company directors on improving financial results.

Bruce has travelled extensively for business and pleasure. He enjoys researching travel opportunities, planning trips, and writing between trips.

Bruce and Lynda have visited approximately 100 countries and territories, as defined by the Century Travellers Club, including 70 United Nations countries.

They live near Sydney, Australia.

Bruce enjoys applying his passion for financial analysis to the travel industry and writing guides to help people travel in luxury while on a budget.

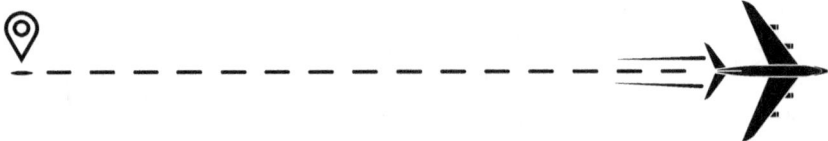

You may contact Bruce directly at budluxtravel@gmail.com or visit his website at www.budluxtravel.com and download his free resources. Register for his newsletter to stay informed of the latest updates in the budget luxury travel industry and future publications.

www.ingramcontent.com/pod-product-compliance
Lightning Source LLC
Chambersburg PA
CBHW071231070526
44583CB00017B/2131